Perspectives on
Teacher Professional Development

Issues in Education & Training Series

Editors: **Stephen J. Ball,** King's College, London and
Ivor F. Goodson, University of Western Ontario, Canada

Issues in Education and Training Series: 11

Perspectives on Teacher Professional Development

Edited by

Mary Louise Holly and Caven S. Mcloughlin

Kent State University

 The Falmer Press

(A member of the Taylor & Francis Group)
London. New York. Philadelphia

UK   The Falmer Press, Falmer House, Barcombe, Lewes,
East Sussex, BN8 5DL

USA   The Falmer Press, Taylor & Francis Inc., 242 Cherry Street,
Philadelphia, PA 19106-1906

First published 1989

Library of Congress Cataloging in Publication Data

Perspectives on teacher professional development/edited by Mary Louise
     Holly and Caven S. Mcloughlin.
       p.   cm.
     Bibliography: p.
     Includes index.
     ISBN 1-85000-345-9 ISBN 1-85000-346-7 (pbk.)
     1. Teachers — In-service training. 2. Teachers — Training of.
     I. Holly, Mary Louise. II. Mcloughlin, Caven S.
     LB1731.P46 1988
     371.1'46 — dc 19

British Library Cataloguing in Publication Data

Perspectives on teacher professional development.
     1. Teachers, Professional education
     I. Holly, Mary Louise II. Mcloughlin,
     Caven S.
     370'.7'1

     ISBN 1-85000-345-9
     ISBN 1-85000-346-7 Pbk

Jacket design by Caroline Archer

Typeset in 11/13 Bembo by Graphicraft Typesetters Ltd., Hong Kong
Imago Publishing Ltd, Thame, Oxon

*Printed in Great Britain by Taylor & Francis (Printers) Ltd,
Basingstoke*

Contents

Contents

Acknowledgements

We would like to acknowledge the contributions of:
Pat Balazs
Kathy Erickson
Clella Fouts
Judy Granger
Dick Hawthorne
Bonnie Heaton
Brian Holly
Jim Jenkins
Jackie Katz
Crysann Kelly
Linda Lee
Pat Little
Patricia McLoughlin
Steve Snyder
and of Christine Cox and Falmer Press

Dedication

This book is dedicated to teachers, and in particular to Helen Hulbert and Louise Sause.

Preface

Teacher professional development, at both pre- and in-service education levels, stands as a major challenge facing contemporary education. Teacher education and continuing teacher education have changed relatively little over the last several decades. Most modern classrooms look surprisingly like they did when this book's authors attended schools as students. Yet, we are on the threshold of new images of teachers and new directions for teaching and schooling. The isolated practitioner, schooled and 'certified', ready to 'sink-or-swim' for the next 30 years is soon to be extinct. Recent pre-service preparation changes, as well as changes in continuing education for the experienced teacher, all signal the genesis of a 'new professional'. From *training* to *development* educational discourse slowly shifts from teacher-as-information dispenser to teacher-as-researcher. Scholarly and influential journals like the *Harvard Educational Review* now have sections devoted to teacher's practices written by teachers. This is in sharp contrast to the recent past when specialists from both outside and inside the field of education, designed 'teacher-proof curriculum materials'.

The field of professional education is in transition. Both broader and narrower visions of teachers and teaching are prevalent. In most states in the USA, for example, experienced teachers are 'tested' to prove their 'competence' to remain in the classroom. A national examination for educators is emerging. In the UK, school organization and national curriculum development are proceeding at what many would call 'a rapid pace'. Teachers are more highly educated than they have ever been, yet they are also more narrowly accountable for their practice. In-service education, once thought of as a major vehicle for professional development, is now addressed as only a small part of a much larger process. It is this larger process, and the contexts which frame it, that this book is designed to address.

Overview

This book addresses teacher professional development from several perspectives, from: the practitioner's viewpoint (chaps 4, 6, 7, 8, 12, 13); broader social, and historical contexts (2, 3, 5); professional education and developmental perspectives (4, 5, 6, 7); administrative and organizational orientations (9, 10); and from philosophical and practical vantage points (7, 8, 12, 13).

In the first chapter, Charles Blackman introduces several contemporary issues which currently challenge educators involved in teacher professional development. Normand Bernier and Averil McClelland discuss the factors which make up the social context of professional development in chapter 2 which begins the section: *Contexts of Professional Development.* Martin Haberman then traces three competing cultures which hold significant sway over current practices in chapter 3.

In Part II, *Beginning Teaching and Professional Development,* Jane Applegate and Les Tickle present contemporary and heuristic conceptions and practices in the professional preparation and early socialization of teachers. (What changes in teacher preparation are underway? What do we know about the first-year teacher and how might 'induction' be consonant with professionalism?) The third section, *Teachers and Professional Development,* begins with Sharon Oja's chapter on adult developmental perspectives on teachers. What, for example, do we know about the developmental characteristics of adults and of teachers that might provide insights into professional development, and give indications of the kinds of environments that might support and contribute to lifelong development? In the next two chapters Jennifer Nias and Mary Louise Hulbert Holly explore the perceptual worlds of practicing teachers in England and the United States of America: What do we know of the evolving identity of a teacher? What do teachers have to say about their own professional development? What is perceived to be facilitating, stimulating, meaningful, and useful? To whom do teachers turn for assistance and colleagueship? With whom do they identify? Part IV, *Support for Professional Development,* begins with a discussion by Roy Edelfelt of the roles of professional organizations in teacher professional development. This is followed by a presentation, authored by John Smyth, of administrators' responsibilities in teacher professional development.

In the culminating section, *Teachers and Teaching: New Images and Directions,* directions for professional development are explored. This section begins with a description of the teacher as a professional who approaches teaching as a moral science, and thus as one who engages in continuing, 'systematic, self critical inquiry'. The next chapter builds upon these images and practices as Holly and Mcloughlin present portraits of teachers who inquire into their practice through writing and collegial discussion. In the final chapter, Holly and Carl Walley discuss teachers' theorizing, evaluation, and collaborative curriculum development as processes for perspective transformation.

This book has been designed to look at professional development from different vantage points — historical, sociological, psychological, pedagogical, and from cross-cultural perspectives, in the hope that using multiple lenses to conceptualize educator growth can enable us to integrate what has seemed disjointed, to understand what is occurring, and to shape a professional future.

Professional development, now viewed as a career-long process, is, at last, being viewed as a major factor in efforts to improve schools. Lawrence Stenhouse said: *'It is teachers who, in the end, will change the world of the school by understanding it'.* He said that this would take a generation to bring about. That was over ten years ago. Today it is happening.

Mary Louise Holly
and Caven S. Mcloughlin
December 1987

1 Issues in Professional Development: the Continuing Agenda

Charles A. Blackman

Throughout the history of schooling, teachers have sought ways to work with learners in more appropriate and effective ways. They have searched for answers to questions concerning school purposes, the relationship between schooling and broader educative functions of the society-at-large, the teacher's role, and the nature of knowledge. As we have come to institutionalize the function of schooling, we have become more attentive to matters of the organization and management of schools — and of teaching. But, no matter what the era, teachers have been learners (Henry, 1957).

We have come to refer to the new learnings of teachers and others associated with schools as *professional development*. Some of it occurs under the auspices of schools. Some of it is individually directed. In most instances an agenda is being consciously addressed. That agenda can come from many sources. The nature of professional development may vary, depending upon where one is in one's career: early, middle, or late. Professional development occurs in social and historical contexts and the nature of these affects it. How one views the roles of the persons involved also has an impact on professional development. Are teachers professionals? Are they technicians? Professional development requires resources of time and money. How and from where these are acquired affects the nature and extent of professional development efforts. What is the role of leadership? From where does leadership come? These questions, issues, and challenges are among those explored in the sections which follow.

Professional Development and Conceptions of the Teacher's Role

How we view professional development is a direct outgrowth of the way in which we view teacher roles (Wise, Darling-Hammond, McLaughlin and Bernstein, 1984). If we view the teacher as an applier of a craft, then we will focus professional development primarily upon the methods and techniques of teaching. If we view teachers as functioning in isolation from one another, we will focus professional development upon the activities of the classroom. If we view the teacher as a functionary, then managers of the school system will be the sources for the agendas of professional development.

If we view teachers in these ways, we are also apt to focus upon what the teacher can *do*, rather than upon what the teacher *is* and can become. On the other hand, if we view the teacher as a professional, we will address issues related to decision making, practice, and professional knowledge — about human development, learning, and school purposes, for example. If we view teachers as members of school building staffs, of school system staffs, and as members of the profession-at-large, we will address not only matters of classroom practice, but matters related to the school building and its sphere of the education program, matters related to the school system which might include questions involving long-range planning, and issues of concern to the profession-at-large.

If we view teachers as professionals, we also consider them capable of creating their own agendas for professional development. Thus, as we alter our views of the teacher's role, from that of technician to that of professional, the focus of the agenda for professional development is altered, the locus of concern is broadened, and the sources of the agenda changed. The view of the teacher as professional permits us to get beyond the technologies of teaching to gain a fuller understanding of what we seek to do in schools, and why. Debate over teacher roles has been with us for a while, as confirmed by Tickle in chapter 5, who explores contrasting views of teachers and teaching. He also draws implications for the teacher as learner depending upon the view held of teacher roles. In chapter 11, Elliott elaborates on two conflicting images of teachers which frame current debate over professional responsibilities and evaluation.

Bernier and McClelland (chap. 2) make reference to Broudy (1973) and his observation that 'the difference between technicians who can merely implement a guide to activity and an educator who can utilize and interpret policies according to the needs of learners and the realities of the school setting is a significant one'. Significant indeed! *This* difference can guide our rethinking of what we mean by professional development. But even more importantly, this difference can be the focus of teachers as they re-examine their roles.

The Teacher as Person: Implications for the School's Curriculum and for Professional Development

The teacher brings both a conception of role *and* a view of herself or himself *as person* to the classroom, school, and school system. The teacher is not only a professional, but a professional *person* with a unique life history and psychological being. Teachers arc persons living and working in specific settings: settings with historical, social and cultural qualities which influence teaching, learning and professional development. For example, those with whom teachers are able to (and chose to) communicate professionally influence their personal identities as teachers, as Nias discusses in chapter 7. She makes the observation that *'who and what people perceive themselves to be* matters as much as *what they can do'*. Teachers are subject to the same characteristics of adult development as other professionals, yet there are also unique considerations related to teacher development and learning. Oja addresses teachers from a developmental perspective in chapter 6. This *person-as-professional* brings values, beliefs, knowledge, attitudes, and insights to whatever professional role he or she may play. Thus, any significant change in what the school means to learners has been influenced by changes, not only in professional understandings of the teacher, but by changes in the teacher-as-person as well. Whether or not one subscribes to the idea that 'the teacher *is* curriculum' or as Nias (chap. 7) writes 'that which gets taught is the teacher', the central role of teachers and teaching to the quality of the lived curriculum is apparent (see, for example, Woods, 1983).

Accepting the interrelationship of teaching and curriculum to learning leads us to view curriculum development as much more than *product* development, much more than a set of agreements about what should be taught. Curriculum development is, in many respects, *people development* — or, as we are describing it here, professional development. Another challenge, then, on our continuing agenda will be to so reconceptualize the processes of curriculum review and development that these become facilitators of personal–professional growth and staff development.

New Dimensions of Professional Responsibility: Multiple Roles for Teachers

How the teacher-as-person feels about her or his professional contribution can be a key factor in determining the satisfactions derived from teaching. As a teacher becomes more comfortable with the management of teaching, there may well be a desire to contribute beyond the classroom. The importance of a sense of personal fulfillment is a factor to keep in mind as we think about staff roles and opportunities for continued professional development.

Multiple or extended roles for teachers can be a means through which experienced and mature teachers can extend and develop their professional expertise. Multiple roles can take many forms:

- A half day teaching and a half day assigned to a curriculum or staff development activity (or some other division of roles);
- an extended year contract which would provide similar opportunities, but after a regular full-year teaching assignment;
- a full-year non-teaching assignment to provide leadership for program or curriculum development in a teaching field or at the school level (similar to practices in British schools such as 'secondment' described by Holly in chapter 8);
- an extra duty assignment for which additional compensation (salary or professional travel reimbursement, for example) is provided; or
- the voluntary assumption of a leadership role in curriculum or staff development.

Recent discussions with teachers while conducting a study in Michigan (Hatfield, Blackman, Claypool and Mester, 1985) confirm that there is a significant number of teachers who do not wish to leave teaching to follow the traditional path of 'promotion' to administration, but who would like both the stimulation and the sense of contribution which accrues from professional activities beyond the classroom. From this research, it is estimated that between 10 and 15 per cent of teachers in Michigan are now involved in some type of beyond-the-classroom role. This number does not include those in athletic coaching. Eight categories were identified within which these multiple or extended roles fell: grade-level chair, department chair, coordinator, consultant, staff developer, teacher trainer, committee chair, and master teacher. While several of these roles have been with us for some time and may be heavily focused upon maintenance or administrative support tasks, the potential is there for these — particularly department and grade-level chairs — to increase in significance. People in these roles can contribute to a growing professionalism through curriculum development, professional development or staff support dimensions which could help to integrate and coordinate functions which have been disparate and limited operations before.

There is further evidence from the Michigan data (and consistent with Lortie, 1975) that financial reward is viewed as much less significant for the teacher participating in a multiple role assignment than are the psychic or intrinsic rewards. There is also increasing evidence which suggests a wealth of untapped talent among teaching staffs. For many persons there is considerable interest in a greater sense of efficacy, and professional contribution to schooling and education.

Both the disposition to continue professional growth, and to contribute to the growth of others, could be supported through appropriate institutional structures. Opportunities for multiple, extended or restructured role assignments could provide means to contribute to learning from working with colleagues (Devaney, 1987).

Professional Development: Who is Responsible for Agendas and for Support?

If we start with the proposition that continuing professional development is a life-long endeavor, where does the responsibility rest for its design and support? Typically, we have assumed that attributes of continued learning which accrue to the individual teacher — graduate degrees, meeting certification requirements, preparation for other roles in education — fall to the teacher for planning and support. In turn, activities which address institutional agendas — curriculum development, instructional improvement, school improvement — fall to the lot of the school system. This may be too simplistic a division.

In each case our measures or indicators of responsibility are based on *products* — degrees, entry credentials, curriculum guides, instructional procedures. This focus may have kept us from looking at qualities, dispositions, risk-taking, emotional support — at those matters which defy quantification, but which may be among the most important determiners of the quality of learning opportunities for all. In the United States, this division has also led us to teacher contracts in which the number and length of staff meetings are clearly specified, and in which a number of additional components appear which are based upon unstated assumptions about teacher roles. Again, *who is the responsible agent* becomes inextricably linked with our conceptions of teacher's role.

Our investment — and it is just that — in professional development is a fraction of what it needs to be. In the United States, for example, a district which approaches 1 per cent of its budget expended for staff and school improvement is lauded. For most, the amount is only a portion of that. A few states have now made support for professional development a line-item in state funding of schools. Increased support from whatever source will come about only when professional development is recognized and acted upon as *the* key ingredient to the maintenance of a vital and dynamic school.

Who is responsible for professional development? Rather than to respond by dividing up tasks, which Lortie (1975) and others (Little, 1982; Nias, 1984) might suggest would contribute to isolation rather than colleagueship and collaboration, perhaps the response should be a corporate one for which staffs have collective responsibility. One possibility lies in the extended contractual year (10 per cent longer?) — within which there is corporate time for long-range planning, curriculum development, and instructional improvement. These endeavors could be jointly planned with recognition that they *all* have significant professional development outcomes. One measure of the quality of our school's program can be found in the items we talk about — that is, what our agendas include. In chapter 9 Edelfelt describes ways that professional organizations contribute to teacher professional development, not the least of which are the ways in which teachers work and learn together, and their engagement with political questions and processes outside their immediate environments.

Contexts for Professional Development

Contexts for professional development relate both to locale and to qualities which characterize the environments, whatever the locale, in which professional development occurs. Researchers who study the culture of schools and the complexity of social interactions and constructions of reality within them, are slowly changing our understandings of educational change and the meaning of school life to participants (Sarason, 1971; Woods, 1983).

Much has been reported about the desirability of making the individual school building the primary unit for both staff and curricular development (Goodlad, 1984). The principal has often been identified as a key to the quality of both types of development efforts. The case can easily be made that the personalization of staff or professional development activities is best accomplished closest to the individuals involved. Mounting evidence suggests that the quality of the relationships among and between staff members is a major factor in school program success (Little, 1982). Collaboration and colleagueship in developing ways of working as a staff, and in creating agendas for discussion and action are associated with successful schools. Commitment to creating agendas is part of viewing the school-as-laboratory, as a place in which there is constant re-examination of 'how well we're doing' and 'whether we're doing what we aim to be doing'. As Stenhouse (1975, p. 142) put it, 'each classroom is a laboratory, each teacher a member of a scientific community'. This searching behavior can pervade the classroom and contribute to an environment for all learners which makes *questioning* central to learning.

The school system context for professional development can be characterized by resources allocated — both time and money — as well as by agendas which provide a total system focus. The delicate management of individual, individual building, and school system concerns and needs is a challenging task.

More broadly, there are both the school community and the professional community which provide the backdrop for current foci of professional development. One major challenge is to help community members to understand the centrality of strong professional development programs to the quality of education offered in schools. Unfortunately, we often perceive teachers' roles as limited to the institutional activities of the classroom. Somehow, we must foster within the community images of the teacher as a professional person who is constantly searching for more appropriate and effective ways to teach, a person for whom professional development is not a luxury but a necessity.

The profession-at-large provides a major context within which issues that transcend the local school are identified. These issues combine with those at the district and building levels, with those of the individual professional, and with those of the community to generate the context and the agenda for continuing professional development.

The relevance and importance of history in understanding and framing discussions of professional development are addressed in chapters 2 and 3. Bernier and McClelland (chap. 2) provide an in-depth discussion of the social context of professional development, while Haberman (chap. 3) traces the roots of competing cultures on teacher professional development in the USA, both at pre-service and in-service levels.

Teachers as Colleagues: Dialogue as Stimulus for Growth

'Schools are ideas that are kept alive by dialogue.' That is the way a teacher in a middle school which has a long history of collaborative efforts among staff summed up the importance of collegial sharing of ideas and of opening discussion and debate. How do we come to regard fellow teachers and administrators as colleagues — as persons with whom we are comfortable sharing our concerns, our doubts, even our sense of uncertainty and inadequacy, as well as our joys, our bright ideas, and our inclination to 'venture'?

The stimulus and support for personal–professional growth which emerges from an environment in which professionals regard one another as colleagues is powerful — and empowering. The quality of the relationships among faculty is central to professional development. The isolation of teachers from one another, classroom by classroom, coupled with the widely held perception that classroom 'instruction' and 'outcomes' are really all that matters, have combined to discourage collegial dialogue. There are schools, however, in which desired openness, exchange, and collaborative planning and action do occur (see, for example, Little, 1982; and Oja, chap. 6).

What are some of the fundamental components that contribute to colleagues' sharing, collaborating, and inquiring together? Conscious efforts to get to know one another can be as beneficial as they are simple. Finding and taking the time to share is a beginning. A look toward how time is spent when staff members are together can move a group toward dialogue and generating agendas representing common concerns. As Holly (chap. 8) found, spending time in another teacher's classroom is one of the most often requested and beneficially perceived resources (by teachers, administrators, and teacher educators in both the USA and England) for teacher professional development.

The principal can be a major facilitator in helping to connect people with common interests. The principal is also a prime determiner of how staff meeting time is spent. Controlled meetings with one-way communication send quite different messages than those in which agendas are developed collaboratively and in which open discussion is not only encouraged but is accepted as 'the norm'.

It is important that open dialogue not be viewed as an end in itself, but as a means by which colleagues can think with one another about practice. The quality of professional development is determined, in large measure, by the nature of the questions being addressed and by the resources drawn upon to address these questions. Holly and Mcloughlin (chap. 12) provide examples of how teachers can document their inquiry and encourage conscious reflection on practice through journal writing. With this method, teachers can return to past practices and see how personal and collective questions, projects, and concerns develop and change over time. Elliott (chap. 11) provides examples of teachers' inquiry and relates the importance of teachers' dialogues and discussions of practice, of 'using the collective wisdom' of their professional groups 'to guide their judgments'.

Leadership for Professional Development: Some Principles for Principals

As a significant part of the human context for professional development, the building principal (or head teacher) faces many challenges. Not the least of these, at least in the USA, is the tension between responsibility for staff evaluation and the responsibility to contribute to a positive growth-oriented environment. Somehow the focus must be on knowing the members of one's staff and upon understanding the basis for each person's functioning as a professional person. This collective knowledge and understanding not only provides a base for designing, collaboratively, professional development agenda, but it also sends clear messages to staff members that they are highly regarded.

Taking time to get to know staff members as persons is but one illustration of time use which sends strong messages. One principal in Michigan spent his morning in the staff lounge — because this was the place where teachers would congregate. It became a place where some very important faculty dialogue occurred — a dramatic change from the conversations typical of many staff lounges. What this principal was 'saying' by his time use was 'it's important that we talk and think *together* about what we're doing'. He was also affirming the regard with which he held the staff. He had an office manager who could take care of administrative details *and* who understood the importance of the way this principal chose to spend a portion of his time. Being visible in halls and classrooms also conveyed interest in staff and students, as well as contributing to a knowledge base for professional development activities. It also extends access for the quick question or sharing an observation — all a part of helping to create an open and collegial climate.

How time is used for faculty meetings can be revealing of leadership and other staff members' values. Is the focus on dialogue and discussion? Is it on one-way information sharing? A faculty which uses its time together for sharing, for agenda-drafting, for serious considerations of professional issues, is more apt to be a growing, learning faculty than is one used to sitting and receiving at faculty meetings.

Another part of the principal's (or the head teacher's) role in meetings is to create a climate in which a *continuing* agenda is the norm. A part of conceiving of the school-as-a-laboratory is that of having a continuing agenda — a list of challenges which both spurs discussion and contributes to a dynamic and vital environment — a list which never ends.

The principal is also a key link between the building and the school system. Two-way communication contributes to the agenda-building process at both the building level and at the system level. Played well, this linking role can be a means through which teachers come to see themselves as members of a system staff — a staff responsible for addressing system-wide issues and concerns.

All of the roles presented here point toward overarching functions which principals are in a position to serve: To empower teachers to help themselves, each other, and the profession. Smyth, in chapter 10, presents an impassioned plea (and rationale) for administrators to 'lead' through 'empowerment'.

While the focus here has been upon the principal as contributor to an environment in which continuing professional development thrives, it is important to note that administrators too have their own agendas for professional development. While they are, hopefully, very much a part of the staff with whom they work, and thus involved in addressing corporate agendas, there are some matters of particular concern to the principal.

Enlarging the circle for professional development involves being mindful of matters of concern to all the employees of a school system and of those matters of concern to each class or group of employees. The significant roles played in a school environment by the secretary, custodian, and volunteers are reminders that continuing growth and learning are for all persons who contribute to the quality of schooling.

Integrating Initial Preparation and Continuing Professional Development

Current discussions about initial preparation programs for teachers will, no doubt, result in some changes in those programs (see, for example, the Carnegie group report, 1986; Holmes Group, 1986; Griffin, 1985; Tickle, 1987). No matter what changes are contemplated, whether a major reconceptualization or tinkering with requirements, however, there will be a continuing need to relate initial preparation to the process of induction — one's entry to the full-time role of teacher — and to a professional lifetime of learning. As Applegate (chap. 4) illustrates through portraits of teacher education students and alternative teacher education programs, there are many factors to address when considering program change. Tickle (chap. 5), based on his experience and research in teacher preparation, presents a rationale and program for the systematic introduction of new teachers to the profession.

Unfortunately, too often the 'induction' process is left to chance — chance that the hiring school district will make appropriate and adequate provision for the support of the neophyte teacher. More appropriately, there are cases where professionals (such as Tickle) seek to achieve a collaborative effort between schools and colleges by systematically extending professional development through at least the first three years of full-time practice. An acknowledgment of further study might be given through granting college or university credit or by recognition in the certification process. Whatever the mode, the key is to convey to the new teacher that the induction period is viewed as a time for intensive continued learning — and that there is support available to aid one in that learning.

Collaborative efforts between schools and colleges may be a way through which both types of institutions can come to address a wide range of issues within the profession-at-large. Given the fast pace of an increasingly technological world and the demands placed on educators, it is too easy for us to become two separate worlds, each dealing with its own agenda, and each with its own vocabulary. Though this might be more efficient, it will not work. The issues facing the profession-at-large demand joint attention. As we address teacher induction, we may rediscover common aims.

Resources which contribute to continuing professional development are vast. There are resources represented by the involvement of individual faculty members in professional organizations, as Edelfelt (chap. 9) discusses. There are individuals who serve as staff within such organizations who may be called upon as resource persons. There are college and university staff members who value their opportunities to work collaboratively with schools. There are state department of education consultants, as well as regional or intermediate school district staff to whom we can turn. And there is a growing number of individual, independent consultants whose services are available.

While the individuals, groups, and institutions mentioned above are all within the professional field of education, there is also an array of human service agencies within school communities. Personnel of these agencies serve the families of students. We have much to learn from them — and to share with them — concerning our common clients.

While the earlier discussion about agenda sources for professional development was focused primarily upon the individual teacher, the staff collectively and the school system, the question of sources external to the system is also critical to put into the context. Individuals and institutions external to the school have their agendas. Their work is often useful to a school staff. Professional associations of disciplines or teaching fields periodically publish position statements concerning professional issues. These can serve as a stimulus for faculty dialogue.

Exerting leadership in developing and carrying out the agenda should be a matter of concern to local schools. Turning the agenda over to a resource person or to an institution external to the school can leave a staff devoid of any sense of ownership of ideas and not disposed to follow-through. Balancing new ideas, which we all need for stimulation against the maintenance of control over our own agendas, is an ever-present challenge.

The Broader View

Looking toward the next century, the continuing agenda for professional development will be interlocked with our efforts to re-examine and redefine the roles of teachers. With extended or expanded roles will come new demands for continued learning (Hatfield, Blackman, Claypool, and Mester, 1985). Debates over career ladders and merit pay will lead further toward reconceptualizing teacher roles, with greater acceptance of *the teacher as learner* as an accepted part of any role definition. The profession will support teacher learning in a variety of ways which build on the many dimensions of professional practice and principles of adult development (Loucks-Horsley, Harding, Arbuckle, Murray, Dubea, and Williams, 1987).

The workplace will be marked by professional relationships between and among colleagues — colleagues who view one another both as stimulus and as resource for continued professional development (Lieberman, 1986; Rosenholtz, Bassler, and Hoover-Dempsey, 1986). The teacher as searcher, researcher, colleague, consultant, leader, child advocate, and even social and educational critic and schooling transformer — all of these, in some measure — will describe the teacher of the twenty-first century. And, we will have accepted continual questing as a quality of the school-as-laboratory — a place where the agenda is constantly changing — and never completed.

Technology will enable us to free ourselves from some of the time-taking, but less creative, parts of our role. It will enable us to access resources heretofore unavailable to many of us. It will enable us to address more fully some of the challenges for individualization and collaboration in learning, both for our students and for ourselves. The computer and its uses will be a recurring item on our continuing professional agendas — no doubt a threat to some, a stimulating challenge to some, and an indispensable tool for others.

Leadership roles will be spread more widely, with the principal serving as manager, facilitator, and along with others, visionary. Teachers will be 'playing from strength' as they make contributions in their areas of expertise and as they take leadership roles in educational change.

And, certainly not of least importance, we will address the issues of resources: time, and money. Added community involvement and understanding will support our efforts for longer contractual years.

On the pages which follow, chapter contributors address various aspects of the continuing agenda for professional development. Hopefully, they will provide you, the reader, with a means for reexamining your own agendas — and a resolve to contribute more fully to the corporate agenda before individual schools, and before us as a profession.

References

BROUDY, H. S. (1973). The role of foundational studies in the preparation of elementary teachers. In M. Gillet and J. A. Laska (eds), *Foundation studies in education*. Metuchen, NJ: The Scarecrow Press.

CARNEGIE FORUM ON EDUCATION AND THE ECONOMY. (1986). *A nation prepared: Teachers for the 21st century*. New York: Carnegie Forum on Education and the Economy, Carnegie Corporation.

DEVANEY, K. (1987). *The lead teacher: Ways to begin*. New York: Carnegie Forum on Education and the Economy, Carnegie Corporation.

GOODLAD, J. (1984). *A place called school: Prospects for the future*. New York: McGraw-Hill.

GRIFFIN, G. A. (1985). Teacher induction: Research issues. *Journal of Teacher Education, 36*(1), 42–6.

HATFIELD, R. C., BLACKMAN, C. A., CLAYPOOL, C., and MESTER, F. (1985 November). *Extended professional roles of teacher leaders in the public schools*. Paper presented at the National Council of States for Inservice Education (NCSIE) Conference, Denver, CO.

HENRY, N. B. (ed.). (1957). *Inservice education for teachers, supervisors, and administrators*. Fifty-sixth yearbook, National Society for the Study of Education. Chicago: National Society for the Study of Education.

HOLMES GROUP. (1986). *Tomorrow's teachers: A report of the Holmes Group*. East Lansing, MI: The Holmes Group.

LORTIE, D. C. (1975). *Schoolteacher*. Chicago: The University of Chicago Press.

LIEBERMAN, A. (1986). Collaborative work. *Educational Leadership, 43*(5), 4–8.

LITTLE, J. W. (1982). Norms of collegiality and experimentation: Workplace conditions of school success. *American Educational Research Journal, 19*, 325–40.

LOUCKS-HORSLEY, S., HARDING, C. K., ARBUCKLE, M. A., MURRAY, L. B., DUBEA, C., and WILLIAMS, M. K. (1987). *Continuing to learn: A guidebook for teacher development*. Oxford, Ohio: The Regional Laboratory for Educational Improvement of the Northeast and Islands, and The National Staff Development Center, co-publishers.

NIAS, J. (1984). Definition and maintenance of self in primary education. *British Journal of Social Education, 5*(3), 267–80.

ROSENHOLTZ, S., BASSLER, O., and HOOVER-DEMPSEY, K. (1986). Organizational conditions of teacher learning. *Teaching and Teacher Education, 2*(2), 91–103.

SARASON, S. (1971). *The culture of the school and the problems of change*. Boston: Allyn & Bacon.

STENHOUSE, L. (1975). *An introduction to curriculum research and development*. London: Heinemann Educational Books.

TICKLE, L. (1987). *Learning teaching, teaching learning: A study of partnership in teacher education*. Lewes: Falmer Press.

WISE, A. E., DARLING-HAMMOND, L., McLAUGHLIN, M. W., and BERNSTEIN, H. (1984). *Teacher evaluation: A study of effective practices*. Santa Monica: Rand Corporation.

WOODS, P. (1983). *Sociology and the school: An interactionist viewpoint*. London: Routledge & Kegan Paul.

PART I

CONTEXTS OF PROFESSIONAL DEVELOPMENT

2 The Social Context of Professional Development

Normand R. Bernier and Averil E. McClelland

Programs for the professional preparation and development of teachers in the United States of America have a brief history. Concern for the education of teachers followed the nineteenth-century development of tax-supported public education under the leadership of advocates such as Horace Mann, James Carter, Calvin Stowe, and Thomas Gallaudet. Indeed, during the early nineteenth century most teachers did not received *any* formal preparation for teaching. Most teacher selection was determined primarily on judgments of moral character rather than upon teaching competencies. Although a few private schools, such as Phillips Academy in Andover, offered some courses in pedagogy, most teachers completed little more than an elementary education.

The first Normal School — a term taken from the French *école normale,* meaning a professional school for the preparation of teachers — in the USA was established in 1838, and many more were founded in the following decades. Standards of admission were minimal. 'Applicants for admission had to pass (whatever that meant) an examination on the basic school subjects, be of good moral character, and declare an intent to teach' (Saylor, 1976, p. 40). Similarly, Meyer (1957) writes:

> The new schools were scarcely more than primitive. They received girls at sixteen and boys at seventeen, and they put them through a one-year course. In rare cases, the ambitious continued for another year. Normally, the would-be schoolman was drilled in fundamentals. In addition he had a cursory glimpse at some of the subjects usually found in the better-stocked secondary schools .... For extra measure he was instructed in Christian piety and morality.

Finally, of course, he was grounded in rudimentary pedagogics (pp. 205–6).

Meyer adds: 'Actually, the normal school itself was often little more than a higher elementary school' (p. 207). Opponents to the normal school idea were numerous. 'Among some of the most ferocious adversaries, oddly enough, were the schoolmasters themselves, who regarded the demand for professional training not only as so much piffle, but as a slur on their competence, and hence their dignity' (p. 206).

After the Civil War (1861–5), collegiate institutions began to offer courses in pedagogy and, toward the end of the century, teachers' colleges appeared on the scene. It was not until the end of the World War I, however, that the two- and three-year normal or teacher training schools were replaced generally by four-year teacher preparation programs that culminated in the granting of a Bachelor's degree. During the depression years, when the supply of potential teachers exceeded demand, standards were improved. Increasingly, professional agencies such as the National Council for the Accreditation of Teacher Education established national standards. While states constitutionally hold the power to determine policies and practices relating to teacher education, the efforts of professional organizations to establish national standards for accreditation and certification should not be underestimated.

Clearly, the history of teacher education in the USA reflects a primary concern for initial or preservice preparation of teachers. Struggles to establish professional standards have focused upon the need for baccalaureate degree programs, a system of institutional accreditation, and the establishment of state certification requirements. All of these efforts centered primarily on pre-service education and this emphasis has not abated appreciably in recent years. For example, in the influential task force report on 'New Horizons in Teacher Education and Professional Standards', a committee of the National Commission on Teacher Education and Professional Standards (NCTEPS), the emphasis on preservice education is clearly stated: *'The three essential processes of enforcement of professional standards are accreditation of preparatory programs, licensure of professional personnel, and rigorous application of standards of practice'* (Lindsey, 1961, p. 238).

This emphasis continues to dominate debates concerning the improvement of teacher education. Within this context, in-service educational programs and staff development activities have been a

secondary concern, lacking a shared conceptual base, consistent attention, and committed resources. Indeed, the professional development
of teachers has been called, with some accuracy, 'a shadow world'
(Cole, 1982, p. 370). In testimony before the US Senate Subcommittee on Education in 1967, Don Davies reflected the frustration experienced by in-service advocates. He write: 'In-service teacher education
is the slum of American education . . . disadvantaged, poverty strick-
en, neglected, psychologically isolated, whittled with exploitation and
broken promises' (cited in Harris, 1980, p. 30). Most concerned educators, however, correctly identify its place in contemporary education as crucial, and 'absolutely necessary if schools are to develop their
most important resource, their people' (Burrello and Orbaugh, 1982,
p. 385).

Nevertheless, recent activities in the field of teacher education suggest that a new enthusiasm is in the air. Griffin (1983), offers four
factors which seem directly related to an increased emphasis on professional development in teacher education: an expansion of the
knowledge base with respect to effective schooling; an increase in
research attention to staff development practices; higher expectations
for schooling expressed by members of the society; and, general
agreement among disparate groups that schools as social institutions
must be changed or improved (p. 3).

In addition, in teacher education as in other professional fields, the
notion that professional development is properly a career-long activity
appears to be taking root (Dodd and Rosenbaum, 1986; Nash and
Ducharme, 1983). Moreover, the numerous recent proposals and
programs designed to improve schooling in general, and teacher
education in particular, offer some promise that changes in perspective
will translate into useful policies regarding the importance of professional development as an integral part of the life of teachers.

Knowledge, debate, and even significant social change, will not by
themselves ensure an effective commitment to professional development. As Burrello and Orbaugh (1982) note: 'what we know is often
compromised by a multitude of other factors that affect planning and
delivery' (p. 385). Whatever the outcome, changes in the professional
preparation and advancement of teachers will occur. The nature of
those changes, however, will depend on a variety of factors: the tenor
of the times, the power which individual ideological groups possess,
the outcome of political conflicts within the society and within the
profession, as well as economic conditions. The purpose of this chapter is to explore some of the factors that will influence the outcome of

current efforts in teacher education to reconceptualize and redefine professional development for teachers.

The major foci of this analysis are grouped into three major areas of concern: the socio-political forces within the society which influence the development of educational policies relating to professional development in education; the ideational elements which serve as ideological orientations in determining educational practice in the professional development of teachers; and, the cultural environment within the profession of education which provides the context for programs and activities.

Educational Policies and Professional Development

Since teacher education, whether pre-service or in-service, is the deliberate and conscious effort to intervene in the personal and professional development of an individual or groups of individuals, both ethical and practical considerations require some policy statement to guide practice. Indeed, it is a fundamental professional assumption that effective education programs rest upon a teaching-learning process that is rooted to a consciously developed plan, and that effective education programs in turn rest upon well-developed educational policies (Standards for Academic and Professional Instruction in Foundations of Education, 1978).

Policy formulation and implementation cannot easily be achieved in a pluralistic and democratic society characterized by rapid technological and social change. Education in the USA is rooted to a variety of socially constructed ideologies or belief systems which, when internalized, influence the perception and behavior of individuals, and thus, the development of educational policies and the direction of educational practices. Since belief systems held by individuals and groups of individuals may contain dissonance and incongruity (Bernier and Williams, 1973; Bernier, 1981) and since ideological perspectives in the American democratic polity may and often do compete freely, conflict is reasonably assured. While such conflict may provide nearly insurmountable barriers to agreement on the resolution of serious educational issues, it is rarely attended to in any systematic inquiry. Suffice it to note that matters of educational policy are always complex and typically the sources of both reasonable and unreasonable disagreement.

Several attributes of USA educational policy are germane to a discussion of the professional development of teachers. First, the term *educational policy* has a variety of meanings, depending on the context in which it is used and on the purpose for which it is intended (DeVitis, 1976). Rich (1976–77), for example, cites three definitions: educational policy as *goals and purposes;* educational policy as *programmatic decisions;* and educational policy as *a form of rules for conduct, action, or usage.* Ruscoe (1976) also defines educational policy as a course of action, and additionally defines it as the (provisional) answers to a set of questions regarding the nature of man-and-society upon which specific decisions about a particular issue are made.

Generally, educational policies include both descriptive and normative elements. They may be general or specific and may contain implicit or explicit suggestions for action which may or may not have contractual and/or legal dimensions. They may relate to the selection of participants in the educational activity, the content to be presented, the mode of instruction to be followed, the aims of the activity, and/or the processes of evaluation (Guba, 1984; Lyons, 1976; Reagan, 1976).

A second attribute of USA educational policies is that they are generated from a variety of sources including all levels of government (Elmore and McLaughlin, 1982; Green, 1980; Thomas, 1975). Because the USA does not have a national educational policy-making body, educational policies may and do arise from a number of different sources (Sarason and Doris, 1982; Zigler and Kagan, 1982). One of the most prolific of these sources in recent years has been the federal government, acting in both legislative and judicial capacities to establish social policies which implement Constitutional guarantees (Fischer, 1982; Heath, 1976; Thomas, 1975).

Many of these policies have educational consequences in both school and community settings. Social policies regarding personnel needs, the rights of children, and equal opportunity employment and housing, for example, have generated the development of educational activities and policies in the workplace, in counseling agencies, welfare departments, in the real estate and banking industries, as well as in public schools and teacher education programs. While staff development literature in education rarely mentions programs in other settings, there is an observable tendency in staff development practice to utilize personnel across settings for teacher development programs. Indeed, a reconceptualization of the educational community is necessary and seems to be occurring. The diversity of sources of educational policy leads to a third attribute of educational policy: Educational policy-makers occupy a variety of roles (Cistone, 1977; Hansot and Tyack, 1982; Monsen and Cannon, 1965).

These roles may be assumed by individuals close to the educational scene or far away from it; by persons trained in education or in some other field or profession; and by individual citizens responding to single interest groups who may or may not share ideological perspective and purposes (Monsen and Cannon, 1965; Stanley, 1953). It is part of the natural evolution of educational policy in the USA that various competing ideological groups will participate in the development of educational policies. While some of these groups may represent narrow ideological interests, others reflect the values of the majority. Whatever the consequences, educational issues are matters of public scrutiny and subject to public debate. The professional change agent who ignores the values and opinions of community leaders and interest groups is unlikely to successfully introduce innovation into American education, regardless of how urgent or reasonable the intent may be. Education is not only a social activity; it is also a profoundly political one.

A variety of issues have emerged as a consequence of the manner in which educational policies are generated in the USA. Since educational policies often emerge from social policies, their educational directives are frequently described in terms of social rather than educational aims (Sarason and Doris, 1982). Thus, educational policies and practices which stem from public concerns are often established without thorough analysis of their *educational* implications. Writing about his concern for philosophical/pedagogical issues in teacher education, Greenberg (1983) notes that recent emphasis on accountability in education (a concept which often implies that the teacher is expected to 'produce' a satisfactory 'product') introduced a new ideological bias into teacher education and staff development:

> I am referring ... to the technology of pedagogy, and to the conceptualizations undergirding that pedagogy, which have begun to dominate the language and the scene in both policy and practice domains. Since the origin of public demands for 'accountability' we have been overrun by the 'technology' of behavioral objectives, minimum competencies, mastery learning, individually prescribed instruction, basic skills, and standardized test score competitions. At times, it seems that measurability has become more important than substance, and that results of normative tests have replaced values as the prime determinants of curriculum (pp. 39–40).

Calling for a balanced approach to thinking about both pre-service and in-service education for teachers, Greenberg underscores the need for a unified sense of purpose among professional educators that will inform the development of policies and practices.

Another example of a case in which overriding social goals influenced educational services to students and teachers is the mandate for equal educational opportunity, which struck down as unconstitutional the 'separate but equal' rule. This mandate was part of the social policy stemming from the Civil Rights movement and had widespread effects on many areas of public social life in addition to schools. The term 'desegregation', however, while not essentially an educational term, has acquired an educational meaning which is more-or-less unrelated to teaching-learning processes. Because they were related to fundamental constitutional issues rather than educational activities, and were often under judicial control, desegregation policies in many school districts often left little room for purely educational considerations. Indeed, 'educational policies' regarding desegregation in the public schools were more often administrative logistical decisions to ensure compliance with court orders in terms of placement of students and teachers than they were policies about aims, activities, and evaluation of teaching and learning. Moreover, both because they were powered by a social value and because they, in fact, had the force of law, it was often impossible for educators to interpret them according to educational knowledge. Social policies in a democratic and pluralistic society characterized by rapid technological change, when applied to educational activities, often supersede purely educational goals.

The implementation of staff development programs designed to assist teachers to carry out social mandates has a cyclical character that does little to enhance the integrity of staff development in the minds of many. Indeed, unfortunately, it may create the view that staff development is largely intended to disseminate the latest political ideology or educational fad.

Even when social policies have specific and legitimate implications for schooling, educational policies developed to implement them often result in conflicting educational goals. Thus, for example, the goals implied in desegregation decisions are in direct conflict with educational goals implied in bilingual/bicultural education. Similarly, goals related to mainstreaming handicapped children as mandated by Public Law 94–142 seem in conflict with goals related to pull-out programs for the gifted. Current emphasis on excellence in education (often defined according to traditionally established criteria), while obviously a clear priority, also may produce conflicts with goals regarding the removal of sexism and racism in educational programs and the encouragement of cultural diversity.

These conflicts reflect authentic ideological differences among individuals within the USA who are involved in policy matters. These conflicts also are a consequence of the fact that professional educators are infrequently involved in the policy-making process (Hall and Loucks, 1982). Policy formulation that does not include those individuals who will be directly involved in the implementation of policies often results in both open and covert resistance to change (Lieberman, 1982; Sarason and Doris, 1982). The difference between a technician who can merely implement a guide to activity and an educator who can utilize and interpret policies according to the needs of learners and the realities of the school setting is a significant one (Broudy, 1973). Indeed, the call for participation of teachers in policy making at local, state, and national levels is a current and welcome concern in staff development, and one that offers promise of opening avenues for collaborative efforts in the further professionalization of teaching.

Deeply rooted traditions as well as powerful social changes are the bedrock of educational policy, and influence the procedures through which policy is formulated. The American experience in education has been a unique and complex social activity. Unlike most nation-states, the USA does not have a centralized system of education. Indeed, the American Constitution is unusual in that it does not mention the term 'education' at all, leaving to states the authority to develop policies for schooling. The decentralization of the schooling function is made more complex by the fact that since Colonial times schools have been largely funded and controlled locally.

The 'Old Deluder Satan Act' which established schools in the theocratic Massachusetts Bay Colony in the seventeenth century was a prototype, not only for the political organization of schooling in the USA, but also for the role of the teacher as servant to the prevailing beliefs of the community. Louis Rubin (1979) identifies an important way in which teaching differs from other professions and crafts:

> Teachers and administrators are beholden, not only to the ethics of their craft and their personal convictions, but to the expectations of their clients and the general good of the social order. It is this dual

allegiance, among other things, that tends to distinguish them from other professional practicioners (p. 31).

The school is, in part, a socio-political system which is the center of society's competing ideological forces and structures, and professional development activities for educators reflect the tensions among these competing forces.

Public education in the USA remains largely under state control. Local school districts working within state mandates establish school district policies. Pre-service teacher education is also under the jurisdiction of the states. Applying standards established by professional organizations and in compliance with state directives, schools and colleges of education prepare individuals for certification as teachers. Policies governing schooling in general and teacher education in particular reflect a variety of directives. These directives include federal legislative and judicial mandates, state regulations, standards established by professional organizations, and individual university and college requirements. Thus, a basic policy-making and policy implementation structure exists.

While most areas of educational activity have been clearly institutionalized and placed under well-developed systems of control and regulation, in-service education is an area that as yet does not show clear patterns of structure, governance, and delivery. Harris (1980) observes:

> There is a growing and urgent need for a legal framework for inservice education in many states that is more comprehensive and more internally consistent than the present statutes (p. 201).

> Local district policy regarding in-service education tends to be nonexistent or fragmentary in most school systems. This is true in spite of the widespread delegation of authority by state law or policy to local school districts (p. 210).

In such a context, in-service education is more subject to the pull of competing ideological forces and more likely to be designed according to current social or political pressures rather than reflect a systematic structure or educational policy. Also, the fact that in-service education continues to be the 'stepchild' of professional education results both in limits on funding and erratic funding patterns. While in some states remarkable programs exist, grounded on a growing body of research, in-service education remains fragmented and devoid of any dominant educational policy to guide it.

Thus, discussions about in-service education represent the search for appropriate governance procedures amid conflicts among competing political factions, advocacy statements representing a variety of ideological viewpoints, and consistent exploration for ways to establish effective and appropriate institutional means to generate policies, controls, and guidelines for practice. As interest in in-service education grows, various groups involved in the educational endeavor are competing for political control or for ways to establish an effective collaboration system.

Some Changing Paradigms and Their Ideological Assumptions

Reality is socially constructed. In their seminal work on the sociology of knowledge, Berger and Luckmann (1967) observe:

> What is 'real' to a Tibetan monk may not be 'real' to an American businessman. The 'knowledge' of the criminal differs from the 'knowledge' of the criminologist. It follows that specific agglomerations of 'reality' and 'knowledge' pertain to specific social contexts, and that these relationships will have to be included in an adequate sociological analysis of these contexts (p. 3).

Further in their analysis they note that some forms of secondary socialization occur when individuals become members of professional groups and adopt the appropriate 'realities' that dominate the group. They write:

> Secondary socialization requires the acquisition of role-specific vocabularies, which means, for one thing, the internalization of semantic fields structuring routine interpretations and conduct within an institutional area. At the same time, 'tacit understandings', evaluations and affective colorations of these semantic fields are also acquired (Berger and Luckmann, 1967, p. 138).

The knowledge base which serves as ideational legitimation of a professional field will reflect historical patterns, intellectual predispositions, social prejudices, and influences exerted by referent groups and will contain elements which can be either functional or dysfunctional as members perform their activities.

The complex ideological system that serves to legitimize and maintain schooling has been labeled *educationism* and its history parallels the development of formal education. Teacher education serves in large part to socialize individuals who desire to become teachers into the folkways and 'realities' of the profession. Increasingly, however, as professional educators move towards the twenty-first century, some of the assumptions inherent in the knowledge base which informs the professional socialization of teachers are being called into question.

Some of these traditional ways of viewing schools have served to inhibit rather than enhance the development of effective in-service education programs. When aspects of belief systems which serve as the ideational base for professional activity fail to change with changing conditions, they should be obviated or transformed. Schools have been particularly resistant to change (Goodlad, 1983; Sarason, 1971), in part, because of ideological ossification. The purpose of this section is to identify and discuss briefly four of the paradigms and the ideological assumptions that serve as conceptual anchors in describing educational activity that seem to inhibit effective professional development efforts. The paradigms each employ a conceptual distinction which limits the construction of a 'nomological network of ideas' (Gage, 1963, pp. 63–4) which can describe the interaction of many factors in a social context. Along with their ideological and institutional underpinnings the distinctions are as follows: between school and society; between pre-service and in-service education; between teaching and learning; and between individual and social aspects of identity.

School and Society

At the heart of policy issues and problems in education generally, and staff development in particular, is the school-and-society model which represents the school as *the* educational institution in the social milieu and focuses on schooling as if it represented *the total educational function* in society.

Within the school and society model are diverse and often conflicting conceptions of the relationship between schools and the society of which they are a part. Some, for example, assume that the school is a mirror of society. Others envision it as a fortress characterized by a resistance to social change. And, still others regard it as an agency charged with the reconstruction of society. In addition, the school and society model may lead to a view of the school as a processing center through which input matter is transformed into a desired product. While there is some truth in each of these perspectives, they can and do form the basis for conflicting policies and programs. Whatever positive consequences have been generated by utilizing the school and society model, one cannot escape the fact that it leads attention away from important educational forces which influence teachers and learners. The model of the school as an island in a cultural sea distorts accurate perceptions of the educational life of the community and serves to camouflage significant aspects of the educational function in society. It has been especially dysfunctional in dealing with those educational forces which are a consequence of American cultural diversity (Yeakey and Gordon, 1982). The fact that the school exists in a dynamic relationship with other educational institutions, some of which may also influence learners significantly, is often ignored in educational research. Minimizing or negating such influences when studying systems of accountability, for example, especially when some of these institutions may reflect goals which are antithetical to schooling, is unconscionable.

The centrality of public schooling in modern societies cannot be denied, nor should it be ignored. However, to generalize this centrality into a monistic model of education is to ignore educational reality and to threaten the effectiveness, if not the survival, of public schooling.

As the USA moved from an agricultural society toward an urbanized industrial system, the relationship between the educational function and other socialization functions of the society changed. The school, especially the public school, emerged as a dominant structural adaptation to the more complex socialization necessitated by industrialism. This change was accompanied by the emergence of an educational ideological thrust which supported public, compulsory, and comprehensive schooling. The common school tradition devolved into a popular and profoundly effective educational ideology rooted to the school and society paradigm. This paradigm not only served as a conceptual foundation for popularizing public schooling, but also generated numerous scholarly works which supported and extended the professionalization of teaching.

As the American civilization moves rapidly from an industrial towards a high-technology society, a shift in institutional patterns can also be detected. The shift away from the biological nuclear family as the dominant family structure, for example, has been well documented (Ginsberg, 1960; Ross and Sawhill, 1975). Similarly, the social organization of economic, religious, and political institutions has altered significantly in recent years. The exponential growth of educational programs and activities in multiple settings represents a similar structural shift which is, in part, an adaptation to the realities of a technological society. The school as reflecting and supporting an industrial model of society must be relegated to the dustbin of history.

These shifts do not necessarily imply a diminishing role for compulsory schooling, although some advocates of voucher systems and home-based education suggest such a goal as desirable (Catterall, 1984; Holt, 1983). It does imply, however, that the role of the public school system *vis à vis* a changing society will be altered. It implies significant changes in the curricula of schools as well as a reconceptualization of the purpose of schooling in the society. Such a reconceptualization is especially needed in efforts to adapt the American high school to the exigencies of a high technology society. It may imply, for example, that public schools emerge as agencies for assisting learners in selecting, analyzing, and monitoring educational activities which influence their development. It may also imply an altered role for teachers, one which requires effective in-service education.

Because of the dominance of the school and society model our usual definition of education is distorted in that it equates schooling with *deliberate education*. Cremin (1976) broadly defines deliberate education as: 'The deliberate, systematic, and sustained effort to transmit, evoke, or acquire knowledge, attitudes, values, skills, or sensibilities, as well as any outcome of that effort' (p. 27). It is obvious that education occurs in a variety of settings. Indeed, the setting becomes an integral part of the teaching–learning process. Unfortunately, by equating schooling with education we have virtually destroyed the chances of developing a realistic educational approach to significant social issues especially as they have an impact on children and youth. Not only does the focus upon schooling distort our perspectives but it also limits our research potential. Unfortunately, most research on education focuses upon the school and confuses the folkways of schooling with the dynamics of the educational process. In contrast, Howe (1977) provides a perspective which may be more suited to new models of professional development in the post modern world. He writes: 'Many forms of learning which are given little or no attention in educational institutions have a vital role in adult life .... It is undeniably important to know about learning which normally occurs in everyday life, away from schools and colleges' (p. xiii). In-service education activities that either focus solely on institutional realities or the individual-as-a-professional and do not take into account the complexity of learnings which an individual brings to the activity are doomed to failure.

While some studies of educational processes as they occur in other settings (e.g., home or church) do exist (Leichter, 1979), rarely are these studies related to research about education as it occurs in the school. Since many in-service programs are designed to bring about changes that are affected by educational activity in these other settings, a broadened perspective of education is needed. As Cremin (1976) observed, the educational configuration that includes such deliberate education settings as the home, the school, the church, or the community center is virtually ignored in research. He writes:

> I mean rather to urge that we go beyond studies that analyze the family or the church or the school or television in isolation and then pronounce on their educational effects, and beyond studies that scrutinize people through a single lens of class or race or religion or ethnicity and, once again pronounce on educational outcomes. Individual institutions and individual variables are important to be sure; but it is the ways in which they pattern themselves and relate to one another that give them their educational significance, and the ways in which their outcomes confirm, complement, or contradict one another that determine their educational effects (p. 128).

The isolation and insulation from other forces of education as it occurs in schools distorts our perspective and creates a fortress mentality when confronting a call for changes from outside agencies. Education as a social institution in the USA is not confined to schooling, but is comprised of a network of diverse educative and educational settings. Such networks of educational configurations (Cremin, 1976), or patterns of educational content and resources which exist on many levels, are important but little regarded factors in shaping educational services. Relations among educational settings and professional educators can provide the basis for on-going dialogue and collaborative efforts or they can serve as pathways and channels for conflict and competition. Issues of schooling cannot be understood effectively in isolation from the patterns of educational activity of which they are a complementary or competing part. This may be particularly true of professional development, which often reaches outside the school for content and personnel. Indeed, observance that 'new configurations of staff development purpose and activity have emerged' (Griffin, 1983, p. 5) supports the notion that the changing nature of educational perspectives requires a broader view of the educational enterprise than is traditionally taken.

The nature of the way we have conceptualized educational activities and research questions about education reflects ideational predispositions. For example, influential sociological studies about education such as the Coleman Report (Coleman *et al.,* 1966), which influenced significantly the character of educational debates and legislation in the late 1960s, were based on process-product research models. Hallinan (1985) observes:

> One area of sociology of education that has commanded considerable attention over the past two decades is *educational productivity.* The use of this term and its associated *input-output model* shows the influence of economists on schools (p. 35).

> Moreover, the theoretical weaknesses of the research make it extremely difficult to interpret the results in a consistent way so as to infer policy decisions about schools and schooling. The state of the research is such that empirical results can be used to support whatever political position is being espoused by persons making decisions about schools (p. 49).

Many current reform proposals utilize such a basis for determining whether schools are effective. In some cases, such as in the document *A Nation at Risk* (National Commission on Excellence in Education, 1983), a model is utilized that compares American student achievements to those of students in other nations. This approach, when it does not take into consideration both the perceptual realities of participants and the critical analyses of an observer trained in ethnographic skills, serves to distort rather than clarify the condition of education.

Pre-service and In-service

A second major assumption that has guided teacher education has been the view that successful completion of a pre-service teacher education program provides an individual with the status and knowledge required to be a teacher. A correlate of this assumption is that such a status, once achieved, will establish positional authority for the duration of one's career. This assumption is rooted to the distinction between pre-service and in-service education. Because of the manner in which teacher education developed in the USA, with a focus on the accreditation of teacher education pre-service programs within college and university settings, and the licensing of students upon completion of pre-service teacher education programs, the link between preservice and in-service education has been tenuous. Even in those cases where teacher educators provide in-service educational programs either in the university setting or in the school, programs generally remain organizationally and conceptually separate from preservice activities. Rarely do pre-service and in-service students meet one another in planned activity within a university or school setting. Margaret Lindsey (1978) observed this unfortunate state of affairs in relationship to the neophyte teacher. She writes:

> Current developments suggest redefinition of certain notions about teacher education. Traditionally, the line between preservice and in-service teacher education has been arbitrary and distinct. For the most part, college and university personnel have assumed responsibility for preparation of a young person during his college years and have abruptly ceased concern for his welfare once he was placed in his first year of teaching. At this point, school personnel have taken over responsibility. The gap between preservice preparation and first years of teaching has long been recognized as undesirable (p. 138).

This bifurcation of professional development continues to the present day and is a major source of problems in conceptualizing and designing realistic and effective professional educational activities. For example, the belief that pre-service education *fully prepares* an individual to teach is unfortunate, in that it serves to encourage resistance to in-service programs by individuals who view such efforts as questioning their competence. Moreover, because shifts in assumptions about professional development accompany current debates about education, concerns about accountability, merit pay, bonuses, differentiated staffing and national testing of teachers necessitate a re-evaluation of the separation of pre-service and in-service education. An ideological shift in conceptualizing the professional education of teachers appears to be occurring and offers promise of generating significant changes in the way that educational policies and practices will be developed in the years to come. One basis of this ideological shift is rooted to significant changes in the infrastructure of society.

Three dimensions of social life influence the way in which human activities are conducted. First, the infrastructure of the society, that is, the technological base, defines not only the modes of production but also the way in which information is processed and designed. Second, the structure of the society, that is, the various institutions and the way they are related, defines the social mechanisms by which the society both reproduces itself and handles change. Finally, the superstructure, that is, the belief systems, values, and directives, provide the ideological foundation for defining social processes and social goals.

Changes in any of the three dimensions force changes in other dimensions. While the degree to which change is necessitated by shifts in technology, for example, is problematic, it is undeniably the case that influences are felt throughout the social system when new technological innovations are introduced.

Peter Berger (1977) has identified two major characteristics of the modern and post-modern era: *bureaucraticization,* and *technological complexity*. Innovations in both areas have had an impact on education, but technological innovations may be the more fundamental. Perhaps the most important of these have been the effect of a mediated culture on the society, the changes in which information is processed, and the utilization of mediated ways of effecting individual development.

The move toward a more complex technological society, for example, has altered assumptions about learning. Increasingly, education is viewed as a lifelong process, both because individuals may be preparing for a succession of work and/or professional roles in their lifetimes (Sarason, 1977), and because rapid technological change itself creates the need for continuous education and re-education. One result is that all professional fields are moving toward a continuous professional development model. For example, changes generated by the technological and information revolutions necessitate that physicians and other medical personnel undergo continuous updating in medical technology. Realtors are required to participate in on-going training in order to remain abreast of changes in legal as well as technical bases of their occupation. And, the environments in which business and industry in the country operate are changing so fast that a whole new entrepreneurial education/training industry is emerging to satisfy demand for educational services in the corporate world, some of which are being shared by schools (Houston, 1987).

Accompanying the increase in technological complexity is the belief that society is dependent upon professionalism and expertise to function properly. However, the definition of expertise depends more heavily on achieved than on ascribed status, and achievement increasingly rests on continuous education. Evidence of licensing does not suffice as a sign of competence in a high-technology society characterized by exponential growth in information. This is perhaps most apparent in the case of the 'expert', whose authority may very well rest not on the completion of a degree program at some past date, but rather on participation in timely and quite contemporary educational development activities. Expertise in many fields is no longer a status conferred, but a condition that must be maintained throughout one's professional career. 'Even if a fully qualified, ideally competent staff were available, *time* would gradually erode that competence as conditions change and old competencies become obsolescent' (Harris, 1980, p. 14).

The definition of expertise also depends, in part, upon one's ideological convictions. An example from schooling may make the point. Is the expert defined as an individual who has carefully and competently researched the relation between various teaching techniques and outcomes, or is the expert the individual who is the successful teacher demonstrating effectiveness in the classroom? Greenberg (1983) identifies a major and continuing tension in teacher education between the university and the classroom educator. He writes:

> Too often in the history of teacher education, higher education and local schools have been isolates, if not adversaries. The issues of control and status, as well as differences over substance, have been big factors. Moreover, the larger political and governance context in which each sector operates has incorporated an orientation or 'list' of priorities largely foreign to the other (p. 43).

This tension creates barriers to collaboration between teacher educators and classroom teachers which must be resolved. Indeed, much recent literature on staff development emphasizes the need for such collaboration (Dodd and Rosenbaum, 1986; Greenberg, 1983; Hanes, Wangberg and Yoder, 1982; Nash and Ducharme, 1983; Parkay, 1986). Current efforts to socialize and instruct teacher-researchers (Cross, 1987) are welcome and may help to alleviate some of the tension. However, clear problems exist for teachers who adopt new roles in the school, and one of the most severe is the question of mixed loyalties to the school, the university, and the profession. This concern will be explored in the final section of this analysis.

Teaching and Learning

The third distinction that has significantly influenced the development of educational policies and practice relates to the tendency to separate the teaching function from the learning activities within an educational activity. As formal educational activities become more complex and structured, the teaching–learning transaction is often analyzed by separating some of its elements. We all know, for example, that efforts to define accountability for teachers according to learning outcomes are often resisted by teachers. While it is commonly accepted that such resistance is due to the insecurity which such an evaluative scheme generates (which may or may not be the case), it is rarely attributed to the obvious transactional character of the teaching– learning process. Again, the input–output model serves to distort the quality of human transactions during teaching–learning interactions.

The reasons for this bifurcation of the teaching–learning transaction are due, in part, to a misconception about the foundations of education which are generally described as the academic disciplines devoted to the study of the nature of society, the nature of the individual, the nature of the learning process, and the nature of knowledge. Thus the 'Foundations of Education' courses offered by most teacher education programs are conceived as the sociology of education, the psychology of education, and a plethora of other formalized academic disciplines. This conception implies that the educational foundations are exclusively academic in nature, a perception that has been at the heart of persistent efforts to diminish the role of practice in teacher professional education. Margaret Lindsey, in 1978, asked:

> I wonder whether the real foundation is not to be found in professional practice. Is not *practice* the core and are not the *disciplines* now called foundational actually the supporting fields, the knowledge and methods that facilitate study of practice? (p. 5)

The foundation of education *is* the teaching–learning process as it occurs within an educational setting. It is the *transaction,* in all its complexity, which should be the focus in studying the fundamental nature of the teaching–learning process. 'Since the teaching–learning transaction exists in order to bring about some alterations in the perceptual world of the participants, it behooves researchers to analyze the nature of the dynamic transactional process in such a way that shifts in meaning, perceptions, and intentions can be detected and analyzed' (Bernier, 1981, p. 292). A naturalistic–ecological perspective based on qualitative phenomenological hypothesizing offers a fruitful approach to the study of education. Unless one maintains a rigorous hold on the contextual reality of teaching–learning, our research is in danger of becoming as gargoyles on the structure of knowledge.

As a consequence of the separation of the teaching and learning aspects of the educational transaction, a mode of perceiving the transaction which has dominated the field of education is one in which teaching is viewed as the act of doing something to someone else. Based on the transaction between a parent and child, this mode suggests that the teacher is an active agent while the learner is a passive recipient of knowledge. While this perspective has been effectively challenged by Progressives, it continues to dominate the educational arena. Invariably, teaching is defined as pedagogy. Malcolm Knowles (1978) has observed that educators often assume that adults learn in the same way as they perceive children to learn:

> These assumptions and beliefs (and blind spots) persisted through the ages well into the twentieth century. There was only one theoretical framework for all of education, for children and adults alike — pedagogy; in spite of the fact that pedagogy literally means the art and science of teaching children (p. 27).

Indeed, he goes on:

> Considering that the education of adults has been a concern of the human race for a very long time, it is curious that there has been so little thinking, investigating, and writing about adult learning until recently (p. 27).

Even a brief survey of library holdings dealing with educational psychology reveals that the adult learner continues to be a 'neglected species'. In schools and other educational settings adult learners have been infanticized and often denied the opportunity to participate actively as fully functioning individuals in the teaching–learning trans-action. Criticisms directed at in-service education activities often reflect resentment on the part of learners at being omitted from the planning process, or at the way in which the in-service activity is carried out. In either case, the learner is treated as a child. In recent years, a proliferation of books and research dealing with adult de-velopment has developed. Adult education programs gradually are appearing in various settings. It can be anticipated that as the median age of the population increases, concern for the adult learner will increase and that androgeny will become a foundation for teaching and research and the basis for inservice education. Androgeny requires that the unique learning styles of the participants serve as a base from which to develop educational opportunities. As Harry Kay (1977) observed:

> Without entering the controversies of learning theory, we can say with confidence that by the age of 18 the adult has not only established many of his patterns of learning, but that these are bound up with his individual personality. It is this link between the cognitive and affective elements that contributes to making the process permanent (p. 14).

Hope Jensen Leichter (1973) also stressed the importance of educative style and related it to the ways in which individuals 'initiate, search for, absorb, synthesize, and critically appraise the various educative influences in their environment' (p. 240). Included in her conception are 'modes of temporal integration, process of selecting for retention and re-examination, speed of learning, rates of interaction, manner of combining experiences, responses to cues, manner of appraising values, attitudes and knowledge, the scanning and searching for edu-cational opportunities, and individual strategies for dealing with embarrassment' (pp. 240–3).

As social systems become more complex, educational practices be-come more sophisticated. Unfortunately this process of refinement generally leads to a focus upon teaching rather than upon learning. Androgeny places learning at the center of the teaching–learning pro-cess and requires that teachers possess the flexibility and the percep-tiveness which enable them to adapt to the idiosyncratic learning styles of students. As biographies become more elaborate with age, so too do learning modes become more complex. Indeed, the phrase 'you cannot teach an old dog new tricks' should be viewed as a judgment on the inadequacies of the teaching mode rather than as a condemnation of the adult learner's capacity.

Individual and Social

A final distinction that informs professional education is a distinction between individual and social aspects of identity. It is a distinction which rests on a dependency in the field of education upon the discipline of psychology. Even a cursory analysis of teacher education programs and the content of the materials utilized in them will reveal that psychology as a discipline dominates educational literature and serves as a foundation for a preponderance of educational discourse. This dominance is historically rooted and should not be surprising since the focus of education has generally been on efforts to influence the development of individuals. This emphasis has served, however, to distort the relationship between education and social context. Social contextual factors are often ignored or distorted when filtered through the conceptual lenses of individuals nurtured within the discipline of psychology, or through education courses which are founded on psychological interpretations of behavior. Seymour B. Sarason, in his insightful work, *Psychology Misdirected* (1981), writes:

> Built into psychology, part of its world view, is the polarity man *and* society. Call it a polarity or a dichotomy or even a distinction, it makes it easy for psychology to focus on one and ignore the other, to avoid dealing with the possibility that the distinction is arbitrary and misleading, that it does violence to the fact that from the moment of birth the individual organism is a social organism, that social means embeddedness in patterned relationships that are but part of an array of such relationships, rooted, among other things, in a social history and a distinctive physical environment (p. 175).

The problem with this view is obvious and important, if little attended to. Indeed, Dewey (with Childs, 1933), who infrequently used strong language in writing, indicated his feelings on the subject with somewhat uncharacteristic emphasis: 'Social', he writes, 'cannot be opposed in fact or in idea to *individual*. Society *is* individuals-in-their-relations. An individual apart from social relations is a myth — or a monstrosity' (p. 291).

It is a characteristic of modern society that traditional boundaries between institutions and organizations are blurring and becoming indistinct (Schoen, 1971). In such a context, individuals-in-their-relations are less able to be perceived, or to perceive themselves, as apart from the plurality of contexts in which they function on a day-to-day basis. This means, among other things, that both teachers and learners bring with them to educational transactions not only the individual patterns of knowledge and learning which they have acquired in the past, but also the on-going influences that are increasingly difficult to ignore just because the individual is in a particular context for the moment. Perhaps nowhere is this more clearly seen than in the relations which teachers have with the professional cultures of which they are a part.

Cultures within the Profession

Patterns of activities which characterize organizational life 'constitute symbolic constructions which embody significant networks of meaning, through which patterns of social life are enacted, understood, and sustained' (Morgan, Frost and Pondy, 1983, p. 18). Schools are similar to other organizations in that they are culture-bearing settings. Louis (1983) writes: 'Organizations provide regularly-convening settings in which cultures may develop; and thus, an organizational setting is analogous to a petri dish' (p. 46).

Teachers belong to an occupational community and also perform their professional activities as actors in an organization. While the manifest functions of the school as an organization and the professional commitments and skills of the teacher are often in consonance, the latent functions of school organizations often conflict with professional educational goals. The literature concerning the hidden curriculum reveals clearly that latent functions of schools often serve to inhibit educational aims. While much of this literature focuses on the impact of the hidden curriculum on students, it also implies significant influences on teachers.

As schools have become more complex in structure and more bureaucratic in function, rational structural assumptions about the role of the teacher often create a context in which professional and organizational goals are at odds with one another. Lortie (1975) suggests that organizational realities rather than professional affiliation define the perceptions and behaviors of teachers especially in elementary schools. He also observes: 'The absence of a refined technical culture is evident in the talk of elementary school teachers' (Lortie, 1985, p. 232). He suggests that a professional culture has not yet developed. 'In view of the truncated nature of professionalization among elementary teachers, it seems highly unlikely that collegial ties play a major role in reducing the potency of hierarchical authority' (p. 232). Indeed, the phenomena of social isolation and social distance frequently experienced by teachers are in large measure a result of the organizational climate of the school and may serve to inhibit the emergence of an effective professional culture. Utilizing the concept 'locus of culture', Louis (1985) suggests that organizations are the seedbed of developing cultures. Thus, while Lortie did *not* find a professional culture in the elementary schools he studied, it is possible that such a culture may be in the process of developing. Louis (1985) continues: 'The term "locus of culture" rather than "unit of analysis" was chosen to reflect that there may or may not be an indigenous culture at any particular site. The term "locus" is used to signal that the specific site in question is *potentially* a site of a distinctive culture' (p. 78).

Staff development programs have been especially affected by this conflict, particularly in the areas of content and control. Nor are professional and organizational issues the only sources of difficulty. Teachers belong to and must consider their membership in a variety of cultural worlds which, for purposes of analysis, can be described in the following way. First, teachers are members of the organizational culture of the school, which has become ever more bureaucratic in structure. Second, they participate in the professional culture, as reflected by their membership in professional organizations, some of which are increasingly adopting industrial labor–management orientations toward school boards and administrators. Third, as they continue to participate in advanced formal education, they are members of the culture of teacher education, which is influenced significantly by pressures to assume greater academic disciplinary emphases.

While manifest conflict of intent, purpose, and direction among these cultures is relatively obvious, some important latent conflict is not. Although each culture group has the continuing improvement of education as a central priority, the modes and methods which each perceives as necessary for accomplishing such improvement may differ in significant and conflicting ways. Thus, a major issue confronting the emergence of professional development among teachers deals with the definition of phenomenological boundaries which will operate in shaping their programmatic direction and, ultimately, their effectiveness.

A major dilemma in education as a political enterprise rests on the conflict between organizational and professional or occupational assumptions. Recent suggestions for improving the effectiveness of schools and the competencies of teachers have focused largely on a utilitarian and organizational perspective (Feiman-Nemser, 1980; Fenstermacher, 1980; Zimpher & Ashburn, 1985). This perspective fits comfortably with the ideological assumptions of American society and thus has considerable popular support. Raelin (1986), in *The Clash of Cultures: Managers and Professionals,* observes the inevitable conflicts that occur when professionals must adapt to bureaucratic realities while struggling to maintain their professional autonomy. He concludes: 'The ideal is that one day professional accomplishment will become consonant with managerial proficiency' (p. 270). Recent emphasis on differentiated staffing, merit pay, and bonus systems reflect this general move from a communitarian (*gemeinschaft*) structure towards a bureaucratic/organizational and rational/utilitarian order (*gesellschaft*).

Van Maanen and Barley (1984) define occupational communities in a way which may clarify the struggle between organizational and occupational cultures:

> Our definition of occupational community contains four elements. Each is separate analytically but interconnected empirically. By occupational community, we mean a group of people who consider themselves to be engaged in the same sort of work; who identify (more or less positively) with their work; who share a set of values, norms, and perspectives that apply to, but extend beyond, work related matters; and whose social relationships meld the realms of work and leisure (pp. 294–5).

Much criticism of teachers is related to the fact that they perceive themselves as isolates within the school and that they choose to remain isolated within the school organization (Lortie, 1975). Teacher isolation is viewed both as an unfortunate characteristic of the teaching role, and as a result of the teacher's own choice. Perhaps, this isolation is not as dramatic as is frequently stated. Teachers, for the most part, remain professionally active through a variety of associations, through friendship networks as well as in personal professional development. Van Maanen and Barley (1984) observe:

> The ongoing struggle of stable and shifting, formal and informal, large and small groups to develop and occupy some niche in the

occupational structure of society is played out every day in organizations where rational and administrative principles of control
(e.g., codification, standardization, hierarchical discipline, etc.)
compete with traditional or communal principles of control (e.g.,
peer pressure, work ideology, valued symbols, etc.) (p. 290).

In considering the professional development of teachers, it is imperative that these two major thrusts in the lives of teachers be distinguished. Both represent important work realities, yet any analysis that
utilizes only one perspective (and organizational perspectives currently
dominate the field) distorts what is actually occurring and prevents the
development of broader and more realistic assessments of staff development.

Another aspect of the discrepancy between organizational and occupational perspectives is illustrated by Van Maanen and Barley (1984).
They write:

> From an organizational standpoint, most people are seen to regard
> their work careers largely in terms of movement (or lack thereof)
> within a set sequence of hierarchically ascending positions, each
> position offering more or less prestige, power, money and other
> rewards. Observers employing an occupational perspective imply
> that persons weave their perspectives on work and career from the
> existing social, moral, physical, and intellectual character of the
> work itself. Individual assessments of work and career are cast in
> terms of one's getting better (or worse) at what one does, getting
> support (or interference) from others, exerting more (or less) in-
> fluence over the nature of one's work, and so on (p. 289).

It is important to note, at this point, that the occupational (i.e.,
professional) perspective among teachers as it relates to staff development is clouded by the fact that a third significant party is often
involved in the process of staff development, the college of education.
While assumptions are often made, and at least lip service given, to
the 'shared professional culture' of teacher educators and teachers, the
organizational forces at work on members of teacher education faculties differ significantly from the organizational pressures on teachers.
In the academically oriented organizational milieu of the college or
university, for example, teacher educators struggle to maintain a professional identity when the praxis that is at the heart of their work is
viewed by many academic colleagues as lacking intellectual rigor

(Ducharme, 1985). On the other hand, classroom teachers must struggle to maintain a professional identity in a school organization often dominated by social and bureaucratic pressures which emphasize non-educational goals (Lytle, 1983), or educational goals that are non-academic. Pratt (1980), for example, notes that teachers value what he calls 'socialization goals', for pupils (e.g., extrinsic motivation, close attention to directions, careful completion of assignments and homework, and frequent testing) 'at least as as much as they value academic learning' (p. 77). Citing a study by Stake and Eisley (1978) he notes that 'teachers use academic content as a vehicle to reach socialization goals and often place these goals above academic learning' (Pratt, 1980, p. 77).

When teacher educators become involved in the professional development of teachers, whether in the college or university or in the school, the parties often find themselves at odds. Pratt (1980) writes: 'Because of the socialization demands, teachers seem to be caught between two systems, the scholarship system and the educational system, but they are much less at the mercy of the scholarship system' (p. 82).

For the teacher educator, the 'ivory tower' of the college of education is less a safe haven than an often dangerous parapet from which to participate in the ideological battle between academe and community, a battle in which the teacher educator may become the object of a fusillade from either or both seemingly opposing forces.

The reward systems and cultural expectations imposed on teacher educators are such that they will have difficulty sustaining their membership in the same occupational community that attempts to encompass teachers at all levels of the teaching profession. The move to establish teacher centers, and for teacher organizations to assume responsibility for staff development programs reveals, in part, a belief that teacher education institutions are *not* part of the school teacher community. Tragically, perhaps, this issue is being fought in the political and economic arena rather than at the philosophical or communitarian level.

At the same time, membership in a professional group does not imply that a sense of community exists. The psychological sense of community (Sarason, 1974) reflects a form of consciousness, a sense of belonging, a 'we-feeling'. Thus, community represents a form of affiliation and generates a sense of loyalty. While dominant loyalty may be to the organizational culture of the school, it may also extend beyond the school boundaries, resting in professional identification with subject matter specialty organizations. For example, the science teacher may have greater affiliation to a group of fellow science teachers than to other school colleagues. Some professional development activities, such as the science curriculum projects of the early 1960s, were based on this assumption. This may explain, in part, why effective building-level staff development programs in secondary schools may be more difficult to achieve than in elementary schools, where self-identification with the world within the classroom is shared by others in the school. Edelfelt (1978) observed:

> Engaging an entire faculty in inservice education on a voluntary basis probably does not happen easily in a school where most people have operated largely as individuals or members of small groups or departments. There is not much tradition for building a faculty as a team. The subject-centered curriculum, the size of many schools, the self-contained classroom, and teacher education contribute little to a conception of a group of teachers in the same building as a coordinated team (p. 9).

Similarly, teacher educators who work extensively with schools and classroom teachers may find that their membership identity in the university community is weakened both in their own view and in the view of their higher education colleagues, since prestige memberships within universities differ significantly from those within elementary and secondary schools.

Conclusions

The current social context of professional education reflects a variety of conflicting forces. Rapid technological changes have been accompanied by dramatic changes in institutional life. These changes, reflecting both commitment to democratic and pluralistic ideals and the need to adapt to rapidly changing environmental conditions, have produced a rich and sometimes confusing dialogue about American education in general and about teacher education in particular. Robert B. Howsam (1982), in *The Future of Teacher Education* explored possible scenarios concerning power and control in teacher education. He suggested three possible futures that could emerge based on three different perspectives: a professional perspective rooted to a collaboration among campus and field-based scholars and professionals; a workforce perspective dominated by the workplace reality and reflective of an organizational control model; and, a state monopoly perspective dominated by state agencies that would define the role of the teacher as a functionary. Calling for collaboration among professional organizations, Howsam expressed a belief that the traditions and institutional forces that favor a state monopoly model can be obviated. He hoped: 'Some, including this writer, have believed that those occupations with the essential characteristics of professions, including teaching, have a manifest destiny and will come into their own regardless of forces that are unfavorable' (pp. 5–6).

Ronald G. Corwin (1969) explored the character of the tension between bureaucratic-employee expectations and professional-employee expectations and observed that two variables significantly influence the process: the complexity of the organization, and the technical specialization of the employees. The greater the degree of complexity, the greater the control exerted by administrators and, conversely, the greater the degree of specialization the more control is placed in the hands of professional employees. In observing the move toward a more elaborate system of specialization in the field of education, and a concurrent increase in the complexity of the school as an organization, one can conclude that the issue of control remains problematic. Corwin observed, however, that some patterns were emerging, patterns that reveal a third significant factor, the issue of public influence and control over schooling. He wrote: 'Lay control is challenged simultaneously by the development of both conditions; and at the same time the concurrent development of specialization and complexity has fertilized the soil for conflict between administrators and professional employees' (pp. 218–19).

It is important to note, in this context, that proposals for reform of schooling reflect that conflict. In some areas, the public will continue to exert an important influence in American education and this influence will often be exerted at the local level. While such influence may reflect provincialism, and may inhibit, to some degree, rapid educational change, it serves both a democratic purpose and an educational ideal. As Raelin (1986) notes:

Over-professionalized professions may attempt to set up an artificial barrier between themselves and lay persons. They may become arrogant and paternalistic in their dealing with so-called nonexperts who may attempt to help solve problems using their intuitive judgment in a trial-and-error method. It has been shown, however, that nonexperts can make significant contributions to technical knowledge in four major areas: 1) problem identification, causal awareness, and diagnosis; 2) traditional knowledge, as in folk remedies; 3) inclusion of cultural elements and community needs in evaluating interventions; and 4) intuitive and personal knowledge (pp. 102–3).

Clearly, the solution in not in sight. Indeed, the data are not all in, and perhaps never may be. Forecasting the future based on the current ferment is a dangerous proposition. Economic and political factors can change rapidly and redefine the manner in which a society will adapt its educational system to changing needs and social conditions. What appears to be certain, however, is that the continuous professional development of teachers through in-service activities will become an established expectation and that legal and institutional factors which are currently emerging will form the base of a structure that will characterize such efforts in the future.

Professional staff development in education is at a crossroads. In one direction lies an arbitrary, imposed, pedagogically designed and bureaucratically structured delivery system that would result from political and economic debates rather than dialogues about educational policies and practices. In another direction lies participant-involved planning, collaborative efforts, shared authority and responsibility among the various educational communities and the public, and programs designed according to a view of lifelong learning designed for self-affirming adults who view their professional development as a vital aspect of their personal growth.

At stake is the development of a strong professional culture that is rooted to knowledge about the educational endeavor; that reflects a recognition that educators in all settings form a vital force both as individuals and collectively; that can serve to expand the application of democratic principles, extend educational opportunities and guide a pluralistic society towards a very promising future.

References

BERGER, P. (1977). *Facing up to modernity: Reflections on society, politics, and religion*. New York: Basic Books.

BERGER, P., and LUCKMANN, T. (1967). *The social construction of reality: A treatise in the sociology of knowledge*. Garden City, NY: Doubleday.

BERNIER, N. R. (1981). Beyond instructional context identification — Some thoughts for extending the analysis of deliberate education. In J. Green and C. Wallat (eds), *Ethnography and language in educational settings* (pp. 291–302). Norwood, NJ: Ablex.

BERNIER, N. R., and WILLIAMS, J. E. (1973). *Beyond beliefs: The ideological foundations of American education*. Englewood Cliffs, NJ: Prentice-Hall.

BROUDY, H. S. (1973). The role of foundational studies in the preparation of elementary teachers. In M. Gillett and J. A. Laska (eds), *Foundation studies in education*. Metuchen, NJ: The Scarecrow Press.

BURRELLO, L. C., and ORBAUGH, T. (1982). Reducing the discrepancy between the known and the unknown in inservice education. *Phi Delta Kappan, 63*(6), 385–8.

CATTERALL, J. S. (1984). *Education vouchers*. Bloomington, IN: Phi Delta Kappa Educational Foundation.

CISTONE, P. J. (1977). Educational policy making. *The Educational Forum, 42,* 89–100.

COLE, R. W., JR. (1982). 'Inservice' is not a verb. *Phi Delta Kappan, 63*(6), 370.

COLEMAN, J. S., CAMPBELL, E. Q., HOBSON, C. J., MCPARTLAND, J., MOOD, A. M., WEINFIELD, F., and YORK, R. L. (1966). *Equality of educational opportunity*. Washington, DC: U.S. Government Printing Office.

CORWIN, R. G. (1969). Professional persons in public organizations. In F. Carver and T. J. Sergiovanni (eds), *Organizations and human behavior: Focus on schools*. New York: McGraw-Hill.

CREMIN, L. A. (1976). *Public education*. New York: Basic Books.

CREMIN, L. A. (1978). The education of the educating professions. *Teachers College Research Bulletin, 18*(3), pp. 1–8.

CROSS, K. P. (1987). The adventures of education in wonderland: Implementing education reform. *Phi Delta Kappan, 68*(7), 496–502.

DEVITIS, J. L. (1976). Educational policy studies: Quest for consistency? *Educational Studies, 7,* 345–50.

DEWEY, J., and CHILDS, J. C. (1933). The underlying philosophy of education. In W. N. Kilpatrick (ed.), *The educational frontier*. New York: Appleton-Century.

DODD, A. W. and ROSENBAUM, E. (1986). Learning communities for curriculum and staff development. *Phi Delta Kappan, 67*(5), 380–4.

DUCHARME, E. R. (1985). Establishing the place of teacher education in the university. *Journal of Teacher Education, 36*(4), 8–11.

EDELFELT, R. (1978). Considerations for developing local inservice education programs. In R. A. Edelfelt (ed.), *Inservice education: Demonstrating local programs*. Bellingham, WA: Western Washington University.

ELMORE, R. F. and MCLAUGHLIN, M. W. (1982). Strategic choice in federal educational policy: The compliance-assistance trade-off. In A. Leiberman and M. W. McLaughlin (eds), *Policy making in education: Eighty first yearbook of the National Society for the Study of Education, Part I* (pp. 159–94). Chicago: National Society for the Study of Education.

FEIMAN-NEMSER, S. (1980). Growth and reflection as aims in teacher education: Directions for research. In G. E. Hall, S. M. Hord, and G. Brown (eds), *Exploring issues in teacher education: Questions for future research* (pp. 133–52). Austin, TX: University of Texas Research and Development Center for Teacher Education.

FENSTERMACHER, G. D. (1980). What needs to be known about what teachers need to know. In G. E. Hall, S. M. Hord, and G. Brown (eds), *Exploring issues in teacher education: Questions for future research* (pp. 35–49). Austin, TX: University of Texas Research and Development Center for Teacher Education.

FISCHER, L. (1982). The courts and educational policy. In A. Leiberman and M. W. McLaughlin (eds), *Policy making in education: Eighty-first yearbook of the National Society for the Study of Education, Part I* (pp. 56–79). Chicago: National Society for the Study of Education.

GAGE, N. L. (ed.) (1963). *Handbook of research on teaching.* Chicago: Rand McNally.

GINSBERG, E. (ed.) (1960). *The nation's children.* New York: Columbia University Press.

GOODLAD, J. I. (1983). *A place called school.* New York: McGraw-Hill.

GREEN, T. F. (1980). *Predicting the behavior of the educational system.* Syracuse: Syracuse University Press.

GREENBERG, J. D. (1983). Connections and tensions: Preservice-beginning teaching-inservice. *Journal of Teacher Education, 34*(2), 38–43.

GRIFFIN, G. A. (1983). Introduction: The work of staff development. In G. A. Griffin, (ed.), Staff development (pp. 1–12) *Eighty-second Yearbook of the National Society for the Study of Education, Part II.* Chicago: University of Chicago Press.

GUBA, E. G. (1984). The effect of definitions of policy on the nature and outcomes of policy analysis. *Educational Leadership, 41,* 63–70.

HALL, G. E., and LOUCKS, S. F. (1982). Bridging the gap: Policy research rooted in practice. In A. Leiberman and M. W. McLaughlin (eds), *Policy making in education: Eighty-first yearbook of the National Society for the Study of Education, Part I* (pp. 133–58). Chicago: The National Society for the Study of Education.

HALLINAN, M. T. (1985). Sociology of education: The state of the art. In J. H. Ballantine (ed.) *Schools and society* (pp. 33–51). Palo Alto, CA: Mayfield.

HANES, M. L., WANGBERG, E. G., and YODER, P. (1982). University/school district partnership in professional development: A model. *Phi Delta Kappan 63*(6), 388–90.

HANSOT, E., and TYACK, D. (1982). Using history in educational policy. In A. Leiberman and M. W. McLaughlin (eds), *Policy making in education: Eighty-first yearbook of the National Society for the Study of Education, Part I* (pp. 133–58). Chicago: The National Society for the Study of Education.

HARRIS, B. (1980). *Improving staff performance through in-service education.* Boston: Allyn & Bacon.

HEATH, K. G. (1976). The making of federal education policy. *Educational Studies, 7,* 173–84.

HOLT, J. (1983). Schools and home schoolers: A fruitful partnership. *Phi Delta Kappan, 64*(6), 391–94.

HOUSTON, W. R. (1987). Lessons for teacher education from corporate practice. *Phi Delta Kappan, 68*(5), 388–92.

HOWE, M. J. A., (ed.) (1977). *Adult learning: Psychological research and applications.* New York: Wiley.

HOWSAM. R. B. (1982). The future of teacher education. *Journal of Teacher Education, 33*(4), 2–7.

KAY, H. (1977). Learning and society. In M. J. A. Howe (ed.) *Adult learning: Psychological research and applications* (pp. 5–19). New York: Wiley.

KNOWLES, M. (1978). *The adult learner: A neglected species.* Houston: Gulf.

LEICHTER, H. J. (1973). The concept of educative style. *Teachers College Record* 75(2), 239–50.

LEICHTER, H. J. (1979). Families and communities as educators: Some concepts of relationship. In H. J. Leichter (ed.), *Families and communities as educators* (pp. 2–94). New York: Teachers College Press.

LIEBERMAN, A. (1982). Practice makes policy: The tensions of school improvement. In A. Leiberman and M. W. McLaughlin (eds), *Policy making in education: Eighty first yearbook of the National Society for the Study of education, Part 1,* (pp. 249–69). Chicago: National Society for the Study of Education.

LINDSEY, M. (ed.) (1961). *New horizons for the teaching profession.* Washington, D. C.: National Commission on Teacher Education and Professional Standards, National Education Association of the United States.

LINDSEY, M. (1978). The professional scholar as teacher: A conception. In E. Hunter (ed.), *Margaret Lindsey: A teacher educator speaks* (pp. 53–63). North Bergen, NJ: Friends of Margaret Lindsey.

LINDSEY, M. (1978). Teacher education: Some reflections. In E. Hunter (ed.), *Margaret Lindsey: A teacher educator speaks* (pp. 2–12). North Bergen, NJ: Friends of Margaret Lindsey.

LORTIE, D. C. (1975). *Schoolteacher: A sociological study.* Chicago: University of Chicago Press.

LORTIE, D. C. (1985). The partial professionalization of elementary teaching. In J. H. Ballentine (ed.), *Schools and society* (pp. 226–33). Palo Alto, CA: Mayfield.

LOUIS, M. R. (1983). Organizations as culture-bearing milieux. In L. R. Pondy *et al.* (eds), *Organizational symbolism* (pp. 39–54). Greenwich, CN: JAI Press.

LOUIS, M. R. (1985). An investigator's guide to workplace culture. In P. J. Frost *et al.* (eds), *Organizational culture* (pp. 73–93). Beverly Hills: Sage.

LYONS, C. H. (1976). Educational policy, educational expertise and the AESA. *Education Studies, 7,* 143–68.

LYTLE, J. H. (1983). Investment options for inservice teacher training. *Journal of Teacher Education, 34*(1), 28–31.

MEYER, A. (1957). *An educational history of the American people.* New York: McGraw-Hill.

MONSEN, R. J., JR., and CANNON, M. W. (1965). *The makers of public policy: American power groups and their ideologies.* New York: McGraw-Hill.

MORGAN, G., FROST, P. G., and PONDY, L. R. (1983). Organizational symbolism. In L. R. Pondy, P. J. Frost, G. Morgan, and T. C. Dandridge (eds). *Organizational symbolism* (pp.3–25). Greenwich, CT: JAI Press.

NASH, R. J., and DUCHARME, E. R. (1983). The paucity of the investment metaphor and other misunderstandings. *Journal of Teacher Education, 34*(1), 33–6.

National Commission on Excellence in Education. (1983). *A nation at risk: The imperative for educational reform* (GPO Publication No. 065-000-00177-2). Washington, DC: U.S. Government Printing Office.

PARKAY, F. W. (1986). A school/university partnership that fosters inquiry-oriented staff development. *Phi Delta Kappan, 67*(5), 368–9.

PRATT, H. (1980). Selecting content for inservice education programs. In G. E. Hall, S. M. Hord, and G. Brown (eds), *Exploring issues in teacher education: Questions for future research* (pp. 75–90). Austin, TX: University of Texas Research and Development Center for Teacher Education.

RAELIN, J. (1986). *The clash of cultures: Managers and professionals.* Boston: Harvard Business School Press.

REAGAN, G. M. (1976). Some notes on the uses of social science inquiry in formulating and evaluating educational policy. *Educational Studies, 7*, 155–68.

RICH, J. M. (1976–77). The dimensions of educational policy. *Educational Studies, 7*, pp. 337–42.

ROSS, H. L., and SAWHILL, I. V. (1975). *Time of transition: The growth of families headed by women.* Washington, DC: Urban Institute.

RUBIN, L. (1979). Continuing professional education in perspective. In L. Rubin (ed.), *The in-service education of teachers: Trends, processes, and prescriptions.* Boston: Allyn & Bacon.

RUSCOE, G. C. (1976). Some questions about educational policy and the social sciences. *Educational Studies, 7*, 135–42.

SARASON, S. B. (1971). *The culture of the school and the problem of change.* Boston: Allyn & Bacon.

SARASON, S. B. (1974). *The psychological sense of community: Prospects for a community psychology.* (1977). San Francisco: Jossey-Bass.

SARASON, S. B. (1977). *Work, aging and social change.* New York: The Free Press.

SARASON, S. B. (1981). *Psychology misdirected.* New York: The Free Press.

SARASON, S. B., and DORIS, J. (1982). Public policy and the handicapped: The case of mainstreaming. In A. Leiberman and M. J. McLaughlin (eds), *Policy making in education: Eighty-first yearbook of the National Society for the Study of Education, Part I* (pp. 23–55). Chicago: National Society for the Study of Education.

SAYLOR, J. G. (1976). *Antecedent developments in the movement to performance-based programs in teacher education.* Lincoln, NE: Prepared as a working document for the Committee on Performance-based Teacher Education, American Association of Colleges of Teacher Education, The L and S Center.

SCHOEN, D. A. (1971). *Beyond the stable state.* New York: Random House.

STAKE, R., and EASLEY, J. (1978). *Case studies in science education.* Urbana-Champaign: Center for Instructional Research and Curriculum Evaluation, University of Illinois.

Standards for Academic and Professional Instruction in Foundations of Education. (1978). *Educational Studies, 8,* 329–35.

STANLEY, W. O. (1953). *Education and social integration.* New York: Bureau of Publications, Teacher College, Columbia University.

THOMAS, N. C. (1975). *Education in national politics.* New York: Yeager McKay Co.

VAN MAANEN, J., and BARLEY, S. R. (1984). Occupational communities: Culture and control in organizations. In B. M. Staw and L. L. Cummings (eds) *Research in organizational behavior,* 6 (pp. 287–365). Greenwich, CN: JAI Press.

YEAKEY, C. C. and GORDON, E. W. (1982). The policy implications of status variables and schooling. In A. Lieberman and M. W. McLaughlin (eds), *Policy making in education: Eighty-first yearbook of the National Society for the Study of Education, Part I* (pp. 105–32).

ZIGLER, E., and KAGAN S. L. (1982). Child development knowledge and educational practice: Using what we know. In A. Lieberman and M. W. McLaughlin (eds), *Policy making in education: Eighty-first yearbook of the National Society for the Study of Education, Part I* (pp. 80–104). Chicago: The National Society for the Study of Education.

ZIMPHER, N. L., and ASHBURN E. A. (1985). Studying the professional development of teachers: How conceptions of the world inform the research agenda. *Journal of Teacher Education, 36*(6), 16–26.

3   The Influence of Competing Cultures on Teacher Development

Martin Haberman

Attempts to improve teachers tend to focus on improved pedagogy, more subject matter, individual growth, or in rare cases on general studies for civic responsibility. Pedagogy refers to providing teachers with specific instructional skills as well as knowledge of children's learning, growth and development. More subject matter refers to the persistent and widespread assumption that what teachers really need in order to increase their pupils' achievement is more expertise in the subject(s) they teach. Teacher growth refers to the strong tradition in teacher education that if teachers were better people — more humane, with greater self understanding, more reflective, more sensitive, more empathetic, more fully self-actualized — they would inevitably be better teachers. General studies and civic responsibility refers to the contention that teachers are apolitical, uninvolved in their communities, and essentially non-participants as citizens; to be 'developed', teachers need more knowledge of how the economy, government and society function, as well as the critical thinking skills for integrating this knowledge and applying it to the problems of living.

It is my contention that universities in the USA reflect value theories basic to American society. The liberal arts, professional and general studies which coexist in the modern university are derived from the belief systems which characterize the general culture. I would contend that the university-based study of pedagogy reflects the American value patterns which advocate achievement and success, activity and work, efficiency and practicality, material comfort, science and secular rationality. On the other hand, the development of the liberal arts college and the modern university as the primary societal institution, in which individuals may actualize their potentialities and personal proclivity, reflects the American patterns related to the values of individual personality, humanitarian mores, equality and freedom. Finally, the development of citizen responsibility and critical thinking (i.e., the civic arts) in the general studies programs of universities reflects the societal value patterns which undergird our commitments to democratic institutions and the concept of the common good.

This chapter traces the cultural antecedents which are used to justify the use of these approaches with teachers and will argue that these cultural themes have been a major force in shaping North American universities, the curricula of lower schools, and the content of teacher education programs. Based on this analysis, predictions will be made regarding which approaches to teacher development will continue in the future as dominant practices and which will be of less importance.

Individualism, The Liberal Arts and Teacher Development

In tracing the set of values which comprise the American vision of individualism, several things become clear. There are different versions of individualism which are ambiguous and even contradictory. Bellah *et al.* (1985) discusses four types of individualism: Biblical, civic, utilitarian, and expressive. Briefly, biblical individualism grows out of the responsibility and accountability believed to be lodged in each individual in relation to God. Civic individualism refers to the legal and political rights which are the foundation of the concept 'citizen' in a democratic society. Utilitarian individualism is an economic set of values that undergird the belief that if individuals pursue their economic self interests the society as a whole will best be served. Expressive individualism refers to the search for personal meaning (psychological, artistic, developmental) which has become so very characteristic of modern American society. There is even a fifth definition — mythic individualism — embodied in the legend of the cowboy and in other American folk heroes; the self-made, inner directed person who is supposedly free of restraints.

The values related to individualism were first manifest in the earliest development of the American university. In describing the University of Virginia, Jefferson made it clear that he did not believe any student should study any course unless he felt like it, and although Jefferson was not credited by the students of the 1960s, his view of a self-selected curriculum qualified him as a colonial hippie. In truth Jefferson was simply pre-Carl Rogers in his view that genuine learning must utilize students' interests, predispositions, and little else. It fell to

President Eliot to establish Harvard as one of the first institutions to make the elective course an acceptable part of college students' curriculum (Morrison, 1930).

As far as university organization is concerned, therefore, the spirit of individualism is embodied in the college of liberal arts and to a lesser extent, in the college of fine arts. By definition, professional colleges (e.g., engineering, agriculture, medicine, law, education, etc.) are filled with course and other requirements which must be met before the particular profession will accept a graduate as a *bona fide* practitioner. It does not matter what a future nurse, librarian, or architect 'feels' like studying, as much as what the practicing profession decides the neophyte *must* study. The primary goal of professional education is not the individual fulfillment of the practitioner but the protection of service to the public, and the willingness of those already in the profession to accept as a colleague a beginner who has demonstrated proficiencies similar to their own. This role of the liberal arts colleges as the primary home for academic individualists, therefore, is not only a function of liberal arts faculties reaching out to cultivate students in their individualism, but also the result of professional schools being unreceptive to students whose highest priority is pursuing their own inclinations and finding themselves. Indeed, it is becoming increasingly common for liberal arts colleges to be 'home' for a large body of students who cannot gain admission to professional schools, or who cannot decide on a profession but who are as fixated on an education leading to a job as those admitted to professional schools. For the avowed liberal arts student, however, there is the perception that academic specialization (i.e., majoring in a liberal art) by virtue of not leading to a particular career is evidence that one is doing one's thing and developing inclinations and predispositions without the inevitable impositions that accrue from knuckling under to some form of professional preparation.

In the universities of the eighteenth and nineteenth centuries the very clear and agreed-upon purpose of university education was preparation for leadership. Affluent males studied for the divinity and took the trivium (grammar, logic, and rhetoric) and quadrivium (geometry, astronomy, arithmetic, and music). As ministers or statesmen, graduates were expected to be leaders in this world, in the next, or in both. There were no professions which required university preparation. Only those males who were unconcerned about their immediate support and a future job could afford the luxury of attending a university. It was admittedly education for an elite student body, but an elite whose first purpose was defined as public service. There is a tragic, poignant quality in today's disadvantaged ethnic groups and lower socioeconomic constituencies who seek to become admitted to the status of liberal arts study without appreciating the history of such studies. I currently serve on the board of an inner-city high school which has adopted as its two specialty curricula, preparation for health fields (e.g., medical records clerks, nurses' aides, etc.) and a parallel program in the liberal arts. This liberal arts curriculum recognizes the need for status without an awareness of its historical meaning, or its anti-job training ethic.

In sum, today's liberal arts colleges are comprised of several types of individualists: those who can afford to pander to their interests, those unable to decide on a career, and those unable to enter a professional school. Taken together these individuals comprise a status elite within the university simply by virtue of the station in life held by the original student body and by the history of the American university.

In this century, strange mutations transformed the original subjects taught in the first liberal arts colleges. New fields of knowledge were developed (e.g., psychology, sociology) while other fields 'exploded' and were adopted into the curriculum (i.e., the natural sciences). Most importantly, the subjects that affluent people simply learned in non-university settings were also adopted as bona fide 'liberal arts'. Among these new liberal arts were studies which were the natural acquisition of rich and gentle folk: modern foreign languages, the discussion and writing of literature and poetry, the analysis of art and architecture, the ability to discuss philosophy, and the reading and writing of history.

In large public universities today's liberal arts colleges have as many as fifty departments, or more, including some which bear titles like Comparative Literature, Afro-American Studies, Women's Studies, Literary Criticism, Communication (in addition to Mass Communication) and even more amorphous titles such as Urban Studies, American Studies, and Twentieth Century Studies. The point, of course, is that in spite of the rhetoric about 'liberating' the mind it is possible — and quite common — for students to complete liberal arts majors with an extremely wide variance in the breadth and depth of their knowledge. At one extreme might be the student who spends two years (junior/senior years) 'majoring' in one subject only (e.g., mathematics), while another student becomes involved in broad, interdisciplinary studies with little advanced work in any one discipline. The only generalization that can be made about the liberal arts curricula now offered in over 2,200 colleges and universities is that they are all, by definition, higher status than teacher preparation programs offered anywhere. This status is a function of an elitist history, and in no way a function of who the wide range of present liberal arts students are, or what they know — or who the liberal arts faculties are, or what they know.

For the analysis here it is my contention that the liberal arts and their cultural roots must be understood in order to fully grasp the complex nature of American individualism as it is currently manifest in lower schools and among teachers. That the liberal arts college claims to produce individualists has been a clear and persistent theme. Graduates are perceived as not only having valuable knowledge but an enhanced self esteem; they are viewed as people who should have come to terms with themselves and their potentialities as a result of their liberating educations. Point: *When teacher education, pre- or in-service, permits individual teachers to self select which courses they will take as part of their professional development, it is operating in the cultural mode which emphasizes individual development and in the educational approach traditional in the liberal arts.* Similarly, when teachers regard the most useful *content* of their professional development to be studies which will enhance them as knowledgeable people (i.e., as individual scholars rather than as professional practitioners), they are living out this liberal arts history. The assumptions are clear: if each person is enhanced as an individual human being the practicing professions will be improved in total. On a pedestrian level this plays out as teachers being free to travel, enter psychoanalysis, or take courses in whatever they please as their in-service development since if they become more complete individuals (however defined) their teaching will inevitably improve. In the late 1950s and early 1960s *When Teachers Face Themselves* (Jersild, 1955) was the most popular book and the most popular in-service course. In the 1980s 'burnout' is still frequently cited as a widespread occupational disease. The process of content determination is the teacher's self-selection of courses. The goal of this work is a more fully actualized individual.

There are four confounding trends which enhance this cultural emphasis on individual development: (a) the fact that substantial numbers of liberal arts graduates are still prepared as teachers — teaching is the only major profession in America for which one can still be fully prepared and certified in an undergraduate liberal arts college; (b) the fact that liberal arts courses are still widely advocated as a basis for improving pedagogy (i.e., in-depth subject matter courses are still seriously proposed as solutions to the problems faced by classroom teachers); (c) the fact that liberal arts courses commonly define their major purpose as developing students' understanding of their personal, social, and physical world; and (d) the fact that numerous liberal arts courses actually do provide knowledge useful to teachers under non-pedagogic titles (e.g., writing, speaking, reading, multi-cultural communication skill, etc.).

But in spite of these confounding conditions which place liberal arts in a unique relationship with teaching as a profession, I would argue that the primary *cultural* influence exerted by the liberal arts has not been over the content of pedagogy or even over the curricula of the lower schools, but in its insistence on individual development and in its nurturance of the cultural ideal of the individual as the basic unit of educational analysis. Whether individual is defined in biblical, civic, utilitarian, or expressive modes, the institution which American society recognizes as *the* major preserver of the individualist tradition is the liberal arts college.

In summarizing the influence of competing cultures on teacher development I have tried to trace the relationship between the societal values which deal with individualism and assumptions of how to improve teachers. Following is a summary of these connections:

What are dominant value themes in the American culture which support individualism? Humanitarian values about the worth of each individual; equality as it is related to the law and equality of opportunity are both strong, recurrent value patterns; freedom to pursue a particular occupation and life style; and the worth of individual personality as an entity to be nurtured and enhanced are all basic value themes.

How might these value themes be stated as a goal? Teachers should be fully actualized, healthy individuals.

What type of education is assumed to be most likely to produce such individuals? A university level education emphasizing the liberal arts. In spite of core requirements for everyone there is wide opportunity for electives and an individual choice of major. Much of the content focuses on understanding both the human condition and the physical world as it impacts on individual development.

What kind of students are likely to self-select such education? Students whose highest priority is self development as well as those capable of benefiting from pursuing and developing their own abilities. Students who are not immediately concerned with occupational choice.

What kind of teacher education is offered by this approach? Emphasis is on subject matter mastery. Self-understanding is also assumed to occur as a result of the emphasis on individual development.

How are such teachers evaluated? On the basis of their knowledge of content as well as on their authenticity as people. Their concern with their own development is assumed to translate into a concern for others as individuals.

What kind of lower school curriculum does this cultural pattern foster? Individual achievement of established bodies of subject matter is primary. Children/youth will enhance themselves as people through school learning.

What kind of staff development would these value patterns lead to? Teachers study more liberal arts subject matter based on their specialization interests and perceived needs. Teachers pursue academic interests and advanced training which they determine will make them more knowledgeable and more fully realized individuals.

Teacher educators have, in my judgment, made a common error of separating the individualism which results from pursuing interest in liberal arts disciplines and the individualism which derives from self-study, whether formal psychoanalysis, reflective thinking, or avocational pursuits. All approaches which focus on the cognitive and the emotional development of the individual are assumed to be a fundamental aid to teaching children and youth.

What has been discussed here is an analysis not an advocacy. Practicing classroom teachers who want a salary increase for a junket to Acapulco are not being offered a rationale. This has been an effort to trace connections between fundamental value themes in the American culture to the development of the liberal arts and to what knowledge, therefore, is considered to be of most worth for teachers. Such tracing has led to the explanation that the strong and continuing liberal arts tradition which pushes those who control teachers to constantly advocate more subject matter is supported by an even stronger American value pattern related to various forms of individualism.

The Cultural Theme of Achievement and Success and Teacher Education

The only thing harder than understanding American value patterns is living them. There is a constant tension borne of trying to reconcile extremely strong cultural value patterns which pull in opposite directions. At war with the value pattern of individual development and the liberal arts is an even stronger set of 'shoulds' which lead Americans to behave as if the basic purpose, indeed the only purpose, for publicly supported education is preparation for the world of work. For the poor, this plays out as the basic skill curriculum of preschool, elementary and high school that leads to a job after high school graduation or into some form of post-secondary training. For the more affluent, this value is expressed and lived out as a view of college as a means of entering professional study and the pursuit of a higher status career. All study only has value as it moves students along toward a better job. The only difference among social classes is in the level of jobs being sought and in the amount of schooling that is required for the particular occupational level. There is no longer any widespread debate about this. Americans at every level and from all sectors share an agreed-upon goal for schools: *to prepare graduates for the world of work.* Any real differences which remain among high school dropouts, high school graduates and college graduates is merely the level, power, and salary of the particular jobs for which they are being prepared. The notion that society would tax itself at what it considers to be exorbitant rates to provide schools which develop better people, or which enhance individual proclivities, or which seek to educate active citizens of a democratic society, are 'theoretic' purposes no longer even debated in the media, by political or economic leaders, or by the public at large. In effect, what Americans have come to want of their schools (pre-school through graduate university levels) is no different from what is wanted by non-democratic and even anti-democratic societies. American students continually have their achievement scores compared with students in other societies and no one even raises the question that our schools should have (might have, could have) other basic purposes which are of equal, or even of greater importance, than preparing people for the role of employed taxpayer. As education became available to the masses, mass culture transformed it and substituted the values of pragmatism, utility, and achievement for the values of individual development and the civic arts — pursuits which do not have immediate payoff.

Popular epithets are a good indicator of our dominant social values. Americans more favorite terms of derogation include 'impractical', 'irrelevant', 'frills-and-fads', and 'theorizing'. The public support of secular education does not tolerate learning as an end; that is, learning that leads to more learning. As a result, the education of gentlemen, historical forms of erudition, and classical humanism fare rather poorly in comparison with vocational or scientific training. From typing to physics, and from cooking to chemistry, modern schooling — at all levels — is permeated by a strong utilitarian and pragmatic emphasis. Its basic purpose is not culture, scholarship, a well-rounded citizenry, or the self actualized individual advocated by existential philosophers. Anything other than a curriculum leading to jobs or careers is denigrated as a diversion or amusement. Schooling is a serious business and must answer the popular questions, 'What use is it?' and 'What can you do with it?' And most important of all, the masses who ask these questions and who judge the quality of the answers are not themselves broadly educated people. In effect, it is the people who are uneducated or undereducated who are most demanding of the coming generations with their 'What use is it?' 'What good is it?' This frequently plays out as the unemployed or underemployed parents demanding that their elementary schools put a higher priority on reading skills than on other subjects, or as the high school graduated parents of a college student asking, 'Why are you majoring in that?' 'What kind of job will that get you?'

Conflicting cultural trends are nothing new in American society or in our educational history. With the election of Andrew Jackson in 1828, government by the elite started to decline. Although Jackson was a rich cotton planter and slaveholder, he endeared himself both to the farm hands and the city proletariat. The mass of Americans saw him as one of their own, risen from the ranks. Jackson's election was the first in which almost all states allowed individuals to vote for president: henceforth, all election campaigns were to be addressed to the bulk of Americans. When the land grant universities were initiated in 1964 there was already a well-established pattern of the mass of people controlling the purposes of public education.

The industrial post-Civil War period saw the rise of technical schools, agricultural and mechanical schools for whites and blacks, and most of all, the development of professional schools (including normal schools for teachers) which were all to become twentieth-century universities or colleges within universities. It was inevitable that as the numbers of those engaged in post-secondary education increased, their values would come to dominate. Today, at even the most prestigious private universities, the graduate schools which educate the professionals are large, well-endowed institutions, and the undergraduate liberal arts colleges remain quite small and selective. To the sophisticated educational status seeker, the issue is not where one earns a doctorate or law degree, but where one attended as an undergraduate. How many people, and which ones, can afford to pay $50,000 per year to earn a liberal arts bachelor's degree that does not prepare graduates for a specific job?

The pathetic cry of the 45,000 professors of education who complain that pre-service and in-service teachers want only 'how-to', 'tricks-of-the-trade', and 'hands-on' experiences demonstrates a monumental ignorance. These values of immediacy, practicality, relevance, utility — all of which lead to occupational success and achievement — are precisely what most Americans want, not only from all their professional schools, but also from their elementary and high schools. Indeed, there would be no schools of education without the mundane, vocational, utilitarian values that the education professoriat denigrates in its students.

What this means for elementary and secondary schools is that job training is now a *super* value disproportionately more important than anything else the schools might claim as a goal. There are numerous manifestations of this trend but the most obvious is that the skills perceived as necessary for employment have become dominant to the point of driving out the rest of the school curriculum. Such perceived needs include basic reading and computational skills. Once the epicenter of a general education curriculum, the elementary school was developed to include sciences, social studies, the arts, physical education, even foreign languages. As practiced today, however, elementary schools are essentially little more than skills and remediation centers. The teaching of reading and computation skills occupies almost all of every morning and involves superhuman efforts by teachers using small groups and individualized instruction. These efforts are bolstered by aides, resource teachers, most of the schools' materials and text budgets, and computers. Most of the work offered teachers as in-service or continuing education also emphasizes teaching basic skills.

In contrast, all the sciences, social studies, arts and everything else in the elementary school curriculum is compressed into afternoons when teachers and children are both run down. Studies which are not basic skills are supported with little in the way of materials or equipment. Most of all, the individualization and small group instruction which characterizes the teaching of reading skills in the morning is notably missing in the afternoon programs of the elementary school. In the teaching of physical sciences, social studies and arts, even young children are given whole group lecture-like instruction, largely out of texts and treated as if all the assumptions about how children learn (which are implemented in the teaching of reading) do not apply to how individuals learn in the sciences, social studies, and arts.

Pre-schools, which were formerly the bastion of child development people are now also merely skills centers readying their charges for first grade. The justification for this basic skills curriculum supplanting the general studies curriculum of public elementary schools is that such skills are not only prerequisite to all subsequent learning but quintessential job training. America has transformed the process of education into one of schooling, and elementary schools into skills centers; and the shift is justified by using the rationale that jobs must be the school's primary goal. The counter-argument that a sound, broad general education will lead to a thoughtful, self-actualized, independent minded citizenry who will learn the job skills they need, as and when they need them, is no longer even presented let alone considered. Occasionally a mild dissent is raised when someone admits we do not know specifically what jobs to prepare people for in future, but this dilemma is momentary and is not pursued long enough to connect it to the purposes of genuine education for Americans — one that should lead to a thoughtful, problem solving, critical thinking populace who can adapt to change and take action in its own behalf.

The connection between these value patterns and the pre- or in-service education of teachers is quite clear. More relevant teaching techniques, more hands-on experiences and less theory are all well known teacher 'needs'. The teacher center movement in which teachers could train other teachers is the ultimate manifestation of this approach in practice. Specifics, or the construction of materials, the making of handouts and the exchange of teacher-to-teacher tips are the dominant focus of these teacher centers. For the purpose of this analysis it is important to note two things: this craft approach to in-service training characterizes every profession and results from practitioners being responsible for their own professional development; this form of professional development is also understood and supported by the mass of Americans.

As a summary, the same questions posed in relation to liberal arts are now answered in relationship to professional education:

What are the dominant value themes in the American culture which support professionalism? The commitment of American society to the belief that achievement leads to success; the inherent value attributed to activity and work; the positive values placed on efficiency, practicality, and know-how; the belief that one is entitled to material comforts that have been earned; and the commitment to a philosophy based on scientific knowledge and pragmatic action.

How might these values be stated as a goal? Teachers should know how to get students to learn. They should have the technical know-how to do what they are paid for. Teachers are technical implementers of the curriculum developed by the public.

What type of education is most likely to produce such individuals? A university based education that not only includes the liberal arts but a relevant professional preparation. This means extensive hands-on, direct experiences; observing and working under master teachers; learning the specific craft aspects of teaching.

What kinds of students are likely to self select such an education? Typical Americans who believe college (or any education) should lead to a specific job or career. People who value the fact that their education will be (should be) as specific as possible to the occupation they will perform subsequently. Students who are not searching for 'identity' or who are not overly concerned with exploring the range of university options.

What kind of teacher education is offered by this approach? The same goals as now stated but delivered more effectively. Fewer professionally questionable courses at the university and more direct experiences in schools. More knowledge of direct instruction derived from research and more knowledge of precisely 'what works'. 'In-service' should focus on workshops rather than courses and on specific approaches to discipline rather than theories of classroom management; there should also be widespread use of videotapes on one's own classroom and conferences with teaching colleagues serving as mentors.

How are such teachers evaluated?   Evaluations include both the learning of children/youth as measured on standardized tests *and* the processes followed by teachers. Do the teachers demonstrate the observable behaviors recommended in the literature of direct instruction? Do the teachers implement the practices advocated by the particular school system in which they are employed?

What kind of lower school curriculum does this cultural pattern foster?   Skills learning which is assumed to be 'basic' and prerequisite to future jobs and careers is directly related to this form of teacher training. (This is specific teacher *training* not broad teacher *education*.) Children and youth are expected to work hard, do well in school and be thoroughly prepared for the world of work upon high school graduation, or for the university professional schools.

What kind of staff development would these value patterns lead to?   Teacher centers are one example; hands-on activities and workshops are another. Traditional university courses and advanced degrees are deemed less appropriate since university faculty are perceived as less relevant and too theoretical. The trend in an increasing number of states is to permit teacher groups and school systems to develop in-service academies to offer in-house courses for keeping teacher licenses current. Teacher-controlled workshops designed on a concrete level which deal with the classroom problems perceived by teachers is the essence of this approach. Teachers decide what they need and who the instructors in their workshops will be. The inevitable content is of a very specific, technical nature. Salary increases and professional advancement rather than graduate degrees are the outcome. Training is clearly improved.

The Common Good, and Teacher Education

The value systems discussed previously — those supporting indi-vidualism, and those supporting the pragmatic world of work — are as old as our society. They can be clearly connected to the curricula of liberal arts and to professional education. The third American value pattern — commitment to the concepts of a democratic society — can be directly connected to a curriculum of general studies in an equally clear fashion. Unfortunately, general studies has all but disappeared from the lower schools and from the common core of requirements in the university. General studies are not merely a conglomeration of introductory courses in various disciplines. They are intentionally planned content aimed at producing problem solving, thoughtful citizens.

These studies include physical sciences, social sciences, arts and humanities taught in a manner which leads the students to a fuller understanding of the persistent problems of living in a democratic society. General studies can only be taught in a multi-disciplinary, integrated manner and learned through applications and analysis of knowledge to real-life problems. *The integration of knowledge and the applications of such knowledge to life are not the sole responsibility of students but the effects of a curriculum planned and offered by a faculty committed to general education.* At present, there is no widespread, serious development of such a general studies curriculum on any level of schooling.

In a real sense, education for the common good began with the Mayflower Compact in 1948 when the Puritans established the first common school. Their view of what content was needed to prepare children for meeting life's problems included reading the Bible, learning their code of morality, and little else. But the avowed purpose of the first schools was to acculturate the young into adult society and for more than 300 years this remained the primary purpose of American public education. While content changed — direct Bible study was replaced by character education whereby literature and history were used to shape moral precepts — the avowed purpose of elementary, high school and the first years of college were to offer a curriculum that 'made' Americans. The purpose of schooling was to socialize the young.

This curriculum was in full force between 1890 and 1920 when 30 million immigrants were 'melted' into American society by absorbing this general studies curriculum — a curriculum of history, English, basic sciences and the arts. This was neither a curriculum aimed at jobs nor the study of liberal arts disciplines for their intrinsic worth. This general studies curriculum was conceived and taught as the very stuff for making a participatory citizenry, involved and active in their communities. Jobs were viewed as things individuals were to take care of on their own, or to get training for from a technical school, while the liberal arts were viewed as the domain of scholars devoted to esoteric studies which, by definition, were considered to be irrelevant and therefore, free of social constraints.

The current situation reflects a complete subordination of all curriculum purposes to that of job-career preparation. Liberal arts have been able to withstand this pragmatic pressure because they too represent strong cultural bases (i.e., the commitments to individual development, the maintenance of a high 'culture' and academic freedom). There is also the fact that the graduate training of faculty is in specific liberal arts and not in the interdisciplinary studies required for teaching general studies. While the culture of jobs dominates the culture of individual development, therefore, the liberal arts remain alive and will persist by virtue of their own strong cultural wellsprings. The complete loser has been general studies programs dependent as they are on teachers who are generalists. When all the reward systems for university study and research are for specialists it is not surprising that the faculty who have the potential of offering general studies cannot be prepared in our discipline oriented graduate schools. For example, the number of physicists who want to teach students at all is significantly smaller than those who seek to become engaged in some form of theory building or research.

If we consider the small number who perceive of themselves as teachers and then raise the issue of interdisciplinary studies whereby these few physicists would co-teach with social scientists and humanists, the number of teacher-physicists who might be interested in interdisciplinary teaching shrinks even further. Yet, the number of students who can benefit from a general knowledge of physics is significantly larger than those seeking to 'major' in physics. A similar situation exists in the lower schools where teachers are prepared and licensed to teach particular specialities, that is miniature liberal arts subjects (English) or occupational trades (computing). Even at the elementary level, the former generalists prepared as teachers are now criticized as lacking 'in-depth substance'. The almost universally accepted solution to the problems of low achievement in elementary and high school is that teachers need to 'major' (that is, study in depth) in one subject area, thereby becoming even less able to function as generalists with young children. The reasons for the popularity of these widespread disfunctionalities is not simply that people are evil or stupid — as endearing as those explanations sometimes seem. At least part of the explanation should be sought in the trends and shifts among basic American value patterns which undergird (and control) what curricula all schools offer. The dominance of utilitarian values over the development of individuals, and the dominance of both of those patterns over the notion of the common good, indeed the lack of interest in developing any commonalities among Americans, is part of the explanation for the demise of general studies curricula.

There have been notable experiments in teacher education which did make general studies the heart of the professional education offered teachers. New College at Teacher College, Columbia during the 1930s was an integrated effort to prepare citizen teachers who would understand the world and the nation, as well as the states and localities that employed them. These future teachers experienced a curriculum that advocated problem solving and the activity concept as the essential pedagogy for educating youngsters.

During this period the University of Chicago and other institutions experimented with general studies that would occupy the entire four years of undergraduate college. Eventually, these efforts, whether offered as teacher preparation or in arts and science colleges, dried up. The usual reasons offered were philosophical. In truth, there were also mundane and bureaucratic reasons which may be better explanations. The following are six of the more obvious ones: it is more difficult to define faculty work loads if several faculty teach one course; it takes an inordinate amout of time to plan interdisciplinary course syllabi and faculty believe they have better things to do than go to endless meetings planning courses; it requires more time and effort to decide cooperatively on requirements and grading policies than to offer one's own course; there is a greater tension in teaching with and in front of colleagues than in teaching one's own course; and the amount of effort to do all of this intrudes on faculty members' other priorities. These are just some of the pedestrian reasons why interdisciplinary general studies never 'made it' in higher education. Added to these, of course, are the pressures which derive from the university culture to specialize ever more narrowly. All the status and prestige gradients, as well as all the tangible rewards which the university is capable of bestowing, are given for ever more narrow specializations. English professors study one author, chemists one type of catalytic action, historians become experts in the Bulgarian Revolution of 1876. The very essence of the university value system is to intensify specialization.

There is an analogous situation for the lower schools. It must also be noted that as the university emphasizes more specialization, the teachers it produces will value such study. Even more, the curriculum of the lower schools will attempt to match the university curriculum (it never works in the other direction) in order to enable high school graduates to succeed in their advanced studies.

In sum, education is now perceived by the mass of Americans and offered by the public institutions on all levels, as a personal good. From day-care through graduate study, those who are perceived as directly benefiting from schooling are expected to pay for it, or as much of it as possible. Schooling is now sold as other services or products, in much the same way as gas, water or telephone services are sold to users, only the immediate consumer is perceived as deriving the benefits of educational services. There is some logic in this approach since, if school curricula have been transformed into job/career training programs, why should not those who are going to earn higher incomes pay for such training? The widespread 'need' for local taxpayers relief is a general reflection of the common perception that those without children have no responsibility for other people's children. The cutback in federal loans and grants to students is another indicator that education is perceived as a personal good, essentially career-training. Current public opinion may best be described as a rising tide of public expectations regarding what all schools should accomplish in preparing people for the world of work.

In summarizing the demise of general studies curriculum as an approach to teacher education, the answers to the same questions posed in earlier sections are as follows:

What are dominant value themes in the American culture which support general education? The commitment to democractic values undergirds the notion of the common good. Democratic institutions including representational government, the legal system and all forms of community action are predicated on the assumption that all constituencies of our society are participants in a common heritage. Law and order is predicated on most people being law-abiding; similarly with the tax system. Public response to crises as well as unreflected upon assumptions about appropriate behavior all assume that we are one society — that in the main we can, to a workable degree, predict the actions of others and the responses of others to our actions. Without such a clear set of common agreements about mutual expectations we would not be able to function on an interactive basis in our daily lives.

How might these value themes be stated as a goal? The preparation of an informed, well-intentioned, active citizenry which will not only watchdog antisocial activity but which will initiate activity to solve common problems. A healthy community, state, and nation is the goal.

What type of education is most likely to produce such individuals? School programs and teacher education programs should be based on problem solving. Content is learned primarily as it feeds into solutions to real world problems and not for its own sake. Cooperative learning is emphasized in addition to individual achievement. The integration of subjects and their application to persistent problems of living is the essence of the curriculum.

What kind of students are likely to self select such education? Those who have a social consciousness and who value their own involvement in communal activities would be most compatible with this approach. Also, those who see education as an instrumentality for improving the quality of life in the community. Those who might volunteer for the Peace Corps but who are put off by current school bureaucracies and a curriculum they see as divorced from life problems would be an example of such a population. Those who participated in the university extension activities which have transformed rural America would be another example of a population concerned with applying knowledge to communal improvement.

What kind of teacher education might be offered by such an approach? Teacher education would emphasize the same general education studies advocated for the elementary and high schools only at a higher level. Teachers would be organized into in-service workshops that focused on the problems of living which most affect education in their communities. Examples of topics studied and the activities engaged in might be issues such as setting school policies for students with AIDS, or those who are pregnant. Issues such as job development in urban areas, the community's financial support for schools, how to provide high quality day-care and the impact of segregated housing, are other examples of subjects the citizen-teacher (and ultimately the children) might be involved in.

How are such teachers evaluated? Teachers' participation in community activities is paramount. Most of all, the teachers would deal with problems now frequently regarded as interference into the school curriculum and would make such issues legitimate study for children and youth.

What kind of lower school curriculum does this cultural pattern foster? The school curriculum would include life problems faced by the students which would be organized into themes around which current content could be learned in more integrated, meaningful ways. Searching student lockers, or placing police in the high school, would not be regarded as an intrusion but would become subjects of study — both for staff and students. Issues of the food served, or all manner of school rules, would provide similar opportunities. English teachers who complained that students are nonverbal, or History teachers who complain about lack of interest in studying the Bill of Rights, might discover that students can be vitally interested in participatory learning of actual problems.

What kind of staff development would these value patterns lead to? Again, space does not permit more than a few examples. Teachers' in-service would range from topics such as 'Who is the school's instructional leader?' and 'How should teachers be evaluated?' to 'What is the teacher's role in having students utilize the school's health clinic?'. There would, of course, be in-service programs for teachers on 'How international trade affects the USA dollar', 'Refinancing the rebuilding of the local community's infrastructure' and 'The meaning of recent Supreme Court decisions on school curricula'. In short, the education of the teacher, not merely as a citizen in the abstract, but as an involved citizen of the community and school, would be emphasized. There would be a clear connection and continuity between the topics studied by teachers and students. There would also be a very close connection between *how* such studies are pursued and the nature of the problems studied.

Implications for Teacher Development in the Future

We can be certain that the advocates for professional education will remain dominant. The cultural support for schooling that leads to jobs and careers will continue to support a comparable form of teacher development that emphasizes more effective methods for teachers. It will continue to make sense to all constituencies — including teachers

— that what teachers need most is more relevance to their immediate tasks, more hands-on direct experience, and more attention to the ever present problems of *how* to improve class discipline, *how* to teach basic skills more effectively, *how* to motivate, and *how* to cover more material faster. Such teacher development is less likely to take the form of graduate degrees — or university courses at all — and is more likely to take the form of in-service programs controlled by the employing school systems. In some cases local teachers' unions will offer the training. In effect, teachers have self identified development needs which are most like those identified by the parents of at-risk students and by at-risk students themselves: training rather than education; concrete information rather than abstract principles, basic skills rather than problem solving methodologies; practical competencies which require following directions and completing assigned tasks rather than critical thinking in general.

A second trend, much less pervasive but persistently advocated, will continue to propose more liberal arts coursework. This advocacy will have increasing impact in preservice teacher education programs and almost no influence whatever on in-service teacher development. The reasons are clear: undergraduates can be required to take more liberal arts but most school systems and teachers see little relevance in more liberal arts courses helping them solve the problems they face. Even more important, the overwhelming number of practicing teachers do not have the prerequisites to be admitted to graduate school coursework in the liberal arts and undergraduate courses meet more than once per week. Undergraduate liberal arts courses are also not 'packaged' (i.e., scheduled, priced or located) to facilitate practicing teachers taking them. This experience of liberal arts not reaching into 'inservice' was well documented by over 20 million dollars spent on *National Defense in Education Act* Institutes that ended up as summer offerings influencing few schools and even fewer teachers.

The advocacy for more general education, as a reflection of the shared values Americans hold relative to democratic living will continue to be ignored. University systems will continue to reinforce over-specialization and the existing dichotomy between the liberal arts college versus the professional schools. Teachers will be the victims of this crossfire and will not be prepared to offer general education. Lower schools will continue to emphasize basic skills and preparation for jobs/careers in response to the public perception that education is a personal good (i.e., job training).

The implications of these predictions is that teaching will become increasingly solidified as an occupation with less concern for professional development and greater emphasis on staff training. Such training will focus on the craft elements of teaching and on making teachers more effective technical personnel. These predictions are, of course, not advocacies. They are derived from the basic assumption undergirding my analysis; that dominant American value systems control the nature of schooling which in turn controls the nature of teacher education.

References

BELLAH, R. N., MADSEN, R., SULLIVAN, W. M., SWINDLER, A., and TIPTON, S. M. (1985). *Habits of the heart: Individualism and commitment in American life*. Berkeley: University of California Press.

JERSILD, A. T. (1955). *When teachers face themselves*. Columbia: Teachers College Press.

MORRISON, S. E. (1930). *The development of Harvard since the inauguration of President Eliot, 1869–1929*. Cambridge: Harvard University Press.

PART II
BEGINNING TEACHING AND PROFESSIONAL DEVELOPMENT

4 Readiness for Teaching

Jane H. Applegate

A recurring question in the minds of teacher educators and school administrators alike is 'When is a person ready to teach?' This question carries with it two implicit assumptions: *teaching is a process that requires preconditions in order for it to occur successfully;* and, *teaching is a human endeavor.* Teacher education researchers are examining these assumptions in an attempt to address readiness issues. Models for inquiry and samples of practice are being merged in order to understand more clearly the preconditions and human qualities which enable one to be ready to begin teaching.

The concept of readiness is not new to education, nor is it unique to teacher preparation. The field of reading, for example, has long been engaged in studying the issue of readiness for reading. Surprising parallels can be drawn between learning to teach and learning to read. Preparing to read and preparing to teach place emphasis on similar constructs and suggest alternative approaches to address the tasks. The purpose of this chapter is to examine the character of teacher preparation from four positions adopted from the literature of reading readiness research. Calfee and Drum (1986) suggest four propositions which have guided the progress of reading research:

Reading is acquired naturally, like learning to speak.

Reading is acquired through a series of stages.

Reading is learned through the mastery of a set of specific skills.

Reading is learned by formal instruction in a new domain of knowledge (p. 809).

If one were to replace the word *reading* with the word *teaching* four propositions about how one learns to teach become evident. Although, as Cruickshank (1984) argued, 'it is difficult to identify clear paradigms or scientific communities in teacher education' (p. 43), there are schools of thought within teacher education which share common beliefs about how one comes to the point of readiness for teaching (see Cruickshank, 1984; Iannone, 1976; Zeichner, 1983; Zimpher and Ashburn, 1985, for examples of such conceptualizations). These four positions provide a frame of reference for viewing four vignettes, each developed to illustrate a set of preconditions and human qualities found in the practice of teacher preparation. Each of the vignettes presents a story of a person engaged in teacher preparation. As you read these stories consider the following questions. What characteristics do each of the beginning teachers bring with them to teacher preparation? What variations with both people and programs seem to make a difference to the learners? What contextual attributes seem to contribute to a person's readiness for teaching? I hope that the examples which follow will prompt members of the teacher education community — teachers, school administrators, university faculty members and policy developers — to examine their own beliefs and assumptions about readiness for teaching.

Teaching is Acquired Naturally

Maryann Evans graduated from college in 1968. Her degree in European History was secondary to her desire to see and experience the life of the countries she had studied. From 1968 to 1972 she 'bummed around' Europe. While there she met and married an American journalist. In 1972 they returned to the states and settled in to a comfortable apartment in the city. Her children arrived, David in 1974 and Sharon in 1978. Being with them, watching them grow and change right before her eyes amazed her. How could children learn so much so quickly? As she taught them throughout childhood — read to them, listened to their language patterns and talked with them about numbers and letters, and dolls and trucks — she started to believe she might have something to contribute to others.

When her children began school, Maryann became a parent volunteer. Twice a week she worked in Mrs Klein's sixth-grade classroom assisting her with different kinds of classroom duties. She thoroughly enjoyed being in the school, talking with others about students, observing the children on the playground, assisting in the lunchroom and doing whatever needed to be done. Mrs Klein seemed to really appreciate her help. On occasion, Mrs Klein even asked her advice about how to work with particular children. Maryann began to entertain thoughts of becoming a teacher. One day she asked the principal what she would need to do in order to get a teaching certificate. The principal told her that he could hire her right away as a substitute since she already had a college degree, but if she wanted a full-time regular position she should talk with someone at the State Department of Education. Because of her background and experience perhaps they could work something out.

The State Department of Education issued Maryann with a temporary teaching certificate for secondary social studies teaching, and after reviewing her college transcript determined that she needed four courses and student teaching in order to receive a regular teaching certificate. She enrolled as a part-time non-degree student at a nearby state university. After talking with a counselor there she realized that the university's traditional program required many more than the four courses the state required. But after all, she thought, she knew she could teach. She had already proven herself with Mrs Klein. She was older and knew about children through her own life as a mother. Experience had taught her about teaching. What else could she need to know? She was confident that she was ready to teach.

Commentary

Maryann came to her career as a teacher in midlife. Although not a traditional student in teacher preparation her readiness for teaching came as a result of early life experiences. Her intelligence, as well as her previous knowledge and practice in the context of a school, shaped her career decision and her readiness to begin teaching. In this case, formal preparation in pedagogy was less influential than early influences on learning to teach. Feiman-Nemser (1983) identified three different explanations of the power of pre-formal preparation for teaching: Evolution, psychoanalysis, and socialization. The evolution explanation posed by Stevens (1969) cites natural teaching tendencies acquired by children through observing parents and teachers. The psychoanalytic account referenced by Wright and Tuska (1968) focused on the power of modeling by significant others. The socialization account influenced by the work of Lortie (1975) suggests that the entire school experience of an individual contributes to the models of teaching which are activated when becoming a teacher.

Proponents for the position that teaching is acquired naturally frequently cite these influences as more powerful than other preconditions for teaching success. What the student of teaching brings to the task of learning to teach cannot be ignored.

> The likelihood that professional study will affect what powerful early experiences have inscribed on the mind and emotions will depend on its power to cultivate images of the possible and desirable and to forge commitments to make those images a reality (Feiman–Nemser, 1983, p. 154).

Teaching is Developmental

As early as eighth grade, Jim Adler knew that he wanted to be a band director. After three years of practicing the trumpet with Mr Miller, his instrumental music teacher, he was asked to join the marching band at the high school. What a terrific feeling it was to be part of the band! And Mr Miller was so encouraging. He even talked with him about the possibility of going to college. No one from his family had ever gone to college and he had no idea where he would get the money. Although his parents thought he should quit playing music and get a job, Jim wanted nothing more than to go to State and play in the band. Through the efforts of Mr Miller he got a scholarship and prepared himself for college life.

In his first quarter a program counselor advised Jim to enroll in Freshman Field Experience during the next quarter. The course required that he spend three hours each morning in a school as a teacher's aide. He wondered if he could take that much time away from his practicing but the counselor assured him that the early experience would help him decide if he really wanted to teach music.

As winter quarter began Jim walked each morning to Johnson Junior High School to work with Mrs King, the music teacher. Mrs King told Jim that she was pleased to have him in her class and that she had planned many things for Jim to do. When she introduced Jim to her general music class he felt his confidence grow. She asked him to play his trumpet for the students and after a short number the class applauded! Mrs King seemed to know just what to do. Although this was a lot of time away from campus Jim felt as if the experience in the classroom would help him decide about teaching. Quickly he learned that teaching music was much more than playing music. Some of the eighth graders enjoyed the class but many did not. Mrs King seemed unaware that many students did not care. Jim learned that learning about teaching would be more difficult than he had imagined it would be.

During his sophomore year Jim had no contact with 'real' schools or teachers. His advisor in the school of music was pleased with the progress of his musical abilities. The theory courses were tough and the long hours of practice were necessary for him to earn his way to the marching band.

In the summer between his sophomore and junior years his advisor got him a job as a marching instructor for a high school band camp. The experience working with kids who loved music and marching band was just what he needed. He had almost forgotten that he had come to college to teach music not just to perform.

During his junior year he began taking courses in education: Human Development; School and Society; Principles and Practices of Education; Teaching Music in the Elementary School; Secondary Music: Choral; Secondary Music: Instrumental. All of these courses included an opportunity to practice teaching. Now, Jim felt as if he were going to become a teacher.

In his senior year Jim faced two quarters of student teaching. Music teachers had to work with students from kindergarten through high school. Those were a difficult two quarters. He was disappointed when he had to give up marching band in order to student teach. But he recognized that teaching came first. At the end of this experience Jim felt ready to teach.

Commentary

Jim's experience in learning to teach represents the current tradition of teacher preparation. The belief that learning to teach is developmental and sequential is realized in many teacher education institutions. The notion of development illustrated by Jim's story shows that teacher development begins with a desire to become a teacher, an interest in a content area, and some experiences working with children or youth.

When students enter the university and express an interest in education as a career they are enrolled in an introductory course. This course may be campus-based or school-based. Its focus is primarily career choice. A broad general education, or those courses which provide all students within the university the capacity to examine one's life and the place of knowledge within it, is acquired concurrently. According to Phenix (1964) general education provides a vehicle for the search for human meaning, and understanding that results in a complete person. Unfortunately, from the student's point of view, these courses are labeled 'requirements'; few students see them as valuable beyond their necessary path through the university. In Jim's case, they were not even mentioned as part of his career progression.

In the arena of professional development, students participate in four categories of professional studies: content for teaching, humanistic and behavioral studies, teaching and learning theory, and practical experience. For Jim, the content for his teaching was obvious from an early age; he wanted to teach music. His struggle with the content was a career struggle: Should he perform or should he teach about music? That dilemma is also developmental. His 'education courses' gave him a flavor of teaching. The direct experience in schools became progressively more demanding and contributed to Jim's development as a teacher.

At what point did Jim feel ready to teach? From his account, *at the end of his university education*. But, those who believe that teaching is developmental would say that Jim's learning to teach began long before he entered the university and will continue far past the point of university exit.

Teaching is Skill-Based

When Janet Allen came to college she was not sure what she wanted to study or, for that matter, why her parents thought it was important for her to go to college. Only two other people from her graduating class of 1956 went away to school. Nonetheless, she agreed to give college a try. After three semesters with a variety of courses her roommate talked her into taking Education Block I, the first set of courses for teacher preparation.

In her first class the instructor explained that in their college the faculty agreed that the program for teacher preparation would be competency-based. Instead of taking courses, students in the program would work their way through a series of modules designed to help students acquire specific teaching behaviors. The accomplishment of 'mods' would earn course credits. During Block I she would learn how to make a lesson plan, how to assess student behavior, and how to communicate verbally and nonverbally. The instructor also described the content of the other three blocks and told about the teaching laboratory where progress toward meeting the competencies would be measured. No grades would be given for the 'mods'. Either the competencies would be acquired or not. The only thing that concerned Janet was that if the competencies were not acquired she would have to repeat the mods until she had the content mastered and could demonstrate what she had learned.

Janet had never really thought much about becoming a teacher. In fact, she guessed she had never thought much about any career. If she did not meet a man and fall in love before college ended, she would probably need to find a job. Teaching would be as good an occupation as any.

She did well during Block I with her three mods. Block II had her scheduled into the teaching lab two full mornings a week in addition to her other classes. The whole focus of Block II was acquiring teaching skills. Each morning in the lab she had to teach a half-hour lesson and be videotaped. Over the course of the semester she had to teach 8 lessons in mathematics, 8 lessons in language arts, 8 lessons in social studies, and 8 lessons in science. After she taught the lessons she was required to do a lesson analysis which directed her attention to all of her teaching skills. She also had to turn her tape over to the lab instructor who reviewed the tape and asked lots of questions about content selection, timing, pacing, and activity structures. Janet thought this was a lot of hard work.

During Block III Janet was assigned to Perkins Elementary School. She was required to be there two full days a week. She repeated the lessons she taught in the laboratory with real students. She was quite pleased at the students' responsiveness. The students seemed to like her and her cooperating teacher said that she was impressed with the skills Janet had acquired.

Block III had Janet in the school every day for the entire semester. She was expected to have the full responsibility of teaching. She was visited weekly by her university supervisor who assessed her competencies while she taught. At the end of the experience Janet knew that she was a skilled teacher. Her scores on the National Teachers Examination confirmed this. She knew what she knew and was ready to teach.

Commentary

Performance or competency-based teacher education was a major national effort to reform teacher education in the early 1970s. Assumed within this approach was that if the skills and abilities of good teachers could be identified, they could be taught. Cruickshank (1985) described six alternative ways that competencies were identified:

(1) They could be gleaned from research on those teaching abilities that are related to pupil achievement;
(2) they could be provided by experienced educators judged to be experts;
(3) they could be derived from polls of stakeholders in education;
(4) they could be culled from the literature;
(5) they could be extracted from different teacher roles; and
(6) they could result from task analyses of teaching at different levels and in different curriculum areas (p. 61).

Although the competency-based movement had its roots in the early 1970s, today's teacher education community is well aware of the resurgence of this movement to identify the necessary skills of beginning teachers and teach for them. Accountability in the preparation of new teachers has taken the form of examination. Many states have recently developed tests aimed, in part, at assessing teacher knowledge and skill through paper-pencil and observational strategies. The Carnegie Forum on Education and the Economy (1986) has called for a national examination and licensing policy in addition to local mandates to improve teacher competence.

Critics of this skill-based approach to teacher preparation posit that teaching and learning to teach are complex endeavors that cannot be turned into techniques at the expense of understanding the situational and contextual milieu. As in Janet's case where skills were taught independently, one wonders how satisfied Janet will be as a teacher. Still, her technical expertise gained through a skills approach to teacher preparation enabled her to feel competent and ready to teach.

Teaching is Knowledge-Based

Steve Jabronski lived in nine different countries before settling into college. As an Air Force 'brat' he felt well educated, not just in traditional school subjects but also in the varied cultures of the countries in which he had lived. A highly eager and verbal student, Steve came to college knowing that he wanted to contribute something of himself to the society from which he felt he had learned so much. He enrolled in an interdisciplinary English Studies program hoping that solid background in an array of related courses would help him make a career decision.

'Involvement' seemed to be Steve's theme as he worked his way through college. While taking the journalism sequence he volunteered to work on the campus paper. When taking the speech sequence he tried out for and made the debate team. During his theater courses he landed a small role in the campus production of *A Chorus Line*. His Literature courses inspired him to contribute to the *Sojourner,* the campus literary magazine. To supplement his scholarship he taught Karate to children on Saturdays at the local YMCA (Young Men's Christian Association).

Toward the end of his junior year Steve realized that he still had no vocational direction. As a student he loved learning but knew he could not support himself as a college student forever. As a senior, he still wondered what he would do. He felt the he was well educated, 'liberally educated', his advisor in the English department told him. She encouraged him to think about applying for graduate school. If he stayed on at the university she thought she could get him a teaching assistantship in Freshman Composition while he continued his studies. Teaching, he thought, sounded good — but he also thought he knew nothing about it. How could he learn about teaching?

His advisor assured Steve there was not much to learn. But, if he wanted to pursue the topic he could talk with someone in the College of Education. She knew that the College was in the process of radically changing its teacher education course sequence and was going to a graduate-only preparation format.

Steve was intrigued with the notion of teaching. He followed his advisor's suggestion. He learned that the College of Education was providing a new education option for students like himself who had earned a BA in a discipline and wanted to learn to teach. The College described the program as an experimental two years effort consisting of inquiry-oriented, research-based seminars and experience in schools under the guidance of mentor teachers. The goal of the program, simply stated, was to educate professional teachers. He learned that he would earn both a master's degree and a teaching certificate which would allow him to enter an induction program in the second year of his preparation. There he would be paid as a teacher but would have assistance from a master teacher when needed. He would also be learning to teach with others like himself who had degrees and the desire to learn.

Although a career as a teacher really had not occurred to him before, the opportunity to learn about teaching through a program like this was appealing. The description of the coursework coupled with experience in real schools with expert teachers sounded challenging. Although he was wary of the uniqueness of this approach to learning about teaching, he decided to try. He felt ready to learn to teach.

Commentary

Steve's route to teaching exemplifies a current move to professionalize teaching as a career through developing both content knowledge and knowledge of pedagogy before one enters teaching. First envisioned by B. O. Smith in his *Design for a School of Pedagogy* (Smith, Silverman, Borg, and Fry, 1980) the current standard-bearer of reform in teacher education for the purpose of improving both the education of teachers and the context in which teachers work is the Holmes Group. In their initial reform document, *Tomorrow's Teachers* (1986), members of the group describe their goals as:

(1) To make the education of teachers intellectually more solid;
(2) To recognize differences in teachers' knowledge, skill, and commitment, in their education, certification, and work;
(3) To create standards of entry to the profession — examinations and educational requirements — that are professionally relevant and intellectually defensible;
(4) To connect our own institutions to schools; and
(5) To make schools better places for teachers to work, and to learn (p. 4).

As these goals take shape in Holmes Group member institutions, teacher educators are being challenged to reconsider what is meant by a knowledgeable, professional teacher. What knowledge is most worthwhile to a beginning professional? What forms of expertise are valued? What theories in the social and behavioral sciences have relevance in learning to teach? What kinds of knowledge about clients and context are essential as teaching begins?

Certainly, as one examines and reflects upon one's own practice new questions, new forms and structures, and new knowledge about teaching and teacher education emerge. To prepare a new teacher who is guided by the principle that learning to teach is *learning in a new domain of knowledge* takes a serious effort on the part of many teacher educators. Assumed in this course of action is a total reconceptualization of teacher education. More than simply learning to teach, this view of teacher education holds that the essential required knowledge is deliberate learning to learn-to-teach. Though there may never be a final, finished, perfect teacher there will be a continued effort to examine, and to consider what may be the most appropriate action to take. The complexity of teacher education is reinforced through this view.

Summary

These four views of readiness for teaching illustrate ways that the preparation of new teachers vary according to the human qualities of teacher candidates and particular approaches taken by the teacher education community. As with learning to read, learning to teach involves a complex interrelationship of processes, program components and people. Both Katz and Raths (1985), and Cruickshank (1984), stress in their respective pleas the following: an organized framework for knowledge about teacher education, a mindfulness about program goals, characteristics of teacher candidates, characteristics of education professors, characteristics of cooperating teachers in public schools, subject matter content, teaching methods, time, regulations, resources, institutional characteristics, classroom characteristics, instructional processes and evaluation strategies which all effect, in some way, the impact that learning to teach may have.

The broad and diverse perspectives held by teacher educators about all of the dimensions of teacher preparation allow for — and even encourage — reflective and heuristic contemplation about our practice. The examples provided here cause us to raise questions about the value of selection practices, certification regulation, candidate motivation, course sequencing, field experiences, and student advisement.

Each of these examples illustrated different attributes of teacher candidates and different program structures. The values we hold about the importance of maturity, the motives which prompt people to enter teacher preparation, the importance of content knowledge, the importance of knowledge related to pedagogy, the importance of experience — intentional or otherwise — shape the judgments we make as we speculate about the future success of each candidate.

With Maryann one might question the lack of theoretical preparation and her distance from her content area. Will her natural ability be enough to sustain a career in teaching? With Jim one might wonder about his dualistic sense of purpose. Can there be a shared vision of self as artist and as teacher or will one add to or detract from the other? With Janet one might be concerned about the extent to which her technical approach to teaching will enable her to meet the needs of individual students. And, with Steve questions might be raised about the timing and sequencing of professional preparation. Is graduate preparation for teaching essential? Additional questions could be raised were each of these students faced with alternative program options.

Further examination of the human qualities and preconditions which influence one to feel ready to teach is needed before positions about appropriate teacher preparation can be verified. To understand the complexity of teacher preparation we must be willing to invest considerable time and energy in this endeavor. We must continue to challenge ourselves with hard questions by looking beyond our suppositions and by talking with those directly and indirectly involved. As with learning any new set of actions or ways of thinking, an integrative process needs to occur — be it regarding learning to walk, learning to read, or learning to teach. The conceptual, contextual, and personal dimensions of a complex learning endeavor must be considered for intentional learning to occur.

The further challenge for teacher educators and teacher education researchers will lead toward a more complete understanding of this learning process with real people in real programs. Learning to teach can be satisfying and rewarding. What makes each person *ready* still remains unknown.

References

CALFEE, R., and DRUM, P. (1986). Research on teaching reading. In M. Wittrock (ed.), *Handbook of research on teaching* (3rd edn) (pp. 804–49). New York: Macmillan.

CARNEGIE FORUM ON EDUCATION AND THE ECONOMY. (1986). *A nation prepared: Teachers for the 21st century.* New York: Carnegie Corporation.

CRUICKSHANK, D. R. (1984). Toward a model to guide inquiry in preservice teacher education. *Journal of Teacher Education, 35*(6), 43–8.

CRUICKSHANK, D. R. (1985). *Models for the preparation of America's teachers.* Bloomington, IN: Phi Delta Kappa Educational Foundation.

FEIMAN-NEMSER, S. (1983). Learning to teach. In L. Schulman and G. Sykes (eds), *Handbook of teaching and policy* (pp. 150–70). New York: Longman.

IANNONE, R. (1976). Current annotations in teacher education. In S. Goodman (ed.), *Handbook on contemporary education* (pp. 233–7). New York: Xerox.

KATZ, L., and RATHS, J. (1985). A framework for research on teacher education programs. *Journal of Teacher Education, 36*(6), 9–16.

LORTIE, D. (1975). *Schoolteacher: A sociological study.* Chicago: The University of Chicago Press.

PHENIX, P. (1964). *Realms of meaning: A philosophy of the curriculum for general education.* New York: McGraw-Hill.

SMITH, B. O., SILVERMAN, S., BORG, J., and FRY, B. (1980). *A design for a school of pedagogy.* Washington, DC: U.S. Department of Education.

STEVENS, J. (1969). Research in the preparation of teachers: Background factors that must be considered. In J. Herbert and D. P. Ausubel (eds), *Psychology in teacher preparation* (pp. 119–46). Toronto, Ontario: The Ontario Institute for Studies in Education, Monograph Series No. 5.

Tomorrow's teachers: A report of the Holmes Group. (1986). East Lansing, MI: The Holmes Group.

WRIGHT, B., and TUSKA, S. (1968). From dream to life in the psychology of becoming a teacher. *School Review, 27*(3), 253–93.

ZEICHNER, K. (1983). Alternative paradigms of teacher education. *Journal of Teacher Education, 34*(3), 3–9.

ZIMPHER, N. L., and ASHBURN, E. (1985). Studying the professional development of teachers: How conceptions of the world inform the research agenda. *Journal of Teacher Education, 36*(6), 16–26.

5   New Teachers and the Development of Professionalism

Les Tickle

Imagine a debate between two teacher educators. The first, Joseph Lancaster (1778–1836), pioneered monitorial schools in England for the British and Foreign School Society at the beginning of the nineteenth century. He is about to address Dr Andrew Bell (1753–1832) who developed monitorial schools for the National School Society during the same period. Lancaster is the best known English educator of the last century. In their schools 'the system' was supreme, and it was for the participants in them to work it *systematically* and without deviation to ensure efficiency and success. The underlying assumptions about what should be achieved for the education of the poor in the principles of the established church are not the concern of this introduction. Rather, I am concerned with Lancaster's proposed means for teaching, and hence for teaching the teachers. Like the National Society schools, where individual teachers were forbidden to depart from 'the beautiful and efficient simplicity of the system',[1] Lancaster also tried to ensure that teachers deferred to the external authority of his regime:

> The master should be a silent bystander and inspector. What a master says should be done, but if he teaches on this system he will find the authority is not personal, that when *the pupils,* as well as the schoolmaster, understand how to act and learn on this system, *the system,* not the master's vague, discretionary, uncertain judgment will be in practice (J. Lancaster, *Improvements in Education*, 1808, Appendix; cited in Rich, 1933).

It was, according to Rich, from this attempt to ensure that the educational 'machines' (that is, individual schools) functioned properly in the hands of trained supervisors, that teacher training in England developed. Training was not concerned with the education of the individuals who would become the supervisors of the system, but merely with training them in its operation.[2]

The second advocate in the imaginary debate is Hugh Sockett (1937), deriving much of his case from the work and thoughts of Lawrence Stenhouse (1929–82). Sockett's concern throughout his writing is with the professionalization of teachers, which he sees as being achieved through the education of the intellect and the teacher's search for understanding of teaching and its effects. A central assumption is a belief in the need to change the educational system in order to allow for the individual's emancipation rather than suppression. Again, it is not these issues about the purposes of education which I shall address here, but rather their implications for the education of teachers. In contrast to Lancaster, Sockett (1985) has said:

> (student teachers) live and work in a framework of contrary understanding: To grasp *that* they must not only learn to pay close attention to the content of seminars, to the way they are taught, but set out to *challenge* the assumptions embedded in the pedagogy and the practice they encounter as learners (p. 118).

For practicing teachers, such challenges are to be made to their own assumptions, through systematic self-reflection and the analysis of teaching acts (Stenhouse, 1975). The development of skillful classroom technique, in this view, depends upon a mode of learning represented in the teacher-researcher movement which has developed internationally in recent years.[3] Teacher-research, it is claimed, potentially enhances the long-term professional *self*-development of teachers by subsuming the 'technical' expertise of classroom performance within the realm of professional judgment:

> We can shut ourselves in an empty classroom practicing our blackboard writing. We can have critics or supervisors watch out particularly for the way we handle children's answers . . . but if we must use our judgment when we apply our skills, the route to the improvement of performance lies first in practice with judgment and critical reflection, and later in systematic self-analysis . . . (Sockett, 1985, p. 120).

The gap between the contrasting perspectives on how teachers ought to be taught (or ought to learn), which I have chosen to represent through brief extracts from the writing of different historical personalities, is not merely a product of the passage of time. Rich (1933) notes that as early as 1814 within the British and Foreign School Society it was realized that the culture and skill of the teacher mattered at least as much as the mechanics of schooling. That realization led to the establishment of teacher training in which the education of student teachers in 'subjects' occurred simultaneously with classroom practice and educational studies, establishing an early version of a model recognizable today. But the tension between 'personal education' at levels appropriate to higher education students, classroom practice, and educational and professional studies has continued (Department of Education and Science [DES], 1972, 1984). The relationship between educational studies ('theory') and practical teaching has remained especially contentious. Indeed in the recent past that tension has intensified in Britain with the advent of the Council for the Accreditation of Teacher Education (CATE) invoked by the Government in 1984 (DES, 1984). In particular, the CATE criteria for approval of courses highlight the tenuous position held by critical studies of curriculum in teacher education programs, and raise issues about the relationship between classroom practice and 'theory' to a new, contemporary, level (Tickle, 1987).

It is not possible here to address the detailed arguments. But it is important to be aware of the social and political context of teaching in contemporary Britain to understand the dichotomy of the two broad approaches to question of *what should be done to ensure that professional standards and qualities are enhanced for the improvement of teaching.* The CATE arose within the demands for the accountability of teachers which were launched formally in Prime Minister James Callaghan's speech of 1976: *Towards a National Debate* (Callaghan, 1976). Those demands have been discussed widely since (Alexander, 1984; Graham, 1985; Holt, 1982; Sockett, 1980). They have resulted in a variety of manifestations in policy and legislation, including teacher appraisal, the imposition by legislation on teachers of pay and conditions, interventions by the Secretary of State in determining a national curriculum (DES, 1987), and legislation giving the governing bodies of individual schools power to impose their view of curriculum on the teachers (DES, 1986). These are manifestations of the 'management of teachers' approach, and symptoms of the curriculum power struggle being lost by teachers. Other views of a public education service in which teachers play a central decision-making role seek to improve the material conditions of class size, teacher contact time, and in-service teacher education provision. They see teaching as a profession, with professional responsibilities carried out in a framework of self-determination by teachers within a commitment to education. Accountability and responsibility are conceived as operating in mutual trust and partnership between the various interested parties in the education venture.

Those who hold this view — the Sockett/Stenhouse supporters in this not-so-imaginary debate — are critical of the 'management of the teaching force' approach espoused in recent policy and legislation. The management view — with its suggestions that Lancaster and Bell are not yet dead — has, however, gained in momentum, in mechanisms being used to ensure that particular kinds of curriculum will be im-plemented, controlled, and safeguarded at the direction of central government. And, the initial thrust of accountability which centered on school-wide self-evaluation and curriculum reviews has taken a turn firmly in the direction of an individual teacher's performance and its assessment.

It has been argued that the de-professionalization of teachers could result from increasing bureaucratization, which would turn teachers into technicians charged with specific skill tasks (Elliott, chap. 11; Wallace, 1985). It is feared that in such a system what teachers do would be specified by others. They would participate in decision-making in tightly defined realms, accountable to technical managers for the efficient conduct of their tasks. They would be judged accord-ing to the 'efficient' instruction of pupils toward the 'benchmarks' of pre-specified, packaged knowledge. Tests of pupil performance against those benchmarks would measure 'efficiency'. These are the fears of those who regard education, of teachers and pupils alike, as a process in which inquiry, judgment, questioning, and discovery lead to the personal development of individuals.

Crucially, it appears that the management approach to the control of teachers and teaching assumes that there is a consensus about what constitutes good teaching, and that the mechanisms of controlling and developing it are understood. Those who seek individualized profes-sional excellence, on the other hand, do so by seeking new means by which teaching can be developed, with aspirations towards better understanding of those means: the research of teaching. That view, as I have pointed out, does not preclude the development of technical expertise by the teacher. On the contrary, it subsumes it within inquiry in such a way that technical proficiency would be enhanced within professional action based on research (Elliott and Adelman, 1973; Stenhouse, 1975; Tickle, 1987; Walker, 1985).

The essence of the protagonists' views in my imaginary debate appears to have gained in importance in the not-so-imaginary struggle for the professional development of teachers, as it is being fought in the political arena of the late 1980s. It is the explicit purpose of this chapter to argue that through the adoption of a systematic mode of research-based teacher induction it would be possible to ensure an increase in professionalism of teachers. That would be achieved, I will contend, through *their* improvement of practice based on investigating and understanding that practice. That, I believe, is increasingly necessary in the political context which I have outlined briefly. Elsewhere, I have argued that such an approach ought to begin in initial teacher-education, and have shown how it works in practice at that stage (Tickle, 1987). I will draw upon that work in order to establish the case for systematic links between pre-service experience and the induction of beginning teachers. More substantially, it is my intention to present proposals which would elucidate the educational experiences of new entrants to the profession, and to make recommendations for the education and professional development of new teachers beyond their first year of teaching.

Research-based Initial Teacher Education

I have shown in my work with undergraduate student teachers how the initial encounters with classroom practice were concerned with learning the 'secrets of the trade' (Tickle, 1987). There was a commitment among students to doing the things which teachers do — including the menial tasks. The way to learn what teachers do, for those students, was to work with teachers and take responsibility for doing their work. A biological model of young birds being 'imprinted' with the coping strategies of an experienced nearest adult might at first glance seem appropriate. Yet, it was clear from that study that the process was interactive, as the students adjusted to the professional expectations of becoming a teacher: as they came to know the context of the schools and communities in which they worked; as they mastered subject knowledge within the demands of teaching; as they acquired instructional strategies and classroom management skills;

and, as they developed professional attitudes and perspectives. In those crucial areas of professional conduct, I argued, novice student teachers showed how they were capable of elucidating, examining, explaining, and extending their practical knowledge through reflection on their earliest encounters with teaching. I showed how that reflective capability itself emerged. In the view of a student one year into the four-year program the realization of a 'professional code' had a profound effect (Tickle, 1987):

> *Student:* Really, I mean there's a really strong idea of professionalism I find. I've really extended my idea in the last year about what that professionalism is ... there's something implicit that gives you this idea that there are these strong codes ...
>
> *Observer:* What is this professionalism that you're talking about?
>
> *Student:* Extended professionalism is not just doing it (that is, teaching) but knowing the whys and wherefores and the hows and what next of your doing it .... It's going below the surface of walking into the classroom and doing that lesson because that's what you feel like doing, into all the issues around it. And, I think the professionalism comes into thinking and working out those issues (p. 70).

This does not represent a single instance of the sentiment. I identified a large number of students who were questioning, evaluating, and researching practice, on a wide range of issues. Among students in the final year of the program those issues stretched well beyond individual classroom practice to research contracts negotiated with headteachers and teachers on curriculum matters pertinent to the whole school, or in some cases groups of schools. Students focused on developing and demonstrating competence in research as much as in classroom practice. Those skills and the understanding which accrued from their application provided a new dimension of professional responsibility. Johanna, for example, worked with teachers from four schools to develop their teaching using the curriculum project *Man: A Course of Study* (MACOS;[4] Tickle 1987).

> It's very different. What I'm doing with MACOS is not just to do with my learning. It's helping them learn too about what they're doing. And so it changes the emphasis for me. I think that's a very good thing as far as the teachers and heads are concerned too. I got

talking to Mr. J. (a headteacher) about my assessment course and his immediate reaction was 'Oh I've been trying to do something on that myself for years. Can you come in and talk to me about it and about making up some sort of profile for the children in the school?' *He* had the freedom to say can you do anything for me . . . . Do you see what I mean? It has freed *them* as well to say I need you as much as you need me (p. 138).

The potential for changing not only personal perspectives on teaching and curriculum, but also those of professional colleagues, is clear from this work. And, it is based not just on competent practice, but on the *theory* about which there is still widespread professional prejudice. As Toby explained (Tickle, 1987):

In the first year I couldn't see any relationship between theory and practice and now it becomes more and more clear as I go into schools. And to that extent I can talk on an equal level with teachers if not slightly above because some of the new research they can't expect to keep in touch with . . . (p. 140).

The activities reported in that work depended upon substantial access to schools being provided for student teachers over prolonged periods of time. Such access is readily available to teachers themselves. The potential for research-based teacher induction, in which new teachers reflect on their actions and systematically develop their perspectives on teaching and learning, is apparent from that study of intending teachers. It also raises questions about the nature of induction as conventionally conceived by 'providers' and experienced by new teachers.

The Induction of New Teachers

There is an extensive literature summarizing the experience of beginning teachers (Doyle, 1985; Griffin, 1985; Hall, 1982; Johnston and Ryan, 1983; Tisher, 1982). It is not surprising that in this literature the first year of teaching is clearly portrayed as a period of frantic activity through which personal and professional adjustments aim for classroom survival and the development of coping strategies. What is surprising is the range of claims similar to that made by Hall (1982):

The conclusion of the AERA (American Educational Research Association) forum, and of recent writings in the United States and elsewhere is that little is known about induction beyond the fairly obvious fact that teachers find it difficult, and memorable. There has not been extensive research on the influences or the long term consequences (p. 54).

The aspirations for the period of induction are nonetheless enthusiastic:

Given the current interest in formulating and implementing state and local programs for new teachers, other questions may also be helpful as we try to understand the first years of teaching and make those years an experience that can contribute to the development of an effective cadre of teachers in our nation's schools (Griffin, 1985, p. 43).

Among those questions, to which research up until now has not provided answers, are ones about how teacher decision making and reflection can be promoted through induction programs. Others center on the assumptions underlying existing programs about the nature of teaching, learning, and curriculum in schools, and in teacher education, and the possibilities of formulating theories of teaching and teacher education. Overall, they demonstrate the problematic nature of our knowledge of teaching, and of in-service teacher education at the stage of induction in particular. Optimism about filling some of the gaps is conveyed by Doyle (1985):

The study of how teachers learn to teach appears to be emerging as a specialization in educational research, and substantial progress should soon be made in understanding the knowledge domains in teaching and the ways in which these domains are acquired (p. 32).

In summary, then, it seems that there is no lack of information about the traumatic experiences of new teachers. Research which is available focuses on socialization; on improving the technical functions of instruction; and, on the kinds of formal programs run by employers for new entrants to teaching. There is also evidence that suggests that the administration and management of the employment of beginning teachers is deeply problematical (DES, 1982; Inner London Education Authority [ILEA] 1980). Understanding *what* and *how* new teachers learn from classroom experiences, as well as of the nature of these *educational experiences* is lacking. Little is known about the development of practical knowledge and professional dispositions, or the best means of improving them during this phase. Aspects of practical knowledge of teaching — subject knowledge; instructional strategies; knowlege of pupils; teaching contexts; and curriculum development — have been studied to a limited extent among experienced teachers (Burden, 1982; Clandinin, 1986; Elbaz, 1983; Elliott and Adelman, 1973). Yet, it seems reasonable to suppose that the induction period would reveal important characteristics of teachers' educational experiences, highlighted by what is clearly a period of frantic activity and intense learning. Increasing experience of the 'professionalization' of teachers through a teacher-research mode of in-service education has also been built on work with established teachers — often those in positions of responsibility in schools, or those studying for advanced qualifications. The assumptions of action research have not been examined in the crucial period between initial teacher education and in-service education for experienced teachers.

Given the research on 'survival-and-coping', the question arises of whether the education of teachers during this phase can be about *maintaining the problematic nature of teaching* rather than learning coping strategies and survival techniques. Further questions then arise about the qualitative differences between learning-for-coping, and learning-for-teaching within a notion of long-term professional advancement. Burden (1982), for example, cites numerous studies in support of his conception of the first year of teaching as a 'survival' period in which stress is high, confusion common, and a sense of inadequacy endemic. Once through the fire of induction, he asserts, teachers in their second, third, and fourth years settle during an 'adjustment' period. When they are said to 'know what did and did not work' they become 'less concerned with the teaching situation as a problem area' and 'much more comfortable with their teaching' as they enhance their practical knowledge and gain confidence (Burden, 1982, p. 7). Such settling into coping strategies may be explained partly by the process of socialization of teachers. Lortie (1975) explores the limits of socialization into the profession, identifying three aspects of the route into professional knowledge: *formal schooling; mediated entry* (initial training and induction); and, *learning while doing*. He points out that formal schooling provides powerful models of teaching; that the study of education and teaching for intending teachers is recent, unsophisticated, and organizationally brief and simplistic compared to other professions; and, that 'learning while doing' is confronted largely in isolation. He also notes the abruptness of the transition from studentship to full responsibility — a sudden entry into the isolation of the 'learning while doing' phase: 'Compared with the crafts, professions, and highly skilled trades, arrangements for mediated entry are primitive in teaching' (Lortie, 1975, p. 59).

It is thus, perhaps, that coping strategies are needed and sought. Learning what 'works' for individuals displaces the possibilities of professionally shared and empirically derived practices and principles of pedagogy (Lortie, 1975, p. 79). According to this view, learning what works by trial and error of personally derived coping strategies, and drawing on second-hand models from formal schooling and impressions from experienced peers, leads to a lack of a professional culture and collective status among teachers. It affects their status, while individualism in learning teaching affects the ways teachers regard themselves in relation to their practice. Lortie argues that in occupations where knowledge and ignorance are jointly shared, collective support for the individual reduces doubts about personal efficacy. Recognition of the problematic nature of schooling, in short, would lead to shared empirical search for solutions to common problems rather than individualized, privatized coping strategies.

Crucial to my position, as pointed out by Lortie, is the lack of potency in teacher education and induction, such that:

> teachers do not, apparently, acquire new standards to correct or reverse earlier impressions, ideas, and orientations. Nor does later work experience supplement low impact training with a general conception of teaching as shared intellectual possession (Lortie, 1975, p. 81).

It is towards a system which might bring about that possession through research based teacher induction that I want later to make a case. But first I believe it is necessary to balance these generalized and rather pessimistic views of Burden and Lortie by considering some complexities within a more heterogeneous view of teachers, teaching, and educational institutions.

Zeichner and Tabachnick (1985) consider through detailed case study the degree to which beginning teachers adopt the cultures and traditions of the schools where they worked. Correspondingly, they provide evidence of the extent to which teachers maintained the perspectives brought to their first jobs. The underlying concern of these authors was to determine whether beginning teachers can be viewed as 'making substantial contributions to the quality or strength of their own induction into teaching' (Zeichner and Tabachnick, 1985, p. 4). They adopt a theoretical model of *'social strategy'* developed by Lacey (1977) from his study of the socialization of student teachers. From an empirical study of student teachers' experience of classroom practice, Lacey recognized the need for a concept of socialization which allowed for the autonomous actions of individuals, sub-groups, or groups, and their potential influence over situations. Such a concept would have to take account of, and be capable of explaining, social and institutional change. This represents a development of Becker's (1971) notion of *'situational adjustment'* in which, Lacey argued, institutions remain stable, with change being handed down from the top so that new teachers would be seen as being socialized into the norms and values of the institutions in which they work (Lacey, 1977, p. 72). In order to account for the dynamic of socialization in a way which included the purposes, intentions, and actions of professional inductees, situational adjustment is subsumed by Lacey within a concept of *social strategy*. Three varieties of social strategy are delineated by Lacey (1977, p. 72):

Strategic compliance in which, in my present application of the concept, a new teacher complies with requirements made by others or responds to material constraints, without believing in the resulting actions;

Internalized adjustment in which individuals find themselves in accord with, and believe in, the constraints, expectations, and actions within an institution;

Strategic redefinition in which institutional change is brought about by the activities of the individual.

The category of strategic redefinition is invoked by Lacey in relation to individuals who do not possess formal power to bring about change. His concern is with student teachers, and he argues that *the ability of the performer* is crucial in gaining support for strategies by more powerful individuals — whose view of events, and interpretation and acceptance of what is happening, will enable change to be effected. That raises interesting questions not only about the substantive performance of individuals in relation to an activity, but also their political performance in the management of situations. Indeed the informal power of students and new teachers can be considerable, if only tacitly stated, in circumstances where, for example, 'new blood', new realms of expertise, specific 'shortage' skills, or particular perspectives which support minority views held by those in powerful positions, are directly recruited.

Zeichner and Tabachnick (1985) point out the complexity of notions of 'culture and traditions' of institutions such as schools, recognizing that the 'ethos' and belief systems in particular schools may be either dominant and relatively cohesive, or disparate and splintered. Furthermore, they demonstrate how teachers react uniquely to school situations. With four individuals who were tracked through their first year of teaching they showed how two of them demonstrated internalized adjustment, finding themselves in congruence with the school situation. Two showed a dominance of strategic redefinition in the social strategies adopted; one of them was successful, the other was not. However, Zeichner and Tabachnick (1985) assert that:

> all the teachers engaged in some form of strategic redefinition and introduced at least some new and creative elements into their school (p. 12).

They argue from this that first year teachers can have a creative impact on their institutions, 'under some conditions at least' (Zeichner and Tabachnick, 1985, p. 14). They define clearly the lack of success in making creative contributions where a dominant ethos is encountered in opposition to the new teacher's perspective (see also: Beynon 1987; Gracey 1976). Greater success, they posit, arises where the school regime is a plural one, with diverse or contradictory subcultures potentially generating space for individual contributions from new teachers. In summary, the complexity of the socialization of beginning teachers is outlined:

> there is no one explanation which can describe the entry of beginning teachers into the teaching role. Despite the fact that these four teachers began their first year of teaching with fairly similar teaching perspectives, there were significant differences both in the teachers' abilities and desires to implement their perspectives and in the nature of the constraints and opportunities offered to teachers within each school (Zeichner and Tabachnick, 1985, p. 19).

Implicit in this study is a view of new entrants to teaching who have pre-formed perspectives, brought with them to their school situations. Differences in the abilities and desires to implement those perspectives may well be explained by the degrees to which they *are* pre-formed and stable, or the extent to which new teachers are prepared to modify their beliefs, attitudes, values, and purposes in the light of new experience and understanding gained among professional colleagues. That interplay of individual intent and institutional constraint is a crucial feature of the proposals which I want to make later in this chapter. It seems reasonable that the concept of strategic redefinition should also be applied to introspective activity in the individual teachers' perspectives and practices — not only to the impact of those upon the institutional setting.

Zeichner and Tabachnick imply that where internalized adjustment occurs, and the institutional status is maintained, a 'creative impact' does not occur. I contend that such impact *is* possible, based on self-reflection within an individual teacher's work. Furthermore, we might envisage an institution — a 'creative school' — in which the *status quo* is an ethos of inquiry and change, in which creative teachers experience internalized adjustment directly in relation to expectations for strategic redefinition. That is, the two strategies accord with each other to become a blend. Therefore, the crucial questions I want to address are:

can strategic redefinition be deliberately developed and sustained by individual teachers, for their own teaching, and the work of their schools? *and*

can the problematic nature of teaching be institutionally recognized in a widespread way so as to sanction and even require strategic redefinition in professional practices?

A Rationale and Program for Systematic Induction

To argue that a systematic mode of research-based teacher induction would ensure the increased professionalism of teachers is one thing. To demonstrate it is another. To suggest that such professionalism would be achieved through new teachers' own self-improvement in practice, based upon investigating and understanding that practice, is also subject to empirical testing. The proposals which I want to present assume those outcomes will result. They further assume that their implementation, properly monitored, will elucidate the educational experiences of new entrants to teaching, beyond their first year. They present a challenge to current assumptions about the nature of induction, outlined earlier, in particular in the demands they make for the development of practical knowledge and professional dispositions towards improving it. And, they cater for the interplay of individual and institutional change which has been discussed, and which is intrinsic to the concepts of social strategy, professional development, and school improvement.

Recent concerns to improve the quality of teaching have focused on the three phases of professional development — initial teacher education, induction into teaching careers, and the long-term in-service education of teachers. Perceived inadequacies in each phase appear to be compounded by concern about disparate pre-service, induction and in-service elements in the professional development of teachers. Active pursuit of improvements in initial and long-term in-service teacher education are currently under way, within the developments of CATE and new arrangements for allocating in-service education grants, respectively. The period of induction into teaching as the lynch-pin between the other two phases is in need of constructive development, despite attempts to offer probationary year programs in specific localities. The common theme in concerns with each phase is about improving the practical knowledge of teaching. The challenge which is laid down for the improvement of teaching quality is applicable to each phase — that is, to shift the concerns about basic quality in teaching and professional development into constructive means for transforming professional practice into excellence (DES, 1985).

Seen in these terms, teacher education at all phases is required to develop both the conceptions and the means to achieve high standards in academic subject qualifications, personal qualities, professional commitments, and classroom and school practice. The question remains as to the most effective processes and most appropriate conduct to ensure the development of high standards in this complex range of professional knowledge. Yet, it seems increasingly clear that the inter-relationship between academic, professional and practical elements hinges on using the classroom as the focus of study for professional development.

The White Paper *Better Schools* (DES, 1985) sets out the UK government's conclusions following the review of its policies for school education in England and Wales, incorporating threads of policy for teacher education from earlier documents, especially *Teaching Quality* (DES, 1983) and *Circular 3/84: Initial Teacher Training: Approval of Courses* (DES, 1984). The combination of academic, professional and practical elements in the education of teachers, it is said, will enable them to meet the complex demands made on them. Those demands include the use of a repertoire of teaching styles, from the traditional instructional to the informal guidance role which promotes inquiry and involves sharing discoveries with pupils, professional attitudes 'constantly concerned to increase effectiveness through professional development' (DES, 1985, para. 144), and participation in the corporate development of schools. The latter concept explicitly includes curriculum development as a professional activity which falls directly within the responsibilities of classroom teachers.

The ways in which these characteristics of professionalism are to be developed during initial teacher education, in order that they might inform practice after entry into teaching, are not at all clear from the White Paper. The challenge of developing processes (beyond meeting the prescribed criteria for course approval), by which the complex professional demands can be met, is left to institutions. While much is being done both in response to the CATE criteria and in the development of teacher education processes within individual institutions (for example, Ashton, *et al.,* 1983; Tickle 1987; Wragg 1984), there is universal concern that the 'consecutive route' of the Post Graduate Certificate of Education (PGCE),[5] in particular, cannot adequately prepare new entrants for these complex professional demands. In 'concurrent' BEd/BA(Ed.) routes elements of learning deriving directly from classroom experience are also limited. (Current required minimums for approval of initial training courses include 15 weeks teaching practice for PGCE/3 year BEd, and 20 weeks for four-year programs).[5]

The challenge to develop processes by which professionalism can be enhanced, by building on the period of initial teacher education, is also made to local education authorities in *Better Schools* within its concern for the further professional development of teachers. There is a clear commitment to in-service teacher education during the period of induction, expressed as the employers' responsibility to:

support and encourage professional development at all stages of the individual teacher's career. A newly trained teacher needs structured support and guidance during probation and his early years in the profession (DES, 1985, para. 178).

In relation to that period some important issues have recently emerged. Her Majesty's Inspectors of Schools (HMI), in the 1982 report *The New Teacher in School,* identified 'a number of factors most frequently associated with good practice' in a sample of 294 schools in England and Wales. The factors were:

Pupils' participation, interest, and involvement;

Good classroom organization with a balance and variety of objectives;

Efficient use of materials and equipment;

Good relationships often characterized by a shared sense of purpose and mutual respect;

Productive and lively discussion usually associated with varied questioning techniques;

Good planning and preparation and a choice of content appropriate to the age and abilities of the pupils (DES, 1982, para. 2.60).

Three-quarters of the sampled teachers were said to be adequately equipped (or better) for the work they were assigned in their first posts. HMI rated over half of all newly trained teachers as well or very well equipped for their work (para. 6.1).

Three important issues are immediately apparent. First, for all the teachers the factors associated with good practice were concerned with individual teacher–pupil activities within classroom instruction. The need is clear for large proportions of new entrants to address those concerns in a systematic way during the early stages of induction. Second, the factors do not extend to the wider role of teaching — that is, participation in the corporate development of schools, and the development of professional attitudes concerned to increase effectiveness through professional development — more recently identified by *Better Schools* (DES, 1985) as falling within the responsibilities of classroom teachers. Systematic development of these roles is needed for *all* new teachers. Third, HMI makes it clear that the question of adequacy is related as much to the appropriateness of the appointment, and the context in which newly appointed teachers work, as it is to the quality, style and nature of their initial training. Professional adjustment and development during this period needs to be directly related to the working situations of new teachers. A response to these issues needs to be three-fold:

1   systematic and structured support for the study of classroom practice by new entrants, beginning in their first year of teaching;
2   extension of that support beyond the first year, to incorporate the development of self-appraisal for professional growth and the skills of curriculum development and leadership;
3   location of professional study within teachers' working contexts.

What would such a response need to look like? Within schools, new teachers would need to be attached to an experienced teacher-tutor for the period of the program, which would span the first three years of teaching. The teacher-tutors would advise, support, and act as a mentor to the new teachers in the conduct of practice and school-focused study. In addition, the teachers themselves and the teacher-tutors would follow a systematic, cooperative program of study based substantially on the conduct of fieldwork in their classrooms/schools, to develop the skills of inquiry and curriculum development. The outline of such a program assumes a view of professional development from initial teaching qualification to the broader responsibilities of curriculum leadership. That leadership would be built upon individual, personal excellence in teaching quality, gained through systematic practice, reflection, and modification of the new teacher's own teaching. The structure and content is, therefore, seen as continuous and developmental. That development would focus in turn on particular aspects of teaching which are seen to be in need of development within the profession (DES, 1982, 1983, 1985). Each of five aspects of practical teaching, outlined in the following sections, have consistently been regarded as underdeveloped: analyzing children's work; teaching and its different patterns; self-appraisal for professional growth; curriculum modification for a context; and, developing curriculum leadership. Complementary to the development of their own practice teachers would take account of relevant research literature in each of these areas.

Analyzing children's work

Analyzing children's work would engage teachers in learning to use children's work as a major resource and information source for their teaching, so that teaching is well directed to the needs of individual children, and varied according to particular demands of content/learning processes appropriate to the children at particular times. The careful differentiation of *what is taught* and *how it is taught* in order to match pupils' abilities and aptitudes is a fundamental principle of DES curriculum policy. There is widespread evidence of the need for practical implementation of that principle. Selection of content and teaching method can only be done effectively if the abilities and aptitudes of children are known in some detail, across a range of subject areas by primary teachers, and in depth in one subject by secondary teachers. Evidence is available in children's work, yet knowledge of how to elicit and use that evidence is complex. Teachers in the program would be required to use a range of methods for eliciting evidence — recorded oral group work, written work, observations of problem solving procedures, visual products, etc., and to develop their skills in analyzing the range of evidence.

Teaching and its different patterns

Teaching and its different patterns would explore and develop those patterns of teaching associated with the analysis and use of children's work, and varied content/learning processes, on what by then would be a foundation of knowledge of the children. It would consider elements of the practical knowledge of teaching, its acquisition and improvement, such as subject knowledge, instructional strategies, and the context of learning and teaching (use of resources, school policies, classroom and school milieu). The influence of learning activities and teaching styles on what is learned and how well it is learned has been a theme of HMI reports, and the focus of extensive recent research.

That pupils should learn in a variety of ways according to particular ages, abilities, attainments, experience, and the content of learning, means that no single style of teaching is suitable for all purposes. They also need to be adapted to class size, resources, physical layout of schools, and school ethos. Teachers would be expected to use the evidence of children's work (for instance evidence of individual attainments in mathematics, concept development in science, or capacity for discussion in oral language) to devise teaching and learning activities appropriate to individual development, group work, and whole-class progress. They would be required to monitor the styles of teaching adopted. This would require detailed plans of action with observations of teaching and its effects.

Self-appraisal for professional growth

Self-appraisal for professional growth would focus on devising modes of professional development, and working out with teachers how the effectiveness of those modes would be identified and demonstrated to their peers/others. This aspect not only would focus on the teacher's own professional growth, but also on that of colleagues. It would engage the problem of self-appraisal. Moves toward teacher appraisal recognise that no fully established models exist. The professionalization of teachers encourages them to seek professional excellence in their own practice through a process of self-appraisal and consequent improvement of teaching. This aspect of the program would require teachers to devise ways of investigating their own practice and provide evidence from those investigations which can be made available to other teachers, and from which judgments about improving practice can be made. For example, a teacher recognizing personal weakness in subject knowledge could analyze those weaknesses and build a program to rectify them. One whose teaching style is narrow would monitor changes effected as a result of work on the different patterns of teaching, and so on.

Curriculum modification for a context

Curriculum modification for a context would be concerned with ways in which all aspects of curriculum (not only teaching strategies) could be adapted and changed to meet the needs of particular classroom and school contexts. While it would center on the individual teacher's work, it would assume that modification needs to take account of wider contexts within the school and consider the implications of the modifications. Relevance to pupils' own experience and the needs of particular localities is also a fundamental educational principle reflected in recent curriculum policy. Making curriculum relevant to pupils in particular communities is one reason why a curriculum may need to be modified. Changes also occur in response to new technology, the state of knowledge about teaching, or changes in substantive knowledge. Teachers need to change practices with the advent of new examination requirements, institutional policies, and legislation. This aspect would equip teachers with the skills to judge curriculum needs and make adjustments to practice. For example, the introduction of craft, design, and technology teaching in primary schools invokes turbulence in traditional practice. A new teacher would be able to analyze, modify, and evaluate a school curriculum by taking account of the effects of such change.

Developing curriculum leadership

In developing curriculum leadership teachers would anticipate and plan specific curriculum modifications within the school, including their own teaching responsibilities. Issues of collegial professionalism and leadership, and innovation and change will be directly related to practical proposals for implementation. During initial training teachers are not educated formally for the professional responsibilities which are increasingly part of their role beyond their individual classrooms, as subject specialists advising colleagues in aspects of that subject, as consultants to parents and school governors, and as specialists in understanding curriculum and teaching methods. The opportunity for new teachers to develop leadership experience, skills, and attitudes such that expertise can be spread effectively — for increasingly young teachers are required to take leadership responsibilities — needs to be structured. Teachers would be expected to devise a long-term project for development of an aspect of the curriculum in their school. For example, a primary teacher with skills in science teaching might mount a school-wide program to introduce an aspect of science in other classes, a secondary teacher of history might lead colleagues in the development of teaching strategies using visual evidence, a computer-wise teacher might develop a course for computer-novice teachers, or the use of profiles of pupil achievements might be developed across curriculum areas.

Summary

In a recent 'radical' statement of policy for education's future, the Institute of Economic Affairs (1987) included a proposal that teachers should be trained in an apprenticeship system. Despite the recognized failings of current teacher practices, which would likely be conserved through apprenticeship, and despite the calls for teachers to be capable of regenerating education (DES, 1985), the Lancasterians maintain a strong presence in the debate. I urge, however, that the alternative viewpoint to apprenticeship, with its many recent developments towards research-based teacher professionalism, should be established instead. The essence of that professionalism needs to be included in initial teacher education. Because of the extensive involvement in practical teaching which follows, and the crucial nature of this period of intensive learning, it can be fostered more substantially during the induction of beginning teachers.

I have argued that it is necessary to avoid the slippage into *coping strategies* and ensure the development of *empirically derived practices and principles of pedagogy*. I have set out a proposed program which ought to be capable of leading towards such professionalism. If successful, it would help teachers individually and collectively to meet some of the present criticisms of teaching. Such systematic long-term induction would perhaps rectify the 'primitive' state of teachers' early professional development identified by Lortie (1975). And, it would do so within a framework of interactive socialization, recognizing that new teachers are capable of contributing constructively to the practice of teaching and the debate about problematic issues in education. Reconstruction of the practice of individual teachers and of schooling more generally cannot be achieved by isolated individuals. It requires formal collective support for the development of research-based teacher induction in a way which treats the practice of teaching as a serious realm of professional knowledge. The process of induction itself will need careful monitoring in order to elucidate the educational experiences of new entrants to the profession.

Notes

1. National Society Report 1814, p. 14, cited in Rich 1933, p. 3.
2. Even here, according to Rich (1933), there was dispute about how best to achieve such training, with debate about the relationship between theory and practice. Bell sought training entirely through monitorial apprenticeship in the practical operations of the school as the only means by which teachers were to be 'formed'. He accused Lancaster of promoting incompetence by attempting to form teachers in part through 'lectures and abstract instruction' (Rich 1933, p. 4).
3. See for example Nixon, J. (1981), and Carr, W. and Kemmis, S. (1986).
4. *Man: A Course of Study* (MACOS) was developed by the Education Center, Inc., in the USA during the 1960s. See Dow, 1970.
5. Post-Graduate Certificate Programs leading to qualified teacher status are 36 weeks long and usually immediately follow the award of a university degree in a specific subject. BEd or BA(Ed) programs last four years, during which the equivalent of two years is given to subject study, and two years to education studies, methods, and classroom practice.

References

ALEXANDER, R. J. (1984). *Primary teaching.* London: Holt, Rinehart, and Winston.

ASHTON, P. M. E., HENDERSON, E. S., MERRITT, J. E., and MORTIMER, D. J. (1983). *Teacher education in the classroom: Initial and inservice.* London: Croom Helm.

BECKER, H. S. (1971). Personal change in adult life. In B. R. Cosin, I. R. Dale, G. M. Esland, D. MacKinnon, and D. Swift (eds). *School and society.* London: Routledge & Kegan Paul.

BEYNON, J. (1987). Ms. Floral mends her ways. In L. Tickle (ed.). *The arts in education: Some research studies.* London: Croom Helm.

BURDEN, P. R. (February, 1982). *Professional development as a stressor.* Paper presented at the Annual Meeting of the Association of Teacher Educators, Phoenix, AZ.

CALLAGHAN, J. (October, 1976). Towards a national debate. *Education, 148*(17), pp. 332–3.

CARR, W., and KEMMIS, S. (1986). *Becoming critical: Knowing through action research.* Lewes: Falmer Press.

CLANDININ, D. J. (1986). *Classroom practice: Teacher images in action.* Lewes: Falmer Press.

DEPARTMENT OF EDUCATION AND SCIENCE. (1972). *Teacher education and training.* London: Her Majesty's Stationery Office.

DEPARTMENT OF EDUCATION AND SCIENCE. (1982). *The new teacher in school.* London: Her Majesty's Stationery Office.

DEPARTMENT OF EDUCATION AND SCIENCE. (1983). *Teaching quality.* London: Her Majesty's Stationery Office.

DEPARTMENT OF EDUCATION AND SCIENCE. (1984). *Initial teacher training: Approval of courses.* Circular No. 3/84. London: Author.

DEPARTMENT OF EDUCATION AND SCIENCE. (1985). *Better schools.* London: Her Majesty's Stationery Office.

DEPARTMENT OF EDUCATION AND SCIENCE. (1986). *Education (No. 2) Act 1986.* Circular No. 8/86. London: Author.

DEPARTMENT OF EDUCATION AND SCIENCE. (1987). *The national curriculum: A consultation document.* London: Author.

DOW, P. (1970). *Man: A course of study.* Cambridge, MA: Education Development Center.

DOYLE, W. (1985). Learning to teach: An emerging direction in research on preservice teacher education. *Journal of Teacher Education, 36*(1), 31–2.

ELBAZ, F. (1983). *Teacher thinking: A study of practical knowledge.* London: Croom Helm.

ELLIOTT, J., and ADELMAN, C. (1973). Reflecting where the action is: The design of the Ford Teaching Project. *Education for Teaching, 92,* 8–20.

GRACEY, H. (1976). The craftsman teachers. In M. Hammersley, and P. Woods, (eds) *The process of schooling.* London: Routledge & Kegan Paul.

GRAHAM, D. (1985). *Those having torches ... teacher appraisal: A study.* Ipswich, England: Suffolk Country Council.

GRIFFIN, G. A. (1985). Teacher induction: Research issues. *Journal of Teacher Education, 36*(1), 42–6.

HALL, G. E. (1982). Induction: The missing link. *Journal of Teacher Education, 33*(3), 53–5.

HOLT, M. (1982). *Evaluating the evaluators.* London: Hodder and Stoughton.

INNER LONDON EDUCATION AUTHORITY. (1980). *The ILEA induction scheme: A survey of probationers' experiences and views of the first year of the scheme.* London: Author, Research and Statistics Division.

INNER LONDON EDUCATION AUTHORITY. (1985). *The ILEA induction scheme: Five years on.* London: Author, Research and Statistics Division.

THE INSTITUTE OF ECONOMIC AFFAIRS. (1987). *Our schools: A radical policy.* London: Author.

JOHNSTON, J. M. and RYAN, K. (1983). Research on the beginning teacher: Implications for teacher education. In K. R. Howey, and W. E. Gardner (eds). *The education of teachers: A look ahead.* New York: Longman.

LACEY, C. (1977). *The socialization of teachers.* London: Methuen.

LORTIE, D. (1975). *Schoolteacher.* Chicago: University of Chicago Press.

NIXON, J. (1981). *A teacher's guide to action research: Evaluation, enquiry, and development in the classroom.* London: McIntyre.

RICH, R. W. (1933). *The training of teachers in England and Wales during the nineteenth century.* Cambridge: Cambridge University Press.

SOCKETT, H. (ed.). (1980). *Accountability in the English education system.* London: Hodder & Stoughton.

SOCKETT, H. (1985). What is a School of Education? *Cambridge Journal of Education, 15*(3), 115–22.

STENHOUSE, L. (1975). *An introduction to curriculum research and development.* London: Heinemann.

TICKLE, L. (1987). *Learning teaching, teaching teaching: A study of partnership in teacher education.* Lewes: Falmer Press.

TISHER, R. P. (1982, March). *Teacher induction: An international perspective on research programs.* Paper presented at the Annual Meeting of the American Educational Research Association, New York, NY.

WALKER, R. (1985). *Doing research: A handbook for teachers.* London: Methuen.

WALLACE, G. (1985). Middle schools through the looking glass. In G. Walford, (ed.). *Schooling in turmoil.* London: Croom Helm.

WRAGG, E. C. (ed.). (1984). *Classroom teaching skills.* London: Croom Helm.

ZEICHNER, K. M., and TABACHNICK, B. R. (1985). The development of teacher perspectives: Social strategies and institutional control in the socialization of beginning teachers. *Journal of Education for Teaching, 2*(1), 1–25.

PART III
TEACHERS AND PROFESSIONAL DEVELOPMENT

6 Teachers: Ages and Stages of Adult Development

Sharon Nodie Oja

Connecting the Literature on Ages and Stages of Adult Development with Teacher Professional Growth

Recently, large numbers of researchers and local teacher educators have begun to draw upon adult development theories to aid in their study of teacher professional growth. Various developmental theories — describing predictable sequences of growth, adaptation, transformation, and change in adulthood — are employed to this end. The purpose of this chapter is to review the contributions of adult development theorists and researchers to our understanding of teacher development. The goal in examining the available literature, different educators' practice, and illustrative teacher behavior is to share relevant information with other teachers and with those working with teachers in staff development programs. Specifically, what is known about the needs of teachers at various ages and stages of adult development as well as how such developmental differences influence teacher behavior will be described.

This chapter will describe two primary ways to look at adult development in the education profession. One way is to focus on the age-related life issues and career concerns of teachers. Patterns have been found in age and career issues of concern to adults. Figure 6.1 illustrates age-related life periods. The second way to look at adult development is by focusing on behaviors and feelings. Patterns have been found in adults' thinking, emotions, and behaviors, and these patterns have been called cognitive-developmental stages. Figure 6.2 describes characteristics of different stages of development. Examples will be given of teachers who are the same age, yet behave and feel quite differently when participating in staff

Figure 6.1 Developmental Ages

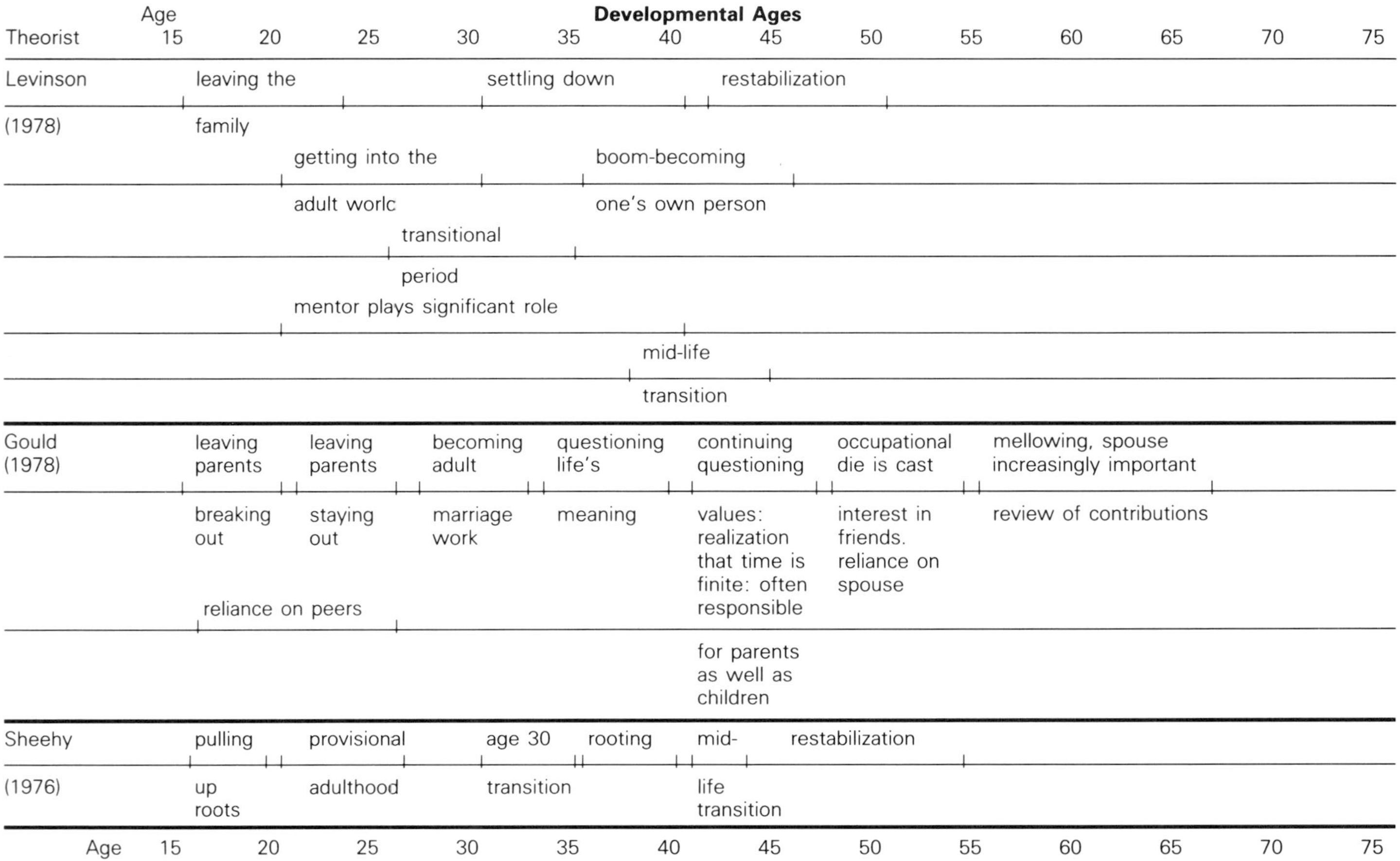

Developmental Ages

Theorist	Age 15	20	25	30	35	40	45	50	55	60	65	70	75
Levinson (1978)	leaving the family	getting into the adult world	transitional period	settling down		boom-becoming one's own person	restabilization						
			mentor plays significant role			mid-life transition							
Gould (1978)	leaving parents	staying out	becoming adult	questioning life's	continuing questioning	occupational die is cast	mellowing, spouse increasingly important						
	breaking out		marriage work	meaning	values: realization that time is finite: often responsible	interest in friends. reliance on spouse	review of contributions						
	reliance on peers				for parents as well as children								
Sheehy (1976)	pulling up roots	provisional adulthood		age 30 transition / rooting	mid- life transition	restabilization							
		transition											

| Age | 15 | 20 | 25 | 30 | 35 | 40 | 45 | 50 | 55 | 60 | 65 | 70 | 75 |

Source: Oja, S. N. (1980). Adult development is implicit in staff development. *The Journal of Staff Development*, 1(2), p. 12.

Figure 6.2   Developmental Stages

Developmental Stages

SELF-PROTECTIVE STAGE

At the *Self-Protective* stage, individuals are able to control their impulsiveness and have learned to anticipate rewards and punishments. Although rules are recognized, at this stage adults use rules for their own advantage. The self-protective individual's main rule is 'don't get caught'. Blame is placed on other individuals or the circumstances when satisfaction is not achieved. Adults who stay at this stage maintain manipulative and exploitive interpersonal relations and thus tend to be opportunistic, deceptive, and preoccupied with control and advantage.

CONFORMIST STAGE

Most people at some time in adolescense move to the *Conformist* stage as they begin to place strong trust for the welfare in the family group, the peer group, or in socially-approved norms. Adults who stay at this stage obey rules simply because they are group-accepted rules. Belonging is of utmost importance. Feelings of disapproval and shame are crucial issues at this stage. Behavior is viewed in terms of external actions and concrete events rather than feelings and inner motives. Personal emotions are expressed through cliches, stereotypes, and moralistic judgments. The adult at this stage is preoccupied with appearance, social acceptance, and reputation.

SELF-AWARE TRANSITION

At the *Self-Aware* transition level between the prior Conformist stage and the subsequent Conscientious stage there is an increase in self-awareness and beginning appreciation and understanding of multiple possibilities, alternatives, and options in problem-solving situations. Growing awareness of inner emotions enhances the capacity for introspection (crucial at subsequent stages), although adults at this stage continue to express feelings in vague or global terms. Growing self-confidence and self-evaluated standards at this stage begin to replace group standards as guidelines for behavior.

CONSCIENTIOUS STAGE

At the *Conscientious* Stage adults are capable of self-criticism. This combined with long-term, self-evaluated goals and ideals and a sense of responsibility form the major elements of the adult conscience, all evident at this stage. Rules are internalized; guilt is the consequence of breaking inner rules. Exceptions and contingencies in rules are recognized in direct relation to a growing awareness of the subtleties of individual differences. Behavior is seen in terms of feelings, patterns, and motives rather than simply actions. Achievement, especially when measured by self-chosen standards, is crucial. Adults at this stage are preoccupied with obligations, privileges, rights, ideals, traits, and achievement, all defined more by inner standards and less by the need for external recognition and acceptance.

INDIVIDUALISTIC TRANSITION

At the *Individualistic* level, a sense of individuality is of utmost concern, especially as it is coupled with heightened awareness of emotional dependence on others. An adult at this level tends to have more complex responses than adults at earlier developmental stages. There is increased ability to tolerate paradoxical and contradictory relationships between events in contrast to earlier stages where adults attempt to eliminate paradoxes by reducing them to polar opposites. There is also greater complexity in conceptualizing interpersonal interactions. Interpersonal relationships are highly valued in contrast to the cherishing of ideals and achievements at the Conscientious stage previous to this one.

AUTONOMOUS STAGE

The distinguishing characteristic at the *Autonomous* stage is the adult's capacity to tolerate and cope with the inner conflict that arises between conflicting perceptions, needs, ideals, and duties. An adult at this stage is able to unite ideas that appear as ambiguous or incompatible options to adults at prior stages. In particular at this stage, the adult acknowledges other persons' needs for autonomy to make their own choices and solutions and to learn from their own mistakes. At the same time, the autonomous stage adult realizes the limitations of autonomy; consequently, mutual *inter*-dependence is highly valued in interpersonal relationships. The person at this stage is concerned with self-fulfillment, differing perceptions of one's role and issues of justice in addition to being concerned about the individuality and achievement issues of prior stages.

Source: Jane Loevinger's Ego Development Stages as summarized in Oja, S. N. (1980). Adult development is implicit in staff development. *The Journal of Staff Development, 1*(2), pp. 22–24.

development activities. This difference results from teachers' different cognitive-developmental stages.

Overview of Ages and Stages of Adult Development

Adult development is paced by cultural and societal expectations as well as by personal values and aspirations. Two broad perspectives can be identified on the issue of what prompts developmental growth in adulthood: (1) life age/cycle, and (2) cognitive-developmental stage.

Life Age/Cycle theorists focus on predictable life events as pacers for growth. Such tasks as establishing and maintaining social and inter-personal roles, as well as dealing with essential intrapsychic tasks, provide the impetus for change and, sometimes growth, in adults.

Cognitive-Developmental Stage theorists, on the other hand, focus on particular cognitive emotional perspectives distinctive to different stages of development. The events that may prompt cognitive development will vary according to the developmental stage perspective a person currently holds. Life Age/Cycle theorists describe transitions and adaptations to life events. Cognitive-developmental theorists describe transformations in adults' ways of constructing and making meaning of experience (Weathersby and Tarule, 1980). Life Age/Cycle theorists consider maturity to consist of successful adaptation to societal expectations through the life cycle. Cognitive-developmental theorists consider maturity to be a developmental process toward types of thinking that are 'more universal and better able to deal with abstract relationships, that more clearly identify psychological and cultural assumptions shaping our actions and causing our needs, that provide criteria for more principled value judgments, enhance our sense of agency or control and give us a clearer meaning and sense of direction in our lives' (Mezirow, 1978, p. 106). Both the age and stage perspectives of adult development can contribute to working with teachers and planning for staff development in schools.

Ultimately, questions arise in how school environments interact with teachers' ages and stages of development as well as whether, and how, interactions designed to foster learning and growth have an impact on teacher performance. Could current problems, such as teacher burnout and teacher dropout, be due to a *lack of fit* between particular teaching environments and particular teacher ages and stages of development? Can schools be adapted to meet the developmental needs of teachers at different ages and stages? How is it possible to design and implement more effective and attractive professional development programs for teachers? This chapter will examine the literature and research practices relevant to such issues and then present case studies of teachers involved in a particular two-year staff development project. The goals and expectations of teachers at different ages and stages, and their reasons for participating in the project, will be described. We found that the reasons 'why' teachers chose to become involved often correlated with their life age and career cycles. On the other hand, we found that 'how' the teachers participated in the groups, and their goals, expectations, and outcomes often correlated with their cognitive-developmental stage perspectives. Both ages and stages of development were important to our understanding of teachers participating in a two-year staff development project. Before describing the teachers themselves, brief summaries of the age and stage perspectives on adult development will be given.

Tasks at Different Ages of Development

Pioneers in the study of ages of adult development have focused on routine 'life events' as prompts for development. Such relatively predictable events as the selection of social and interpersonal roles, the performance of adult tasks, and the adoption of necessary coping behaviors are posited as pacers for adult development. Among theorists taking this functional view of development, one group focuses primarily on age-related tasks (Gould, 1978; Havighurst, 1972; Levinson *et al.*, 1978; Sheehy, 1976), while the second focuses on tasks related to the central issues of different phases of the life cycle (Erikson, 1959; Neugarten, 1963). See Figure 6.1 for the Life Age/Cycles perspective.[1]

The work of the Life Age theorists has been criticized on various grounds, so while we consider their implications, we are also aware of their limitations. Their accounts are based on clinical/biographical data from adults at different ages. The groups employed by Levinson *et al.* (1978) and Gould (1978) consist primarily of white middle-class men. One must wonder whether the life pattern exhibited by these individuals can provide a schema of development which will adequately describe the experience of those from different ethnic and social backgrounds. Also, there are questions of whether the schemes provide a good fit to the lives of most women. More recent studies have studied the age-related issues of women, and Levinson is scheduled to soon release a book on the seasons of a woman's life. So while one should be cautious in employing such schemes of tasks in design of educational programs for adults, these theorists do succeed in making the point that the negotiation of certain life tasks in various life periods may indeed have a significant impact upon the functioning of the adult. An awareness of the impact of such events and a sensitivity to the needs of adults at various life-ages could be valuable aids to individuals working in the field of staff development.

The life-cycle theories also have implications for staff development. Adults at certain times may require aid in confronting what Bernice Neugarten has labeled as off-time events such as the unexpected death of a child, spouse, or parent (1963), as well as support in working through or reworking the issues of identity, intimacy, generativity and integrity which Erik Erikson posits as crucial for cycles of adult development (1959). An awareness of these issues and the roles they play in the lives of adults may help to broaden the focus of staff development programs.

Career Cycles and Teacher Concerns

A number of researchers in teacher staff development have related the Life Age/Cycle theories to teacher career cycles. Researchers like Newman, Burden, and Applegate (1980) first used teacher age to describe three linear phases in a teacher's career. Through teacher interviews they described a first career phase, from about age 20–40, as being a time of finding one's place in the profession, a time which may involve considerable shifts in one's commitment to teaching. Then from about age 40–55, teachers in their studies described a second phase characterized by a strong commitment to teaching and high personal morale. Finally, they report a third phase involving loss of energy and loss of enthusiasm as teachers become aware of a pulling away from teaching and from their students. Judy Arin-Krupp's interviews with teachers (1981) defined seven periods of teachers' careers from their twenties to retirement, and helped to further specify and characterize key concerns and the implications for professional development planning at each of the seven career periods. This scheme most closely reflects Levinson *et al.*'s research on *Seasons of a Man's Life* (1978) which will be more thoroughly discussed in the middle section of this chapter as we look at some specific examples of teachers at different ages and career cycles and describe why they became involved in a particular staff development project.

Another Life Cycle approach which explains even further the complex of factors that influence a teacher's career direction is posed by Judith Christensen, Peter Burke, Ralph Fessler and David Hagstrom (1983). They explain both the personal tasks and the organizational factors that have an impact on the various facets of a teacher's career. The 'Teacher Career Cycle Model' shown in Figure 3 uses the Life Age/Cycle principles of adult growth and development and borrows an approach from social systems theory. It views the teacher's career cycle as influenced by and influencing both the teacher's personal environment and the organizational environment of the school. Christensen *et al.* (1983) give a dynamic and flexible perspective to the teacher career cycle rather than one of a static or fixed set of phases dependent on age alone.

Investigation of teachers' concerns at different career points resulted in the development of the Concerns-Based-Adoption-Model (CBAM) by Gene Hall and Susan Loucks (1978) and others from the University of Texas Research and Development Center for Teacher Education. CBAM describes levels of teachers' concerns about change and innovation as a basis for facilitating and personalizing staff development activities and school change programs. Huling-Austin (1981) investigated teachers' concerns in a collaborative research study, and was able to relate their changing concerns to their participation in an extended one-year staff development project involving interactive research and development.

In the developing literature base on teachers' issues and concerns at different career cycles much has been learned in the last ten years. Now it is time to match those learnings with the newer learnings in teachers' cognitive-developmental stages. It is possible to design and implement more effective staff development programs which attract teachers' interest and enthusiasm, result in genuine new learnings for both individuals and the schools, and allow for continuing adult development within our teaching profession.

Cognitive-Developmental Stages of Development

Adult cognitive-developmental stages are best described by referring to specific stages of moral/ethical judgment, conceptual complexity,

Figure 6.3 Dynamics of the Teacher Career Cycle

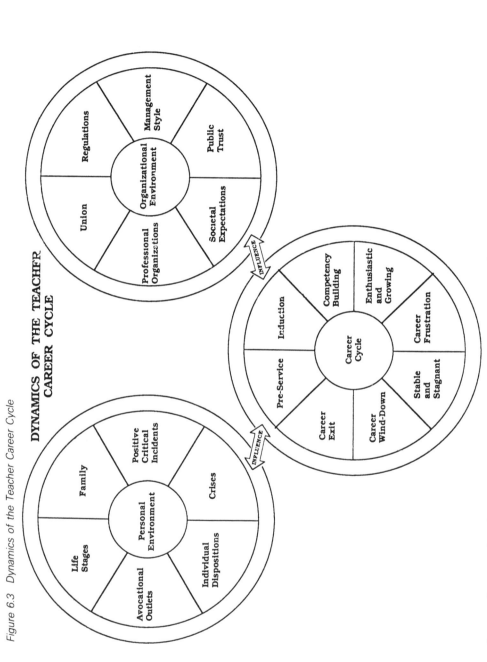

DYNAMICS OF THE TEACHER CAREER CYCLE

Source: Fessler, R. (1985). A model for teacher professional growth and development. In P. J. Burke and R. G. Heideman (eds), *Career-long education* (pp. 181–183). Springfield, Illinois: Charles C. Thomas, publisher

ego development, and interpersonal functioning. This chapter uses primarily Jane Loevinger's stages of ego development since they tend to encompass aspects of cognitive ability, moral/ethical judgment, conceptual level, and interpersonal behavior within the larger umbrella framework of ego stage. In her theory of how one perceives oneself and others, Loevinger (1976) conceptualized seven sequential stages with three transition stages. Each developmental stage is more mature than the last and none can be skipped in the course of development. However, different individuals may stabilize at certain stages and consequently not develop beyond those stages. Among adults there can be found representatives of each of the developmental stages who share characteristics and features specific to that stage. The range of stages of development in adulthood are the self-protective, conformist, self-aware, conscientious, individualistic, and autonomous stages. These developmental stages are summarized in Figure 6.2 presented earlier in the chapter.

The essence of development is the striving to master, to integrate, to make sense of one's experience. Development takes place in a sequence of steps along a continuum of increasing differentiation and complexity. There is a unitary nature to this scheme in describing the stage of development as the frame of reference that structures one's world and within which one perceives the world. The ego stage, then, becomes an 'inner logic' which maintains its stability and identity and its structure by selective inattention to factors inconsistent with its current ego level. The characteristics of the successive stages of development are described in terms of one's impulse control, interpersonal style, conscious preoccupations, and cognitive style. These stages can be compared with levels of moral judgment. At the adult preconventional level, are the Impulsive and Self-Protective ego stages. At the conventional levels are the Conformist, Self-Aware, and Conscientious stages. At the post-conventional levels are the Individualistic, Autonomous, and Integrated Ego stages. In the Loevinger scheme, the Moral Judgment levels and Cognitive stages are included within her more encompassing ego stages. Also, Loevinger claims that the Autonomous and Integrated Ego stages go beyond principled moral thinking by including concern for mutuality and responsibility beyond a single focus on individuality. (This seems to be the same issue which Carol Gilligan (1977, 1982) is confronting in her research on moral judgment differences in women and men, particularly women's conception of self and of morality.) Loevinger and other researchers report the conformist-conscientious transition stage (called the Self-Aware level) to be the most predominant adult ego stage. Staff development studies with teachers found that the predominant teacher stage was the Self-aware Transition stage (Sprinthall and Bernier, 1978) or the Conscientious stage (Oja and Sprinthall, 1978). Jane Loevinger's developmental stage theory along with the work of Lawrence Kohlberg (1969, 1971, 1973, 1976), Carol Gilligan (1977, 1982) and William Perry (1970) in moral/ethical judgment and David Hunt's work (1966, 1970, 1975, 1976, 1978) in the area of teachers' conceptual development have strong implications for adult development programs within teacher education[2].

Illustrations of Teachers at Different Ages and Stages

Following this short introduction and overview of life age cycles and cognitive developmental stages, summaries of teacher case histories provide examples of teachers who represent different life periods, career cycles, and developmental stages. In questionnaires and interviews prior to and at the beginning of a staff development project called *Action Research on Change in Schools* (ARCS), we asked teachers about their life periods and career cycles. In particular we asked teachers their perceptions of (1) their life periods as chapters in an autobiography, (2) stability and transition in their lives, (3) the importance of personal development goals versus career goals in their current life period, and (4) critical key issues that were currently important in their lives (see Figure 6.4). These data from an Educational Experiences Inventory (available from the Collaborative Research Project Office at the University of New Hampshire) were analyzed to investigate the relationship of life phases and career cycles to teachers' participation in a particular staff development activity like ARCS.

Teachers' voices and descriptions can be heard in a different way by using the additional perspective of cognitive-developmental stages. Thus, we asked teachers to respond to three empirical measures of cognitive development stages: the Defining Issues test of moral judgment, the Sentence Completion for ego development, and the Paragraph Completion questionnaire of conceptual complexity. The characteristics of teachers according to their cognitive-developmental stages were used to examine individual teacher participation in and perception of issues related to the ARCS staff development project[3].

Figure 6.4 Life Issues and Concerns

Life Issues and Concerns

1. Separating myself from my family and/or my parent's expectations.

2. Seeing myself as an adult, becoming part of the adult world.

3. Starting a career and/or exploring family or community roles.

4. Parenting . . . raising my children as I'd like to (or deciding to be a parent).

5. Developing my sense of myself as an adult.

6. Making deeper investments in my choices for life and work; setting long range goals and meeting them.

7. Becoming recognized for my contribution and achievement in roles I value.

8. Becoming my own person with identity and direction, not dependent on boss, spouse, colleagues, critics, or mentors.

9. Changing my activities and ambitions to reflect more realistically who I am and what I want from my life and work.

10. Sharing my knowledge and skills, contributing to the next generation, being helpful to younger friends and associates.

11. Sharing everyday human joys with others; maintaining warm relationships with friends, family, spouse, and colleagues.

12. Accomplishing a few important things in the finite period I have left.

13. Accepting what has transpired in my life as 'mine;' valuing myself and my choices.

Source: Oja, S. N. (1983). Life age/cycle characteristics of ARCS teachers. In Oja, S. N. and Pine, G. J., *A two year study of teacher stages of development in relation to collaborative action research in schools: Appendix to the final report* (p. 755). Washington, DC: National Institute of Education. (ERIC Document Reproduction Service No. ED 248 227)

Great emphasis in the documentation of the ARCS project was given to each individual teacher's perceptions and to presenting these perceptions in the teacher's own remarks. Reading teachers' remarks as they have been woven into the analysis helps one to understand the differences in the way in which teachers perceive issues in the collaborative group process and research process. Analysis of different stages of development using the teachers' remarks also helps one recognize how a teacher's developmental stage may be a lens (or world view) through which the teacher makes meaning of his/her school environment and the particular staff development activity.

The following descriptions of teachers are organized chronologically by age period. Each example is introduced with a teacher's pseudonym, age, life/age cycle, career cycle, and developmental stage. With one exception, the life/age cycle of Getting into the Adult World, each life/age cycle is represented by a specific teacher example.

In these examples, the reader will hear why the teacher became involved in a specific staff development activity, and then how they participated in the collaborative group activity.

Life/Age Cycle: Getting into the adult world

'Getting into the adult world' encompasses the early twenties to about age 28. At this time the individual is concerned with exploring new options in the adult world in order to form an inital perspective of him/herself as an adult. Levinson calls this 'forming a life structure'. It is the life structure which continues to be redefined and transformed as the tasks of adulthood are undertaken. As part of this initial life structure, the new adult makes initial commitments to a job and career, gets married (or decides not to get married), decides whether to raise a family, buys a house, moves, and so forth. Between 35 per cent and 50 per cent of our schools' teachers originally indicated interest in the ARCS project, but none of these teachers were in the 20–28 age period. The lack of representation of this age group reflected the current age context of staff in the school project sites; the schools were composed of experienced, older staffs and had not had a major influx of younger beginning teachers. The least experienced teacher originally indicating interest in the ARCS project had 8 years of experience teaching. Teachers involved in ARCS had between 9 and 23 years of teaching experience. Even if the project schools had larger numbers of teachers in this beginning age group, we are unsure whether they would be attracted to a staff development project like *Action Research on Change in Schools*. Research on the beginning teacher indicates concerns most closely tied to the individual's classroom. Problems of the beginning teacher are often quite different from the problems and issues of concern to the more experienced teacher. The beginning teacher studies (for example, McDonald, 1980; Johnston and Ryan, 1983; and Zeichner and Tabachnick, 1985) have information to provide about this early part of the career cycle and, in particular, the needs for beginning teachers to have teacher mentors. Current work by Theis-Sprinthall (1986) illustrates an exciting new program for experienced teachers who learn to mentor beginning teachers and then train other teachers to mentor. For teachers like John, in the examples to come, who wants to mentor younger colleagues, a program like this would be ideal.

LORI (age 34)
Career Cycle: **12 years' experience**
Life Age/Cycle: **Age 30 Transition**
Cognitive Developmental Stage: **Self–Aware Stage**

In the late twenties or early thirties the 'age 30 crisis' confronts the new adult. S/he asks 'what is life all about?'. In confronting this question, the adult re-examines the intial life structure and the commitments made in the previous period. This questioning may result in a change in career or personal relationships. What options exist in the teaching profession for those teachers in the thirties transition who wish to make a change?

Lori has 12 years of teaching experience, 11 of them at the school in which she currently teaches. She says, 'I'm always interested in hearing about innovations in education which will make me a more effective teacher ... and ... I'm determined not to fall into the rut of an experienced teacher whose most important teaching tool is the file cabinet.' Like other teachers in the Thirties Transition, Lori indicates that she has just come through a huge transition in her life and work, and she feels she is on the verge of making a lot of changes. In describing the transition she has just experienced, she suggests what it means to readjust to the status quo of the classroom:

> I recently completed an M.A. degree in Educational Leadership, and I was looking forward to a new position in the district. Unfortunately, I applied for three positions in the district and was turned down for all three. Overcoming these losses was very difficult for me. Now that I'm over them, I'm adjusted to reassuming my role as a respected classroom teacher. However, if the situation arises I will again apply for a position outside the classroom, but only if it's what I *really* want, not for the sake of moving out of the classroom.

Her participation in the ARCS project seemed motivated by her interest in innovation and because she liked the approach of teachers doing action research. Benefits for herself included the possibility of getting a Ph.D. as she explained, 'I was very interested, and I have to agree wholeheartedly with this new approach ... Let's look at what teachers say are their own problems ...' Benefit for self? 'I would really like a doctorate someday and I have been thinking about it in terms of what would I ever write a thesis on and when you brought this up, boy, there would sure be some interesting topics to explore.'

Lori listed work and personal goals as equally important in her life. The key issue she was most hard at work on (from the list in Figure 6.3) was making deeper investments in life and work choices and setting long range goals and meeting them. A second key issue reflected her balance of work with more personal goals: sharing everyday human joys with others and maintaining warm relationships with friends, family, spouse, and colleagues. Research with life age/ cycles suggests that women in their twenties focus more on personal issues than men of their same age, while women in their thirties begin to focus on work choices more. Lori's third life issue was accomplishing a few important things in the finite period she has left. It is unlikely that this issue reflected her growing sense of the finiteness of time which Neugarten (1963) suggests confronts adults at mid-life, but rather that Lori feels the pressure of a career change and the need to take action before too long, a typical Thirties Transition issue. This latter reason also seems more likely when listening to Lori's fourth key issue in life, changing her activities to reflect more realistically who she was and what she wanted from her life and work. Lori titled the period of life she just left as 'Discontent', her present period as 'Thirty and Out', and the next period as 'Nirvana'. A final indication of Lori's Age 30 Transition, with many issues up in the air, was that she was not just working on these five key issues but saw three additional issues as becoming increasingly important: parenting (deciding whether to be a parent), exploring a new position, and accepting what has transpired in her life as 'hers'.

The age-related characteristics and career cycle presented above helped to describe why Lori was interested in becoming a part of the collaborative action research project. As we continued, we found that Lori's cognitive-developmental stage helped describe how she perceived the group proccess and operated within the action research team.

Lori exhibited behavioral characteristics of the Conformist–Conscientious transition level, called the *Self-Aware stage* (see Figure 6.2). Like other teachers at this developmental level, she expressed global and sometimes vague goals when asked about using the project to solve school problems. With the help of others in her team she was able to become more specific. Lori was committed to and highly involved in the project, able and willing to assume responsibilities for tasks on the team, and seemed clearly in transition to the Conscientious Stage. At the end of the project Lori emphasized the value of collaborative action research as a model for staff development. She said,

> I think being introduced to action research as a process has been the most valuable part of the project for me. In fact, as I look back at the work that we've done and the topics we've discussed ... the fact that we have been able to work together within the model made all the difference. Because I see how valuable the model is and see, too, how the model can be used in so many different situations.

Further descriptions of the Self Aware transition stage of development will be given later in the examples as Anne is introduced. Anne was older (in her late thirties) and working on different life age and career issues than teachers like Lori at the Age 30 Crisis; however, Anne and Lori did share the same behavioral characteristics of the Self-Aware developmental stage. But before jumping ahead, it is important to mention the next life period of the early thirties. It is also important to describe Elliot, in particular, because his stage of development was among the most mature of the adults on the collaborative research teams.

Elliot (age 34)
Career Cycle: **11 years' experience**
Age/Cycle: **Settling Down after 30s transition**
Developmental Stage: **Individualistic level**

Having dealt with the issues of the Age 30 Crisis, men settle down in the early thirties, reaffirming commitments and often choosing the career as the most highly valued investment of time and energy. Children are often in school; mother (if she was at home) probably returns to work or school. Settling long-term goals both for work-related and family-related activites becomes important to adults in this phase.

Elliot, a math teacher of 11 years, 6 of them at his current school, was originally somewhat hesitant to commit to the 2 year action research project because he was preparing to 'advance to a role of more responsibility' most likely outside the teaching field. 'Very recently', he says, 'I have questioned my motivation in meeting weekly and discussing educational topics; I'm a little burned out from that as a result of my pursuing the Masters degree in Education I did recently. I'm considering moving out of education.' In deciding to participate he indicates a clear sense of commitment and a conscious decision: 'ARCS will ideally motivate thought and greater precision in my conceptualization of issues relevant in an advanced position.' Elliot also indicates an awareness of his own skills as he adds: 'I derive pleasure from such activities (action research); I am skillful ... I can make significant contributions.' Although only moderately satisfied with previous staff development activities, he said that he definitely enjoyed participating in research type activities in the school during a previously federal funded project. He said he signed up for ARCS because he was interested and excited about it. Elliot indicated that prior staff development activities were somewhat helpful to him in negotiating changes in his life or work in terms of 'motivation to learn and filling voids in knowledge background'.

Elliot felt he was just on the verge of making a lot of changes. The life period he just left he titled 'Frustration'. The present period was titled 'Moving On' and the next period he saw as 'Living Comfortably'. When asked to indicate how hard at work he was on certain life issues he circled three key issues and indicated the rest (out of thirteen listed in Figure 6.3) were 'not an issue now'. This rating is very different from Lori and other teachers who were in the Thirties Transition. There is a sense that Elliot had wrestled with and made decisions on a number of life dilemmas and was on his way in the life period titled *'Settling Down'*. Elliot's three key issues were parenting, starting a career and/or exploring family and community roles, and being recognized for his contribution and achievement in roles he valued. Similar to many men in this age cycle, Elliot pointed to work and career goals as significantly more important than personal goals; he says 'my personal life right now is substantially involved in planning and preparing for professional growth and change'.

Elliot's behavior in the collaborative action research project exhibited characteristics of the *Individualistic* stage of development. Elliot felt skillful in approaching the individual and group goals set by the action research team. He was able to keep his own needs and goals in mind while fulfilling obligations to the group (for example, doing computer programs and data analysis contributed to his own needs to learn more for a course he was teaching while also contributing to the group's goals and needs). Teaching a statistics course allowed him to bring information back to the team to help them clarify goals. This contrasted with another group member (operating at the Conscientious Stage) who had difficulty in maintaining her obligation to the team without submerging her own growing sense of individuality and her need to address personal issues. This other team member almost dichotomized the two so that her sense of responsibility would not overtake her emerging focus on personal needs within the group. Elliot, in contrast, was able to integrate his individual needs with the demands of the group. Elliot was also able to stand back from the group and view it in perspective when needed, whereas the Conscientious Stage teachers like John and Florence, in the examples which follow, tended either to have their values and actions embedded in the group's work or were struggling to differentiate their individual emerging values and perceptions from those of the group.

Even though Elliot's goals were individualistic, he had a sense of obligation to the group, a feeling of contractual commitment which influenced his acceptance and volunteering to carry out team tasks. He talked about being 'flexible' in the group, so that even when he made objections or questioned the research project, he said he did so to enhance the overall project, not to obstruct it. This characteristic was very different from the conformist stage teachers who thought that if they began to question, then they were obstructing the group or causing it to break down. In comparison to the conscientious stage behaviors like tending to use formula solutions to problems, Elliot, like other individualistic stage teachers, was able to generate alternatives, project consequences, and to accept conflicting points of view, seeing when they were equally valid.

Individualistic stage teachers can stand back from the group and analyze the team's process and the individual's contributions to the collective goals. Unlike those in transition from the conscientious stage who tend to get caught up in interpersonal conflicts, Elliot, who was fully operating at the individualistic level, was able to accept individual differences which could have resulted in conflict and work with or around them toward mutually defined goals.

Elliot continued to discuss project outcomes (as he did goals) in terms of his own professional growth. He noted that the best thing about the project was the intellectual and personal excitement in the national conferences as he saw and met speakers whom he may have quoted in his written papers over the last few years. He generalized his experience in the research team to his goals in the future. He thought about the steps the group took in its process and wanted to investigate how a different group could progress under different conditions. He described the research process of the group as 'the crooked path we took in developing research questions and developing our instruments and making our conclusions' and now that 'you've gone this crooked path in your early formula ... then you could do a real rigorous measurement'. In terms of benefits from the project he said 'Personally, I've developed confidence and also interest in pursuing the topics related to action research and, in general, any topics that would broaden my own experience or bring some sort of recognition to me.' Since the project has ended, Elliot has continued to investigate the possibility of further graduate study. Elliot is actively redefining his career; although he sees teaching as a professional career he is not limited by the definitions of duties, performances and work roles that the school as an institution gave rise to. Instead, similar to other individualistic stage teachers he could be viewed as entering the perspective where an interdependent definition of oneself retains primary focus and self-actualization becomes a goal.

Anne (age 38)
Career Cycle: **10 years' experience**
Life Age/Cycle: **Becoming One's Own Person**
Cognitive Development Stage: **Self-Aware Stage**

Career-related goals were important to Anne, one of the teachers in the stable life phase of Becoming One's Own Person (ages 35–9 or 39–42). In most professions, promotions are crucial markers of success. While work relationships are important, the adult seeks to break away from advisors and mentors in order to become more independent in work. At this age as well as at each of the different age periods, the adult is trying to create a better fit between the life structure already defined and the reality of life's challenges.

Anne perceived herself to be in a period of stability, as she described that 'although job security becomes a worry each year, my job and life have not changed much in the past few years. My personal life seems very stable. My husband has worked very hard to earn his degree and improve himself. My children are in high school and seem very independent.' Anne had ten years of teaching experience, all at the same middle school. She titled the life period she just left 'Learning and Adjusting' and her present period 'A Stable Life — A Good Teacher'. The phase of Settling Down and Becoming Her Own Person certainly fit her perceptions. Anne was hard at work on no major life issue (see Figure 6.3).

Anne suggested that modifications were needed as she looked ahead to her next life period: 'A Better Life — A Better Teacher'. Work and personal goals were equally important to Anne. Major issues in her career were to 'bring all my materials and know-how up to date and together ... improve my techniques and become a better teacher'. A need for some change had evidently influenced her reasons for participating in the project. She said: 'I see the ARCS project as an excellent means of incorporating new or 'changing' methods into my classroom. The community and school are in constant change. I seem to be at a stage in life and teaching when change is necessary and needs to be initiated by some outside force.' In terms of the purpose of the project, Anne saw it twofold: 'getting people in touch with change that's going on and ... a way of me working at some problem that I might want to attack this year ... something that needs work in my classroom, working with the children, educating them'. In terms of benefits for herself, Anne shared her expectations of a 'good way for me to realize some sort of improvement or growth and hopefully learn from others and share with them'.

Anne's yearning for change within her own stable life period of Becoming One's Own Person is quite different from the feeling of constant transition that we hear from teachers in prior life ages of the Thirties Transition. Even in the just prior life age of Settling Down after Thirties Transition, we heard Elliot and others speak about yearning for stability amidst so much change in their lives.

Anne operated in the group from characteristics which fit the Conformist-Conscientious transition stage of development, called the *Self-Aware stage*. She was similar to Lori (even though Lori was younger) in her tendency to use global, vague descriptions and the inability to be specific. Like other teachers we knew who operated at the Conformist–Conscientious transition stage, Anne tended to describe the outcomes of the project in terms of what she hoped would come out of it rather than focusing on any specific changes the team did or did not accomplish. Anne, unlike some of the less confident teachers at this stage, was optimistic, perhaps because she had been given a new role by the principal to help her school staff the following year utilize the action research process in addressing other school or classroom problems which individual teachers might want to investigate. One of the indications of Anne's transition stage between the Conformist stage and the Conscientious stage was that her perceptions of the project's outcomes paralleled the Conscientious stage teachers who felt that their experience on the action research team had led them to feel that they are doing things right. She said, 'This was a project that really helped me feel that I had some valuable things that I'm doing in the classroom, different ways that I really could contribute.'

Thus, for Anne the consolidation of her self-confidence seems to have been a result of her experiences in the group project. She started out questioning the value of her own contributions to the action research process and ended up recognizing her own skills and being recognized by others on the team for the skills she was able to contribute. For instance, Lori says of Anne the first year that 'she tended to think that she didn't have much to offer, that her experiences were very limited and she didn't know how to do one thing or another; yet I think she became a much more active member of the group the second year'. Another teacher describes her more active role, 'I think Anne was always the starter, a good spark plug, in the group. She was always sort of "let's get going, let's get it done." ... I saw Anne taking leadership parts in the group many times in the course of the second year.' The fact that the principal designated Anne to take on the additional leadership role in the school in the year following the project further reinforced Anne's capabilities and achievements. These further experiences very likely will encourage her transition to the Conscientious Stage of development. Despite her nervousness about assuming the leadership role the following year, she took it. She had gained self-confidence in her abilities in the school and this confidence is needed before anyone operating from the Self-Aware transition can move ahead and begin fully operating from the Conscientious stage perspective.

Moving along, our investigation looks next at three teachers in their early to mid forties, each of whom seems to fit different life-ages and different cognitive-developmental stages. Once again we point out that although age seems to be fairly consistent with the life periods, developmental stage is not. And sometimes age, too, is not consistent. In the examples which follow, two teachers close in age, 42 and 41, were in different life ages and developmental stages.

JANE (age 42)
Career Cycle: **16 years' experience**
Life Age/Cycle: **Mid-Life (Forties) Transition**
Cognitive Developmental Stage: **Individualistic Level**

Jane exemplifies the need to create a better fit in her goals as a teacher and in her view of herself as an independent person. The Mid-Life

Transition of the Forties occurs as one realizes that life ambitions might not develop. The disparity between the benefits of living within one's stable life structure and the recognition of what else one wants in life urges a person to try to create a better fit between one's life structure and self. The Mid-Life Transition is a time of redefining one's work in conjunction with a deeper understanding of self. Jane, age 42, with 16 years of experience, indicated this sense of redefinition as she gave the following reasons for participating in the ARCS project:

I think this program can make a difference ... also I want to change. In the past, I have always liked to try new things, but in the last three to four years I've slacked off on innovation and become a bit complacent. I want to do something new. I've gotten some systems down pat and working well, I'd like to extend 'down pat and working well' to other areas.

A key issue for Jane was being recognized for her contributions and achievements in roles she valued. She said, 'I want to be the best teacher there is. I'm pretty good already.' Like Anne, Jane looked for change within a stable sense of herself, her abilities, and her accomplishments. As part of her redefinition of the teacher role, Jane was concerned that 'I'm afraid, as I've changed from being a sixth grade elementary teacher, to a sixth grade middle school teacher, to a sixth grade junior high teacher that I am losing sight of the kids because time and production have become so important in the school.' Jane's second key issue at this point in her life was becoming her own person with identity and direction, not dependent on principal, spouse, colleagues, critics or mentors. For instance, in relating issues in her personal life to participation in the ARCS project she said:

All my married life, I've been a docile unadventurous person, and I think it's time I started being more independent ... the meeting with the other group of teachers, 1,000 miles away, would be a breakthrough in that I'd be away from home alone for the first time.

This sense of exploring one's identity apart from family is a common theme at the Forties Transition. Changes in self-perception are typical. Change is both internal and external. As an example similar to others in the Forties Transition, Jane wanted renewal in her teaching and was reexamining her roles to gain a new perspective on herself. Seeing herself as an independent adult was a key issue that was gaining importance. She said, 'I've been dependent too long'. The sense of having already accomplished the life tasks in the thirties called Becoming One's Own Person came through over and over in Jane's professional work. She titled the period she just left as 'Threshold'. Like many women in the Forties Transition she is now concentrating on issues of independence. She titled her current period 'Disequilibrium' and looked forward to a next period of 'Autonomy and Harmony'.

In Jane's response there was also the urgent quality of most transitions as compared to more stable times which we witnessed above in the case histories of Elliot and Anne at the life periods of Settling Down and Becoming One's Own Person. The Forties Transition, in contrast, is often seen as the internal clock shifting from time lived to time left to live. Urgency is expressed by many at this transition. In Jane, however, the professional side is quite stable, 'I feel I have accomplished important things and expect to continue. I feel no pressure or panic about the finiteness of it all'. Although Jane noted that professionally she was in a period of stability, while personally she was in a period of transition, she did seem to be on the verge of making changes in both personal life and work. As with many teachers in the Forties Transition, change in part of one's life will undoubtedly affect other parts.

Jane operated on the team mostly from an *Individualistic* stage of development. She indicated goals for the action research project in terms of redefining her work in conjunction with a deeper understanding of herself. She had a stable professional self and was pleased with her abilities and accomplishments. Jane consistently brought the student perspective to the team discussions. She also presented alternative opinions and perspectives to the team discussions. Jane left the project after the first year. Although she said she left the team because her perspective was represented by others, the documentation of the first year of the project indicates that her perspective on school, classroom, and teaching/learning issues was quite different from others on the team. She seemed to be an outsider to the rest of the team in many respects. In addition to her having been a prior elementary teacher and, thus, having different experience from the other junior high team members, the other four teachers in the group had been good friends and team teachers for some time.

Jane's developmental stage at the Individualistic level was similar to Elliot, eight years younger, who operated in a different school.

Analysis of her interpersonal understanding suggested, however, that Jane viewed the group process quite differently from Elliot. Jane saw the group as needing to be a homogeneous community, in which all good group members have the same concerns. This view of a group means that loyalty to the group is based in members having the same values, so interpersonal relations are based on common groud. But, clearly, Jane's views were different from others in her group. Although she was working on her own 'autonomy and harmony', she may have felt that she could not stay in the group without being totally committed to their ideas for the project.

Elliot, on the other hand, viewed the group process differently. Rather than expecting group members to have the same concerns, he relished their pluralistic perspectives. Had Jane been able to view the group from such a pluralistic perspective she may have been able to remain on the team and find a successful compromise which would have enabled her to use and enhance her own skills and learnings while others did the same in different areas of the project. This example of teachers' differing perspectives of the group organization and process illustrates one of the building blocks to cognitive-developmental stages. Robert Selman (1980) helped us to describe these teachers' different understandings of the group process and interpersonal interactions on the collaborative research teams. Piaget (1972) used the term *horizontal décalage* to suggest that while different stages represent quite different views of one's world, as adults we are continually filling out the stage we mostly operate from, as we also build the support from which we may eventually move ahead to more mature stages. There are ways in which a group facilitator could help teachers like Jane to feel more supported in the group even when her alternative, and often more complex, ideas made her appear so different from the others[4]. In leaving the example of Jane, we note the similarity in much of her problem-solving performance on the team to Elliot, who was much younger, but at the same individualistic stage of development. On different teams, each brought new perspectives and alternative ideas to other team members. In schools it is important to provide opportunities and support for the continuing growth of teachers like Elliot and Jane, who represent some of these highest stages of development.

And at this point we move on to our two last examples, two teachers in consecutive life age periods, but the same cognitive-developmental stage, the Conscientious stage. In these examples of John and Florence, the issue of mentoring becomes important as a growth force and exciting challenge. For John, the excitement comes from wanting formally to mentor younger and beginning teachers, and for Florence, her satisfaction and challenge in growth is felt from an informal mentoring relationship developed between herself and Jane during the project.

JOHN (age 41)
Career Cycle: **19 years' experience**
Life Age/Cycle: **Restabilization after 40s Transition**
Cognitive Developmental Stage: **Conscientious Stage**

After the Forties Transition, one again enjoys a period of restabilization to enjoy one's choices and lifestyle. John reflects the characteristics of a stabilization period. He has the time and energy to become involved in new pursuits, and at the same time he enjoys being an informal advisor and mentor to less experienced teachers.

John had been teaching science at the junior high for 11 years and had 19 total years of teaching experience. He was chairperson of the staff development program for the school and, in fact, was part of the team that designed the current district-wide staff development plan, having to appear personally before five town school boards to negotiate approval. Because of the experience, he said, 'I can deal with administration and school boards better than ever before'. He felt he was in a relative period of stability; evidently this was important to his reasons for becoming involved in the ARCS program. He had come through a transition initiated by a divorce and had total responsibility for raising his junior high aged son for the last few years. There is a sense that in the current period of stability, John could combine study of action research with his family responsibilities and enjoy both. He said,

> I have taught in public and private, small and large schools (and have seen many changes good and bad), and have many ideas of how to improve. In the past my personal life has been hectic so extra time could not be used. Now I have the time.

John's main issue in life was mentoring. Very important to him was sharing his knowledge and skills, contributing to the newer generation of teachers, and being helpful to younger colleagues. During the project on a regular weekly basis, John shared his project journal comments with the principal and at least 25 per cent of the school staff. Important in his career he said was 'what is good for students'. He saw the ARCS group as a potential sounding board for his ideas. In terms of benefits, he said,

> For me, yes, because in dealing with people you're working with, if you're talking with them on a basis in which you are constantly sharing ideas it can't help but help either you or them; even if you may not agree with the idea, if they have a sounding board, if it helps them, it helps you.

One more aspect of the stabilization after either the Thirties or Forties Transition is a response which indicates pursuing long-term goals and accelerating progress or satisfying intellectual curiosity and exploring personal interests. John illustrates this latter facet of stabilization when he said that he's not done much with educational research and 'that's part of the reason why I'm getting involved now to find out more about it'. John titled the life period he just left as 'Trying to Swim' and the current period as 'Surviving'.

John's thinking and behavior in the group exhibited characteristics of the *Conscientious Stage* of development. He emphasized his assumption that the project would solve school problems, 'dealing with students and dealing with teachers within our particular areas — trying to find help with the problems'. While more Self-Aware stage teachers focused on doing a project to address people's needs, John and other Conscientious stage teachers wanted to solve problems within the school as a system. Like other Conscientious teachers John felt skillful in his ability to address problems and assume tasks which led to problem solutions. He felt confident in his ability to approach and talk to other teachers, principal, assistant superintendent, and school board members. He was comfortable directing the team as it carried out data collection and analysis. Even though he originally felt he lacked research skills, he continually found ways to bring the skills he had into the working of the team. This approach was very different from the more Self-Aware teachers who tended not to initiate tasks or compensate for skills they may have lacked. John could list clearly his own strengths, weaknesses, and perceived outcomes from the project. This too was in contrast to the more Self-Aware stage teachers who were more vague in identifying skills they had or lacked and what they gained from the project.

One additional characteristic John exhibited is similar to other conscientious teachers. In order to solve the problems he saw as the team's goal, John tended to find and use formulas, seeking the rules or laws which governed behavior and interactions. While this allowed him to work on the problems identified by the group and move the team along, it prevented him from looking at alternatives or subtleties in the problem situations. It was often up to teachers at the individualistic stage to bring up the alternatives and point out the subtle contradictions to conscientious stage teachers like John.

Participating in the project 'revitalized' John. He said he felt 'more conscious' of what he was doing in the classroom. Another value John found in the project was the use of logs to vent his anger by writing his frustrations down. He said this helped him 'channel the anger and frustration and get it out of the classroom'. John described how he would use some of the skills he gained from the project, specifically using a process of documentation timelines to summarize student work on a writing project for parents and other teachers. He also hoped to capitalize on his increased confidence in writing by working on a paper to be a teacher's view of action research, thinking he might possibly present it at some conference. He emphasised the value of the process the group went through and planned to modify it (to *action inquiry*) for use with science colleagues or other teachers. Another outcome for John was that his increased confidence and skill gave him greater power within the system. 'Doing this has given me a way to write which I did not have to increase that particular power base ... talking at places, conferences, knowing that I can stand up in front of a group and say what I want to say'. John's experience caused him to become more proficient at operating within the conscientious stage.

Our final example is of Florence, older than John and in the next life period, but who thought and operated in a different group in a manner very similar to John, thus both exhibiting the characteristics of teachers at the conscientous stage of development.

FLORENCE (age 45)
Career Cycle: **23 years' experience**
Life Age/Cycle: **Fifties Transition**
Cognitive Developmental Stage: **Conscientious Stage**

The transition into the fifties involves another reexamination of the fit between one's life structure and oneself and often results in change in direction. There is a sense of this need for redirection as Florence (age 45) said she needed a 'shot in the arm'. Florence had taught all of her 23 years at the same middle school. She was single and had no family nearby. 'My friends are my family', she said. The title she gave to her current life period was 'Everything in its Place' and the period she just left she titled 'Aggravation Unlimited'. Although she indicated her current life period to be more stable, her reasons for becoming involved indicated a need for change. She said,

> I would like to explore some new approaches to presentation of language to students at this level (seventh and eighth grades) ... I know there are probably ways that I can be more effective, and I'd like to explore those possibilities. It is important to do this now to alleviate a feeling of monotony I am experiencing.

Comments like this, in periods of relative stability, make one wonder whether, in fact, human life is based on change and those periods of stability are only short stopping places in a cycle of transitions. This certainly seems to be true of the teachers in our projects. Florence added, 'I wanted to find out if there are some ways to institute changes in my methods and still be as effective a teacher as I think I am now'. Like Jane, there was a need for change, but it was the kind of change that retains and increases one's effectiveness. Also, we note Florence's clear sense of her own capabilities, comments not made by Lori and others, who were in the Thirties Transition and still discovering and testing their teaching skills.

For Florence in the Fifties Transition, like Jane who was in the Mid-Life transition of the forties, the ARCS program seemed to provide a setting for redefining one's work in conjunction with a deeper understanding of oneself. While Jane was seeking personal autonomy, Florence was seeking professional autonomy. Florence had for the last 8 years been resident manager of the apartment she had lived in for 20 years. Obviously, this involved extensive duties and responsibilities. In her teaching, however, there was a need, she says, to 'find out for myself that I'm really doing things the right way' and keeping up with the changing times. Her concern with meaningful teaching decisions in the school and her part in making those decisions is also reflected in her comments about the purpose of the project. The project appealed to her because it recognized the capabilities she knows she has. She said, 'ARCS sounded interesting when my principal mentioned it at staff meeting. I was especially interested when she said that this research would not be the usual educator-decides-change type with the teacher-expected-to-institute-it'. She continued by describing why this project was so attractive to her at this point in her life by saying,

> finally instead of saying 'here is a problem, we want you to prove it's a problem', somebody is asking me 'what do you see are the problems in your classroom situation?' ... 'what can you tell us about this problem and how can we work on it so it's no longer a problem?'

Florence's three key issues in life at this period were sharing knowledge and skills with others, sharing everyday joys with others, and accepting what has transpired in life as hers, valuing herself and her choices. Indications of transition were that Florence noted five additional life issues in Figure 3 becoming increasingly important.

Florence's thinking and behavior in the group problem solving showed characteristics of the *Conscientious* stage of development. Her comments reflected her internal sense of competence and achievement which define this stage. Like John and other teachers at the Conscientious stage, she felt confident of her own self within the system of the school and the classroom.

One incident in the school in the second year of the project stands out, in which Florence felt her professionalism and her way of operating in the school was challenged by an imposed (mandated) staff development program. She was unable or unwilling to seek support or validation of her dilemma from Lori who was responsible for carrying out the staff development mandate (a relatively new role for Lori as a part-time staff developer in the school). Lori was unable to offer or suggest alternatives to Florence. It also seemed that Lori's self-aware stage of development limited her in being able to empathize with Florence's dilemma. It seemed after this incident that Florence withdrew a part of herself from the group. She continued to carry out necessary tasks but perhaps lowered her expectations and commitment in order to guard against further challenges. As a result, in the final interviews, she expressed her perceptions of minimal outcomes for the project. Personally, she said she felt satisfied with the work of the team 'I think we did a good job' but she did not express any other impact of the project on herself or the school.

The school mandated staff development program which caused a problem for Florence was an example of a school putting a lid on the growth potential of teachers. Florence had already studied in the area of the mandated staff development program and, in fact, she felt quite skillful. But the school provided no alternatives for teachers like Florence, who already had the skills and knowledge in this area, and perhaps on their own or in a small group could have extended their understandings to new areas. Instead every teacher was required to attend the same set of workshops. Ann Higgins and colleagues (Higgins, 1983, and Howard, Power, and Higgins, 1983) studied the ways in which some school atmospheres put ceilings on the potential development of teachers while other schools promote continuing development for all teachers. For example, they describe a school atmosphere that would be fulfilling rather than frustrating for someone using the same stage of developmental reasoning and, at the same time, challenging for those people using lower stages of developmental reasoning.

In our example, a teacher using conscientious stage reasoning, like Florence, working in a conformist school atmosphere expressed frustration with and alienation from her work. When the teacher's developmental stage reasoning is higher than the environment, he or she ceases to receive developmental stimulation from work. The teacher may become increasingly alienated from the job and/or seek developmentally stimulating experiences more indirectly related to the job itself. We suggest that if the teacher in this kind of mismatched school atmosphere cannot offset the alienation by other stimulating experiences, then conditions of burnout (role ambiguity, negative attitudes towards students, and depersonalization) as described by Richard Schwab (1983) may noticeably increase. To avoid alienation and burnout we need more developmentally appropriate work environments and staff develpment programs in schools.

In Florence's case, she was able to find a developmentally stimulating experience, but not without some difficulty. During the first year of the ARCS project, Florence said that she valued the different perspective that Jane (at the higher individualistic stage of development) brought to the team, and it is well documented in team meetings and her logs that she looked to Jane as a resource and even a catalyst for her own thinking about new perspectives in the group's problem solving. In Florence's first year interview, she said, 'I literally never see Jane except during our ARCS meetings on Wednesday, and I've started to think about a lot of things that Jane has brought up which I never thought of as affecting me before or having anything to do with me at all'. In her final interview Florence said that she thought Jane had made 'an important contribution the first year . . . Jane was sort of the devil's advocate'. Florence continued to value and build up her new friendship with Jane even after Jane left the team in the second year. In her final interview after the second year Florence said, 'Now Jane and I make a point to come to each other's rooms and talk to each other and see each other and it is nice, it's really nice. It's one of the big advantages to me.' Jane's leaving the team may have prevented the team interaction druing the second year from being as growth producing as possible for Florence, however, Florence had gone ahead to seek out the stimulation which Jane provided her. It is clear that Florence had developed a stimulating informal mentoring and peer collegial relationship with Jane that was to continue in the years to come.

Implications for the Professional Development of Teachers

An overview of adult development theories was presented in section one, and descriptive analyses of teachers at different ages and stages formed section two of this chapter. The third and final section of the chapter will summarize recommendations for promoting healthy adult development within in-service staff development opportunities. The overall message to readers concerns the need to match the education and growth opportunities in staff development to the ages and stages that individual teachers have reached.

Age Alone Is Not Enough

Age alone is not enough information upon which to determine a teacher's career cycle, life period, or developmental stage. Although there is a closer consistency between years of age and life period, there is still not a one-to-one correspondence. Rather, the key issues one is currently working on in one's life determine the life period. The listing of thirteen kinds of life issues given in Figure 6.3 were used to help characterize the life periods of the teachers described in this chapter and may be helpful for others trying to plan staff development activities attractive to teachers in different life periods. On the other hand, it is clear from our work that a long-term project like the two-year collaborative action research study was attractive to teachers who were in a variety of life periods from the Age 30 Crisis, Settling

Down, Becoming One's Own Person, Mid-life Transition, Restabilization after the Forties Transition, and Fifties Transition.

In schools in which we have worked thus far, the school staffs tended to be older and more experienced. The career cycle examples of teachers in this chapter fit our experience thus far in the schools in which teachers have begun their careers in their early twenties and followed the traditional teaching pattern. With a variety of older adults entering teaching as their second or third career, this pattern is changing. As more current efforts are made to attract to teaching older adults with teaching as their second career, the person's age alone will tell us even less about their career cycles in the school. We believe that the Career Cycle model by Christensen *et al.* (1983), which is not dependent on age, will become even more helpful as older adults move into the teaching field as beginners.

Why *a Teacher Becomes Involved vs* How *a Teacher Participates*

Age, life period, and years of teaching experience can help explain key issues in a teacher's life and career. These can often weigh heavily as *reasons why* a teacher will become involved in certain staff development activities. But, these are not enough to explain *how a teacher will participate* in a chosen staff development activity. Teachers' performance, thoughts, problem-solving, and group behavior, once they have chosen a certain staff development activity, are based in cognitive-developmental stages. Staff developers may use knowledge of the developmental needs of teachers to identify the relationship between characteristics of adult stages of development and the implications of support and challenge in each of these stages to promote adult learning and growth. The characteristics of different adult cognitive-developmental stages are important to recognize and prepare for. After working with many adults we find that their performances are not simply idiosyncratic and based only in the individual. On the contrary, we have found that it is the cognitive-development stage characteristics which help explain how certain adults think and perform as they do. With this additional perspective and experience we have been able to be better facilitators of the actual staff development activities — the day to day, week to week meetings of groups of teachers. We have been able to understand why certain conflicts or support networks develop between teachers who are at similar or different stages of development. I hope that the teacher examples in this chapter have clearly indicated that cognitive-developmental stage is not related to age or career cycle. Any group of teachers, even with the same age and experience, is likely to have a mix of teachers who are operating at different stages of development. This is part of the exciting, reinforcing, yet sometimes frustrating part of planning and implementing staff development activities. If all teachers were at the same stage, the spirit of change, movement, and adult learning in schools might dissipate. It is exactly because school groups are composed of different stage individuals that a teacher committed to the goals of the group will find the personal challenge to thinking differently, more broadly, more universally, more interdependently, with empathy and understanding of one's own differences and skills compared to those of each other person in the group. This is what moves the individuals and the group forward in their own problem-solving.

Planning for Adult Development

In our teacher examples is it any wonder that Florence sorely missed Jane's participation on the team? Jane had been the person in the group consistently to exhibit the characteristics which spurred on Florence to think about some new and interesting alternatives. I strongly believe in the Piagetian principle that humans yearn for continuing growth and stimulation, and when they feel supported in new learning, they are willing to risk to stretch themselves toward meeting new challenges. For Elliot, another teacher in a different team who also exhibited the Individualistic stage characteristics, another benefit emerged. He found that people began to listen to him in the group and were willing and interested to pursue discussion of ideas and alternatives that he brought to the problem-solving situation. He began to feel more connected and more understood by other colleagues in the school. Staff development programs need to be based upon some key features which allow for more thinking about alternative perspectives, more genuine problem-solving on classroom and school concerns, and more empathic roletaking (the ability to understand another person's point of view, to act 'as if' in a situation, to step into another's shoes to gain alternative perspectives on issues and beliefs). The goal of such programs would be deliberately to design environments which allow for adult development in ego maturity, principled moral/ethical reasoning, and increased conceptual complexity as follows:

Ego Maturity The development of more complex, differentiated, and integrated understanding of self and others, away from manipulative, exploitative, self-protective attitudes *toward* self-respect, mutual respect, and identity formation.

Moral/Ethical Development Development toward principled moral judgments, away from unquestioned conformity to peer, social, and legal norms *toward* self-evaluated standards within a world view framework cherishing individual human rights and mutual interpersonal responsibilities.

Conceptual Growth The development of higher conceptual levels, away from thinking in terms of simple stereotypes and cliches *toward* recognition of individual differences in attitudes, interests, and abilities, and toward increased toleration for paradox, contradiction, and ambiguity.

Notes

1. In previous papers I have presented in depth reviews of all these theorists; see Oja (1980, 1985), and Johnson and Oja (1983).
2. See Oja (1980, 1985) for an in depth review of the literature, and comparison and contrast of these intertwining theories which form the basis of the cognitive-developmental approach to teacher education and staff development. For an additional description of the cognitive-developmental view of the teacher as an adult learner (based in cognitive-developmental studies of children, adolescents, student teachers and experienced teachers) see Sprinthall and Thies-Sprinthall (1983).
3. The reader is referred to Oja and Pine (1983, 1988) for the final report of this project and further descriptions of ARCS school contexts and teachers' attitudes toward decision-making and change, perception of group organization and process, perception of leadership and the university researcher, and perception of authority of the school principal. Oja and Smulyan (in progress) are analyzing the group process issues and adult development potential when teachers in one school are involved in collaborative action research.
4. In a previous paper we have discussed possible supports and challenges which a staff developer or group facilitator could offer to teachers like Jane in situations like this (Oja and Ham, 1984).

References

ARIN-KRUPP, J. (1981). *Adult development: Implications for staff development.* Manchester, CT: Author.

CHRISTENSEN, J. C., BURKE, P., FESSLER, R., and HAGSTROM, D. (1983). *Stages of teachers' careers: Implication for staff development.* Washington, DC: (ERIC Document Reproduction Service No. SP 021 495)

ERIKSON, E. H. (1959). *Identity and the life cycle.* New York: International Universities Press.

GILLIGAN, C. (1977). In a different voice: Women's conceptions of self and of morality. *Harvard Educational Review, 47,* 481–517.

GILLIGAN, C. (1982). *In a different voice:* Cambridge, MA: Harvard University Press.

GOULD, R. L. (1978). *Transformations: Growth and change in adult life.* New York: Simon & Schuster.

HALL, G. E. and LOUCKS, S. (1978). Teacher concerns as a basis for facilitating and personalizing staff development. *Teachers College Record, 80*(1), 36–53.

HAVIGHURST, R. J. (1972). *Developmental tasks and education.* New York: David McKay.

HIGGINS, A. (1983, November). *Recent findings in adult moral development.* Paper presented at the meeting of the Association for Moral Education, Boston, MA.

HOWARD, R., POWER, C., and HIGGINS, A. (1983, November). *At the crossroads of moral development and the sociology of education: Assessing the moral atmosphere of the school.* Paper presented at the meeting of the Association for Moral Education, Boston, MA.

HULING, L. L. (1982). The effects on teachers of participation in an interactive research and development project. Paper presented at the meeting of the American Educational Research Association, New York City.

HUNT, D. E. (1966). A model for analyzing the training of training agents. *Merrill-Palmer Quarterly of Behavior and Development, 12*(2), 137–56.

HUNT, D. E. (1970). A conceptual level matching model for coordinating learner characteristics with educational approaches. *Interchange, 1*(3), 68–82.

HUNT, D. E. (1975). The B-P-E paradigm for theory, research, and practice. *Canadian Psychological Review, 16*(3), 185–97.

HUNT, D. E. (1976). Teachers' adaptation: 'Reading' and 'flexing' to students. *Journal of Teacher Education, 27*(3), 268–75.

HUNT, D. E. (1978). In-service training as persons-in-relation. *Theory into Practice, 17*(3), 239–44.

JOHNSON, D. F. and OJA, S. N. (1983). Review of the literature: Teachers life age/cycles and stages of cognitive-structural development (ARCS Report Vll, pp. 261–310). In Oja, S. N. and Pine, G. J. (eds), Appendices to the Final report: A two year study of teacher stages of development in relation to collaborative action research in schools. Washington DC: National Institute of Education (ERIC Document Reproduction Service No. ED 248 227).

JOHNSTON, J. and RYAN, K. (1983). Research on the beginning teacher. In K. Howey and W. GARDNER (eds), *The education of teachers: A look ahead* (pp. 136–62). New York: Longman.

KOHLBERG, L. (1969). Stage and sequence: The cognitive-developmental approach to socialization. In D. A. Goslin (ed), *Handbook of socialization theory and research* (pp. 347–80). Chicago: Rand-McNally.

KOHLBERG, L. (1971). Stages of moral development as a basis for moral education. In C. M. Beck, *et al.* (eds), *Moral education: Interdisciplinary approaches* (pp. 23–93). Toronto: University of Toronto Press.

KOHLBERG, L. (1973). Continuities in childhood and adult moral education revisited. In P. Baltes and K. Schaie (eds), *Life-span developmental psychology: Personality and socialization* (pp. 180–201). New York: Academic Press

KOHLBERG, L. (1976). Moral stages and moralization: The cognitive-developmental approach. In T. Likona (ed.), *Moral development and behavior*. New York: Holt, Rinehart & Winston.

LEVINSON, D. J., DARROW, C., KLEIN, E. B., LEVINSON, M., and McKEE, B. (1978). *The seasons of a man's life*. New York: Alfred A. Knopf.

LOEVINGER, J. (1976). *Ego development: Conceptions and theories*. San Francisco: Jossey-Bass.

MEZIROW, J. (1978). Perspective transformation. *Adult Education, 28*(Winter), 100–10.

McDONALD, F. (1980). *The problems of beginning teachers: A crisis in training. Study of induction programs for beginning teachers* (Vol. 1). Princeton, NJ: Educational Testing Service.

NEUGARTEN, B. L. (1963). A developmental view of adult personality. In J. Birren (ed.), *Relations of development and aging*. Springfield, IL: Thomas.

NEWMAN, K., BURDEN, P., and APPLEGATE, J. (1980). Helping teachers examine their long range development. *Journal of Teacher Education, 15*(4), 7–14.

OJA, S. N. (1980). Adult development is implicit in staff development. *Journal of Staff Development, 1*(2), 8–55.

OJA, S. N. (1985). *Review of the literature: Adult development and ·teacher education*. Unpublished manuscript, University of New Hampshire: Collaborative Research Projects Office, Durham.

OJA, S. N. and HAM, M. C. (1984). A cognitive-developmental approach to collaborative action research with teachers. *Teachers College Record, 86*(1), 171–92.

OJA, S. N. and PINE, G. J. (1983). *A two year study of teacher stages of development in relation to collaborative action research in schools: Final report*. Washington, DC: National Institute of Education. (ERIC Document Reproduction Service No. ED 248 227).

OJA, S. N. and PINE, G. J. (1988, in press). Collaborative action research: Teachers' stages of development and school contexts. *Peabody Journal of Education, 64*(1).

OJA, S. N. and SMULYAN, L. (in progress). *Collaborative action research and teacher development*. Barcombe: Falmer Press.

OJA, S. N. and SPRINTHALL, N. A. (1978). Psychological and moral development for teachers. In N. A. Sprinthall and R. A. Mosher (eds), *Value development ... as the aim of education* (pp. 117–34). Schenectady, NY: Character Research Press.

PERRY, W. (1970). *Forms of intellectual and ethical development during the college years*. New York: Holt, Rinehart and Winston.

PIAGET, J. (1972). Intellecutual evolution from adolescence to adulthood. *Human Development, 15*(1), 1–12.

SCHWAB, R. L. (1983) Teacher burnout. *Theory into Practice, 22*(1), 21–5.

SELMAN, R. L. (1980). *The growth of interpersonal understanding*. New York: Academic Press.

SHEEHY, G. (1976). *Passages: Predictable crises of adult life*. New York: E. P. Dutton.

SPRINTHALL, N. A. and BERNIER, J. (1978). Moral and cognitive development of teachers. *New Catholic World, 21,* 179–84.

SPRINTHALL, N. A. and THIES-SPRINTHALL, L. (1983). The teacher as an adult learner: A cognitive-developmental view. In G. A. Griffin (ed.), *Staff development, Eighty-second yearbook of NSSE* (pp. 13–35). Chicago, IL: University of Chicago Press.

THIES-SPRINTHALL, L. (1986). A collaborative approach for mentor training: A working model. *Journal of Teacher Education,* 13–20.

WEATHERSBY, R. and TARULE, J. M. (1980). *Adult development: Implications for higher education*. (Report No. 4). Washington, DC: AAHE-ERIC/Higher Education Research (ERIC Document Reproduction Service No. 4 ED 191–382).

ZEICHNER, K. and TABACHNICK, B. R. (1985). Social strategies and institutional control in the socialization of beginning teachers. *Journal of Education for Teaching, 5*(1), 1–25.

7   Teaching and the Self

Jennifer Nias

The claim that teaching is a personal activity is often advanced as a
reason why it cannot systematically be taught to others or fully
brought into the public domain. Yet, this claim is seldom explicated
or justified — to the detriment of mutual understanding among people inside and outside the profession. In this chapter, I argue that to be
a teacher in the primary (and in some instances, the middle) schools of
the United Kingdom (UK) is to work in a historically determined
context that encourages individualism, isolation, a belief in one's own
autonomy, and the investment of personal resources. Each of these
conditions stresses the importance in teaching of *the teacher as a person*
(as distinct from, though not as opposed to, the teacher as the posses-
sor of occupational knowledge and skills). In other words, the self is a
crucial element in the way teachers themselves construe the nature of
their job. In turn, this directs attention to theoretical formulations of
the self — a hypothetical construct which has been explored by,
among others, poets, philosophers, psychologists, social psychologists, and sociologists. In this chapter, I focus upon the sociological and
psychological perspectives provided by symbolic interactionism and
psychoanalysis (especially self-psychology), and in particular upon the
distinctions which may be made between the self as *me*, the self as *I*
and the notion of *identity*.

Most obviously, teaching is a personal activity because the manner
in which each teacher behaves is unique. Teaching, like learning, has a
perceptual basis. The minute-by-minute decisions teachers make within the shifting, unpredictable, capricious world of the classroom and
the judgments they reach when they are reflecting on their work
depend upon how they perceive particular events, behaviors, materials, persons. In turn, these perceptions are determined by schemata

155

('persistent, deep-rooted and well-organized classifications of ways of perceiving, thinking and behaving' which are also 'living and flexible', Vernon, 1955, p. 181) or basic assumptions ('schemata ... organized in more generalized, vague or ill-defined patterns', Abercrombie, 1969, p. 641) which help us to order and make sense of the world around us. Schemata and assumptions are learned; they are slowly built up as, from birth, we develop and exercise the skill of seeing (or hearing, smelling, tasting, touching). They are modified by experience and activity. Since no two people have the same life experiences, we all learn to perceive the world and ourselves as part of it in different ways. So teachers, as people, 'see' and interpret their pupils and the latter's actions and reactions according to perceptual patterns which are unique to themselves. No matter how pervasive particular aspects of a shared social or occupational culture may be, or how well individuals are socialized into it, the attitudes and actions of each teacher are rooted in his/her own ways of perceiving the world.

This biological explanation for teachers' individualism exists side by side with a pervasive historical tradition which emphasizes the teacher's personality. In his study of American elementary schoolteachers, Lortie (1975, p. 79) has pointed to an unchallenged orthodoxy, that 'personal predispositions are not only relevant but, in fact, stand at the core of becoming a teacher'; and more recently, in the UK the same view has been expressed not only by writers such as Woods (1981) and Sikes *et al.* (1985) but also by Her Majesty's Inspectorate of Schools (HMI), and the governmental Department of Education and Science (DES). In 1982, the DES report on *The New Teacher in School* (1982, Section 6.2) claimed: 'HMI found that the personal qualities of the teachers were in many cases the decisive factor in their effectiveness. A similar view was put forward by schools'; and the government White Paper *Teaching Quality* (DES, 1983, p. 26) argued: 'Personality, character and commitment are as important as the specific knowledge and skills that are used in the day to day tasks of teaching.' Small wonder, then, that practitioners themselves perpetuate a largely unquestioned assumption that 'what gets taught is the teacher'.

This stress upon personality is encouraged by allegiance to philosophical traditions which see the personal relationship between teacher and learner as central to the educational process. Two centuries ago Rousseau wrote *Emile* (1762 (1911)), an imaginary account of the education of one child by his tutor. On to this Romantic preoccupation with the individual, practicing educationalists grafted the Christian tradition, expressed by Froebel and Pestalozzi as respect and concern for the whole child, and by Buber as the 'I–Thou' relationship (in which the teacher as a person becomes a resource for the self-activated development of the learner). Still today, many primary school teachers see the personal relationship which they have with individual children not just as a means of establishing control and increasing motivation but also as the means by which education itself takes place (Woods, 1987).

Moreover, throughout their professional education and socialization, teachers are led to believe that they are capable of knowing not just one child, but all the pupils in their care (Alexander, 1984). When Kay Shuttleworth set up the first teacher training college in England at St John's, Battersea, he took many of his ideas from Pestalozzi's work in Switzerland. Among them were the notions that teaching should be inspired by love, and that teachers should therefore live and work among their pupils. This aspiration was itself drawn partially from Froebel's metaphysical concern for the centrality of unity and wholeness and his consequent belief that education should be an organic process, free of artificial and damaging divisions. Teachers socialized into this tradition tend to identify with their classes, talk of themselves in relationship to their pupils as 'we'. Indeed, many teachers derive intense satisfaction from feeling 'natural' and 'whole' in their relationship with children, and from creating a sense of community within classes and schools.

The centrality of the personal relationship between teacher and pupils is further emphasized by the solitary nature of much primary teaching. Until recently, the architectural design of most UK primary schools has unquestioningly followed the tradition, established in nineteenth-century urban elementary schools, that instruction is best carried out in 'box' classrooms occupied by one teacher and a group of 30 or 40 children. These classrooms are cut off from one another, though they are usually linked by a corridor, a staircase, or, in older schools, a central hall. In addition, windows are often placed so that it is difficult for passing teachers to see into one another's rooms. The isolation imposed by architecture has helped to foster an occupational context from which teachers learn to expect that much of their working lives will be spent with children not adults. Further, initial teacher education provides students with relatively few chances to observe their more experienced colleagues in action and, except in open plan schools, the latter seldom see one another teaching. This lack of opportunity to 'sit by Nellie' encourages students and probationers to feel that they must survive by their own efforts and to believe in an occupational *rite de passage* which equates the establishment of competence with suffering (Nias, 1987a).

Altogether, as Lortie (1975) and Hargreaves (1980) have argued, teachers have little opportunity or incentive to develop shared professional knowledge or a collegial sense of the 'state of the art'. Teacher education, experience and conventional wisdom continually underline the uniqueness of the individual, the specificity of context and the primacy of the person.

These tendencies have been encouraged by the relative freedom from political control which primary teachers until recently have taken for granted; although, as Broadfoot and Osborn (1986) point out in a comparative study of French and English teachers, the latter's freedom is restricted in practice by the power of their headteachers. For much of the past hundred years, teachers in Britain have felt it was their responsibility to make far-reaching decisions about the curriculum and teaching methods which they will use in their classes, to the point in some schools, that there is little continuity, communication or agreement between classes in the same school. Teachers often learn to depend upon their own knowledge, interests and preferences in making pedagogic and curriculum decisions. Indeed, this freedom from external constraints and collegial influence is, for some teachers, one of the main attractions of the job (though others deplore the sense of incoherence which it sometimes gives to their work; Nias, 1980).

A sense of autonomy in matters of curriculum and pedagogy is closely related to the ideological freedom which most British primary teachers enjoy. This is particularly important because few of them are satisfied with imparting only knowledge or skills to their pupils. Rather they have always been chosen, or have selected themselves, in part for their concern with religious, moral, political or social values (Rich, 1933; Tropp, 1957). Indeed, in the past many have seen themselves as 'missionaries' or 'crusaders' (Floud, 1962), a tradition which still persists (Nias, 1981). The Ashton *et al.* (1975) study of primary teachers' aims found that the majority thought that aims relating to social and moral education were more important than those which were concerned with intellectual, physical or aesthetic education. Lortie (1975), Lacey (1977), Woods (1981) and this writer have all highlighted the continuing existence within the profession of individuals with strong dedication to religious, political, or humanitarian ideals. Kay Shuttleworth's vision of a band of 'intelligent Christian men entering on the instruction of the poor with religious devotion to their work' (quoted in Rich, 1933) is still, *mutatis mutandis*, a recognizable one in many schools.

However, as studies such as those by Ashton *et al.* (1975) and Hartley (1985) demonstrate, there is little agreement, even within single schools, on which moral or educational values should be transmitted. Indeed, given the different social and curricular traditions (Blyth, 1967) which have shaped the primary system, and into which its teachers are socialized, it would be surprising if there were. Educational writers such as Alexander (1984) and Kelly (1986) have drawn attention to the persistence of this plurality, arguing that conflicting views of the nature of knowledge, and thus of teaching and learning, still bedevil primary schools. The epistemological confusion which such authors describe does, however, allow those teachers and headteachers who have a coherent philosophy to pursue it with relative impunity. Despite recent political developments, the English system still offers plenty of scope to individuals who wish to propagate particular views of the educational process.

Teachers' freedom to make many of the decisions which closely affect their work, and to select within broad limits the values which they seek to transmit, has also been protected in the past few decades by attempts to define teaching as a profession, and therefore to regard it as self-governing. Although 1986 and 1987 political decisions have undermined these efforts in the UK and tend to reduce teaching to, at best, the level of a 'semi-profession' (Etzioni, 1969), habits of autonomy are likely to die hard. Teachers will probably go on expecting to enjoy large measures of personal choice and discretion in matters relating to the conduct of their classrooms.

Finally, there are some teachers who, consciously or unconsciously, reduce the boundaries between their occupational and other lives. For them, teaching is very 'inclusive' (Argyris, 1964), that is, it absorbs much of their time and energy and makes use of many of their talents, skills or abilities. For such people, teaching is particularly personal in the double sense that it draws upon interests and capacities which might, in other occupations, be reserved for non-work activities, and that it allows little space for the development of alternative lives. Indeed, the more demanding it becomes of imagination, insight, problem-solving and professional skills, the more it offers an outlet for creative potential, thereby reducing individuals' need to seek the latter elsewhere. Similarly, when teaching is conceptualized as a relationship between two or more people, rather than as an instrumental activity, it becomes possible for teachers to find personal and emotional satisfactions within their working lives instead of outside them.

The fact that teaching as an occupation is potentially inclusive is compounded by the chronic scarcity of resources from which it suffers. By definition, no teacher ever has enough time, energy, and material resources to meet all the learning and personal demands of a large class of young children. To this shortage are now added recent expenditure cuts at both local and national levels. So, as an occupation, teaching has a bottomless appetite for *commitment* (for example, 'a readiness to allocate scarce personal resources', Lortie, 1975, p. 89). As a result, teachers are easily trapped. The more they identify with their jobs, the greater the satisfaction they receive from their personal relationship with individuals and classes, the more outlet they find in their work for varied talents and abilities, the greater the incentive that exists for them to invest their own personal and material resources in their teaching. They are, in short, beset by the paradox that the personal rewards to be found in their work come only from self-investment in it.

Primary teaching is, then, an activity which for psychological, philosophical and historical reasons can be regarded as individualistic, solitary and personal, inviting and in some senses requiring a high level of self-expenditure. It follows that any understanding of primary teachers' actions and reactions must be based upon knowledge of them as people.

However, this line of thinking leads into poorly charted territory. Surprisingly, an occupation which has for nearly 200 years attached great importance to the idea of knowing and catering for the individual child has paid little formal attention to the concept of the individual teacher. Particular primary teachers have attracted some largely unflattering attention from fiction writers (see for example, Biklen, 1986), but very little from academics or from teachers themselves. There have been a few attempts (notably Elbaz, 1983) to examine the professional or craft knowledge of individuals, to portray their 'ideologies' (Hartley, 1985) or personal constructs (Ingvarson and Greenway, 1984), or to record their feelings (for example, Hannam *et al.*, 1976; Huggett, 1986). One or two life histories exist (for example, Aspinwall, 1987) but there has so far been no work on individuals' lives and careers comparable to that carried out by Sikes *et al.* (1985) or Connel (1985) on secondary teachers. Individuals feature in the work of King (1978), Berlak and Berlak (1981) and Pollard (1985), but their opinions and activities are treated as if they were representatives of groups or sub-cultures. Moreover, studies such as these make more use of observation and questionnaire than of interviews. Few attempts have been made to present a detailed portrayal of the subjective reality of teaching from the standpoint of — and, as far as possible, in the words of — teachers themselves.

To emphasize the personal nature of teaching is also to draw attention to the notion of the 'self'. Yet although terms such as 'self-concept', 'identity', 'self-esteem', 'the ideal self' have multiplied in educational writings, they are, like the notion of the 'self' itself, hypothetical constructs which do not refer to anything tangible or directly observable. Any choice of explanatory system for them is therefore to some extent arbitrary.

One such system which offers many productive insights is symbolic interactionism, a set of ideas primarily associated with two Americans, Charles H. Cooley and George H. Mead. Although the psychologist William James made the distinction in the 1890s between *I* and *me*, it was Cooley (1902, 1983 edn) who argued that through interaction with people to whose behavior we attach symbolic meanings, we learn to take other people's perspectives and so to see ourselves as we think they see us. In doing so we come to have an awareness of ourselves as objects. Mead (1934) elaborated this idea, claiming that the *self* can be an object to itself (that is, *I* (ego) can observe, be aware of and think about *me* (alter)). We experience ourselves in the same way that we experience the people and things with which we come in contact. More than that, by interacting (Mead argued *by talking*) with others we become aware of the attitudes they hold toward us and this in turn shapes the way we see ourselves. Our 'selves' are inescapably social. Deprived of interaction with others we would have no sense of self for 'selves can only exist in definite relationships with other selves' (Mead, 1934, p. 164).

This is not to claim that all interactions are equally important in determining the way we see ourselves. Social psychologists now generally accept that 'significant others' (the idea, though not the term, was coined by Cooley) have a particularly powerful effect upon our self-concept. For, as Cooley (1902, 1983 edn, p. 175) argues, 'In the presence of one whom we feel to be of importance, there is a tendency to enter into and adopt by sympathy, his judgment of myself'. Mead built upon this idea when he introduced the concept of the 'generalized other'. His suggestion was that, in time and through repeated interactions, we internalize the attitudes not just of particular people but also of organized social groups (for instance, churches, political parties, community groups, work forces). When we do this, we supplement with new influences the forms of internal regulation we have acquired through identification with significant others. Our behavior, as adults, is therefore likely to vary not just in relation to the social context of which we are immediately a part, but also according to the 'reference group' (Newcomb, 1950) whom we have in mind in any particular situation. In other words, Mead set the scene for the development of the notion of 'multiple selves', each sustained and regulated by reference to different 'generalized others'.

Yet few social psychologists would wish to defend a totally situational view of the self. Katz (1960) suggested that each individual develops through contact with significant others an inner self or core. Writing as a biologist, Abercrombie (1969) put forward similar views, arguing that through the processes of perception, individuals begin at birth to develop assumptions about the world and themselves as part of it. The most potent schemata or assumptions (including those which are self-referential) are established by close physical contact between the infant and growing child and those in caring roles. Because they are formed before the child can talk, and 'having been made non-verbally are very difficult to talk about' (Abercrombie, 1969, p. 73), it is particularly hard for individuals to uncover the fundamental assumptions they have about themselves. These, therefore, remain relatively impervious to change.

Ball (1972) used the term 'substantial' to distinguish this inner core, which, he argued, is persistently defended and highly resistant to change. It comprises the most highly prized aspects of our self-concept and the attitudes and values which are salient to them. This idea, that we most strongly protect from challenge those attitudes which are expressive of the values by which we define ourselves, finds support from other theoretical perspectives. Rogers (1982) argued from his experience as a psychotherapist and educationalist that individuals need to maintain consistent self-concepts and will reject new ideas which they do not perceive as compatible with the latter. Festinger (1957), observing that people often find it psychologically uncomfortable to hold views which are mutually incompatible or to act in ways which are inconsistent with one or more of them, suggested that we resolve the resulting 'cognitive dissonance' by changing our views or actions so as to bring them into line with one another. Rokeach (1973) went further, claiming that the dissonances most likely to precipitate change in an individual arise not at the level of views but of beliefs and values. By implication, it is against dissonance in values or between values and actions that we most strongly protect ourselves. The group psychotherapist, Foulkes, was also of this opinion. He argued that 'the nuclear family imbues and impregnates the individual from his earliest phase of life and even before birth, with the total value system of the culture of which this family is part' (1975, p. 60). We become habituated to the patterns of behavior derived from these values and very skilled in their defense, to the extent that in new situations we try to recreate the relationships which sustain and perpetuate the values from which our view of ourselves derives. There is, then, support from different disciplines for the idea that we each develop a relatively impervious *substantial self* which can be distinguished from our *situational selves* and which incorporates those beliefs, values, and attitudes which we feel to be most self-defining.

Two further distinctions need to be made with respect to the self as 'me'. The first is between self-concept and self-esteem. It is easy to envisage circumstances under which people are not happy with or proud of the image which they have of themselves. Though the evidence is inconclusive (Hargreaves *et al.*, 1975), it seems in general to support the idea that when there is a conflict between the two, people act so as to maintain a stable self-image, even though this image may not be the one they wish they had. This may be in part because self-perceivers have access to 'privileged information' (Hampson, 1984, p. 192), that is, to knowledge of past and present experience which is denied to their partners in the interaction. Such knowledge may affect their perceptions of themselves and also of the messages being transmitted by their partners. The second is related: social psychologists often distinguish between people's images of themselves as they would like to be ('ideal') and as they think that they are ('real'). However, if one is guided by Thomas' (1931) well-known dictum that 'what people believe to be true is true in its consequences', this distinction becomes blurred. Unless people make it clear when they are speaking self-referentially that they are making a distinction between their 'ideal' and 'real' selves, it may be helpful to assume that they have the latter in mind.

So far, the discussion has been of the self as *me*. Symbolic interactionists also, however, conceptualize the self as *I*, the active subject which initiates and innovates as well as responding to the message about *me* that it receives from others. As a concept, the self as subject is, however, even more elusive than that of the self as object because *I* turns into *me* as soon as the actor is self-conscious, as soon, that is, as his/her actions become the object of reflexive thought. As Mead said:

> The *I* of this moment is present in the *me* of the next moment
> .... I cannot turn round quick enough to catch myself
> (Mead, 1934, p. 174).

Nevertheless, the *I* is important because it is:

> that part of the self which is relatively free of social constraints:
> It is impulsive and capable of inventing new ideas or meanings
> not sent in by the 'others'. It is that most private core of inner
> experience which has a degree of autonomy .... The *me*
> cannot be anything but conformist ... (but when we realize)
> that in some respect we acted against the grain of society, such
> a realization is awareness of the *I* and its capacities (Introduc-
> tion to Sociology Course Team, 1981).

In other words, Mead's notion of the 'ego' makes it possible for us to
reject the concept of a self which is entirely the product of social
conditioning.

But accepting that the self exists as subject, as well as object, brings
us no closer to knowing how we should conceptualize or characterize
the 'ego'. This may in part be, as Holland (1977) has so clearly shown,
because attempts from Mead onwards to explain the social self have
been unable (or unwilling) to come to terms with the powerful,
instinctual forces of the human personality to which Freud drew
attention over a century ago. Freud's analysis of personality structure
provided two hypothetical constructs — the *superego* (the controlling
'conscience' provided by internalized values) and the *ego* (the conscious actor in touch with the realities of daily living) — which fitted
in relatively well with the idea of a socially constructed self. It also,
however, presented us with the *id* (the unconscious, a potentially
explosive mixture of instincts and repressed memories). This aspect of
the self is, by definition, resistant to investigation but because of the
forces which are contained within it, it continually influences every
aspect of human thought, feeling, and behavior. It is obviously difficult to accommodate within a view of the self which emphasizes
socialization, continuity, and conformity rather than individuality,
conflict, and change.

Yet, the *I* is an inescapable part of education. Books such as those
by Jersild (1952) remind us that the encounter between teachers and
learners is an emotional experience. Richardson (1967, 1973) and
Salzberger-Wittenberg *et al.* (1983) both used an explicitly Freudian

perspective to explore the actions and reactions of student teachers and teachers in relation to their pupils and colleagues. Abercrombie (1969) carried her work on the unconscious nature of perception into higher education, increasing the autonomy and responsibility of adult learners by helping 'each participant to understand his own behavior and acquire better control over it' (Abercrombie, 1981, p. 52). Her first project, with medical students, is reported in Abercrombie (1969); the second, with architecture students in Abercrombie (1974); the third, on improving small-group teaching in universities, in Abercrombie and Terry (1978, 1979). In addition, accounts of her work with teachers, guided by the same insights, appear in Abercrombie and Terry (1979) and Lintott (1986). There is, then, growing evidence that teachers' attitudes, actions, and responses are influenced by their unconscious as well as their conscious selves, by the parts of themselves which they have rejected or 'split off' (Holland, 1977) as well as by those which they accept.

However, not all psychoanalysts adopt a view of the *I* which involves the denial and repression of parts of it. Rather, self-psychology (Kohut, 1971) stresses the continuation into adulthood of self-love or narcissism, seeing it as the means by which many admirable human qualities are developed. Kohut presents a view of the self which, drawing upon the infant's apparent inability to distinguish in early life between self and others, argues that nurturant figures in their environments become what he calls 'selfobjects' (Kohut, 1971, p. 27). Since young children are inescapably self-regarding, these extensions of self mirror back to them their own sense of 'narcissistic grandiosity' (Kohut, 1971, p. 25). Infants also expect to be able to control these 'selfobjects' as if they were themselves. With the passage of time, they learn to differentiate self and environment and they realize the limits both of the care provided by their nurturant figures and of their own controlling powers. As this happens, Kohut argues, the qualities detected as missing from their nurturing 'selfobjects' are incorporated into their own egos and adopted as their own ideals. At the same time, their self-love and self-importance become less extreme and unrealistic and are integrated into the ego as conventional aims and forms of ambition. So, early care-providers fulfill both a mirroring and an idealizing function for young children. As these functions are gradually internalized, individuals develop a stable capacity for self-regard and self-regulation and a mature ability to love people and things that exist independently of themselves.

However, as adults, they retain their early tendency to relate to the world and people in it as if these were part of themselves. Indeed, Kohut argues that self-love develops into culturally valuable attributes such as creativity, the ability to be empathetic, a sense of humor, and wisdom. This development is accompanied and in some senses sustained by the fact that we do not lose our need, especially in periods of intellectual, biological, or social change, for relationships which mirror or affirm our sense of self-esteem and present us with an idealized picture of strength and concern for others. The fact that we are able to revert at times of stress and confusion to infantile levels of narcissism enables us to treat these as transitional periods during which we can reshape or rebuild ourselves in a manner more in tune than previously with the external circumstances that caused our distress.

This account of the ego differs from that of classical psychoanalytic theory in positing separate development in individuals of the capacities to relate to their environments both as part of themselves and as independent of them (as opposed to the Freudian view that the normal individual develops beyond narcissism and that the persistence of the former is a sign of regression or dysfunctional dependence on a mother figure). Now, widespread acceptance of Freudian notions has resulted in a socially defined view of the ego, and thus of the individual teacher, from which not only negative emotions but also self-love are largely banished. Yet, the persistent self-referentialism of teachers, their tendency to treat their pupils as 'selfobjects', and thus to seek simultaneously to control and to look to them for reinforcement of their self-esteem, suggests that Pajak (1981) may be right in pressing for fuller understanding among educationalists of Kohut's views. It may well be that a continuing capacity for narcissism underpins the development of many adult aspirations and qualities. Certainly, any view of the *I* which discounts self-love is as incomplete as one which ignores the controlling superego and the instinctual drives of the 'id'.

Notwithstanding lack of agreement among psychologists and social psychologists about the nature of the *I*, many teachers are intuitively aware of its existence. They and others will recognize this expression of it, described by William James in a letter to his wife (quoted in Erikson, 1968, p. 19):

A man's character is discernible in the mental and moral attitude in which, when it came upon him, he felt himself most deeply and intensely active and alive. At such moments there is a voice inside which speaks and says, '*This* is the real me!'

James does not offer a definition of the *I* and his account contains no criteria by which the *I* may recognize the 'real me'. Nevertheless, his is an experience of which writers from diverse fields (ranging from poetry to psychology) are aware. It may be useful to refer to it as an awareness of a sense of personal 'identity'. Notwithstanding the many specific and general meanings which they, and others, have already attached to this word.

None of this, however, is to argue for a static view of the self. To be sure, the heart of the *I* (a sense of identity), and the core of the *me* (the substantial self) are hard to reach even by reflexive activity (for example, introspection and self-examination), are well defined and difficult to change. Yet, as I have argued (Nias, 1987b), both are open to modification, development, and even (as St Paul's experience on the road to Damascus suggests) radical redefinition. However, as the work of Marris (1958, 1974) shows, changes in self-definition reduce an individual's sense of control over self and environment. They are, in consequence, accompanied by feelings of loss, anxiety, and anger, particularly when (for example, in bereavement, tribal dislocation, job loss) they threaten fundamental aspects of the self. In such cases, accommodation to them will be painful and conflictual. It is clear from the work of Woods (1981), Nias (1984, 1985), and Pollard (1985) that teachers, too, being people, are threatened by the prospect of changes in self-definition, that many of the gratifications and dissatisfactions of teaching are related to the maintenance of an individual's self-image, self-esteem, and identity and that they develop situationally specific strategies to protect themselves from the need to alter the ways in which they perceive themselves.

There are, then, good reasons for regarding teaching as an occupation which makes calls upon the personality, experience, preferences, skills, attitudes, beliefs, values, interpersonal qualities, and ideas of the individual practitioner. The culture and physical context of schools, together with the historical and philosophical traditions of primary teaching and the resulting way in which the activity is often defined, all create a situation in which *who and what people perceive themselves to be* matters as much as *what they can do*. There are a growing number of classroom studies which illuminate the latter but as yet virtually no information about the former. To assist preliminary steps in this direction, the theoretical framework provided by symbolic interactionism and self-psychology have much to offer. I have used these perspectives to throw light on 150 interviews made as part of a longitudinal study of early and mid-career teachers in primary and middle schools, looking in particular at the subjective realities of teaching, job satisfaction and dissatisfaction, motivation, staff relationships, and the extent to which teaching as a career is compatible with notions of adult development (Nias, 1988, forthcoming).

Note

This chapter first appeared, in a modified form, in *Cambridge Journal of Education*, 1987, *17*(3).

References

ABERCROMBIE, M. L. J. (1969). *The anatomy of judgment: An investigation into the processes of perception and reasoning.* Harmondsworth: Penguin.

ABERCROMBIE, M. L. J. (1974). Improving the education of architects. In K. Collier (ed.), *Innovation in higher education.* London: NFER.

ABERCROMBIE, M. L. J. (1981). Changing basic assumptions about teaching and learning. In D. Boud (ed.), *Developing student autonomy in learning.* London: Kogan Page.

ABERCROMBIE, M. L. J., and TERRY, P. M. (1978). *Talking to learn.* Guildford: Society for Research into Higher Education.

ABERCROMBIE, M. L. J., and TERRY, P. M. (1979). *Aims and techniques of group teaching* (4th edn). Guidford: Society for Research into Higher Education.

ALEXANDER, R. (1984). *Primary teaching.* London: Holt Rinehart.

ARGYRIS, C. (1964). *Integrating the individual and the organization.* New York: Wiley.

ASHTON, P., HENDERSON, E., *(et al.).* (1975). *The aims of education: A study of teacher opinions.* London: Macmillan.

ASPINWALL, K. (1987). Teacher biography: The inservice potential. *Cambridge Journal of Education, 116,* 210–15.

BALL, S. (1972). Self and identity in the context of deviance: The case of criminal abortion. In R. Scott and J. Douglas (eds), *Theoretical perspectives on deviance.* New York: Basic Books.

BERLAK, A., and BERLAK, H. (1981). *The dilemmas of schooling.* London: Methuen.

BIKLEN, S. K. (1986). *Good morning, Miss Mundy: Fictional portrayals of young female teachers.* Paper presented at the American Education Research Association, San Francisco.

BLYTH, W. A. (1967). *English primary education,* Vol. II (2nd edn). London: Routledge & Kegan Paul.

BROADFOOT, P., and OSBORN, M. (1986). *Teachers' conceptions of their professional responsibility: Some international comparisons.* Paper presented to the British Educational Research Association conference, Bristol.

CONNELL, R. (1985). *Teachers' work.* London: Allen & Unwin.

COOLEY, C. (1983). *Human nature and the social order*. New Brunswick, NJ: Transaction Books.

DEPARTMENT OF EDUCATION AND SCIENCE (DES). (1982). *The new teacher in school*. HMI Series: Matters for discussion, 15. London: HMSO

DEPARTMENT OF EDUCATION AND SCIENCE (DES). (1983). *Teaching quality*. London: HMSO

ELBAZ, F. (1983). *Teacher thinking: A study of practical knowledge*. London: Croom Helm.

ERIKSON, E. (1968). *Identity: Youth and crisis*. London: Faber & Faber.

ETZIONI, A. (ed.). (1969). *The semi-professions and their organization*. New York: Free Press.

FESTINGER, L. (1957). *A theory of cognitive dissonance*. Stanford, CA: Stanford University Press.

FLOUD, J. (1962). Teaching the affluent society. *British Journal of Sociology*, *13*(4), 299–308.

FOULKES, S. H. (1975). A short outline of the therapeutic processes in group-analytic psychotherapy. *Group Analysis, 8*, 59–63.

HAMPSON, S. (1984). The construction of personality. In P. Barnes *et al.* (eds), *Personality, development and learning*. London: Hodder & Stoughton/ The Open University.

HANNAM, C., SMYTH, P., and STEPHENSON, N. (1976). *The first year of teaching*. Harmondsworth: Penguin.

HARGREAVES, D. (1980). The occupational culture of teachers. In P. Woods (ed.), *Teacher strategies: Explorations in the sociology of the school*. London: Croom Helm.

HARGREAVES, D., HESTER, S., and MELLOR, F. (1975). *Deviance in the class-room*. London: Routledge & Kegan Paul.

HARTLEY, D. (1985). *Understanding the primary school as an organization*. London: Croom Helm.

HOLLAND, R. (1977). *Self and social context*. London: Macmillan.

HUGGETT, F. (1986). *Teachers*. London: Weidenfeld & Nicholson.

INGVARSON, L., and GREENWAY, P. (1984). Portrayals of teacher development. *Australian Journal of Education, 28*(1), 45–65

INTRODUCTION TO SOCIOLOGY COURSE TEAM (1981). *Self in social context*. Milton Keynes: Open University.

JERSILD, A. (1952). *When teachers face themselves*. Columbia: Teachers College Press.

KATZ, D. (1960). The functional approach to the study of attitude change. *Public Opinion Quarterly, 24*, 163–204.

KELLY, A. (1986). *Knowledge and curriculum planning*. London: Harper Row.

KING, R. (1978). *All things bright and beautiful: A sociological study of infant schools*. Chichester: Wiley.

KOHUT, H. (1971). *The analysis of the self: A systematic approach to the psychoanalytic treatment of narcissistic personality disorders* (Psychoanalytic study of the child. Monograph No. 4.) Madison, CT: International Universities Press.

LACEY, C. (1977). *The socialization of teachers*. London: Methuen.

LINTOTT, B. (1986). *Group work in a course for teachers*. Cambridge: Cambridge Institude of Education.

LORTIE, D. (1975). *Schoolteacher*. Chicago: University of Chicago Press.

MARRIS, P. (1958). *Widows and their families*. London: Routledge & Kegan Paul.

MARRIS, P. (1974). *Loss and change*. London: Routledge & Kegan Paul.

MEAD, G. H. (1934). *Mind, self and society*. Chicago: University of Chicago Press.

NEWCOMB, T. (1950). *Social psychology*. New York: Dryden.

NIAS, J. (1980). Leadership styles and job satisfaction in primary schools. In T. Bush, R. Glatter, J Goodey, and C. Riches (eds), *Approaches to school management*. London: Harper & Row.

NIAS, J. (1981). Commitment and motivation in primary school teachers. *Educational Review, 33,* 181–90.

NIAS, J. (1984). Definition and maintenance of self in primary education. *British Journal of Social Education, 5*(3), 267–80.

NIAS. J. (1985). A more distant drummer: Teacher development as the development of self. In L. Barton & S. Walker (eds), *Social change and education*. London: Croom Helm.

NIAS, J. (1987a). Learning the job while playing a part: Staff development in the early years of teaching. In G. Southworth (ed.), *Readings in primary management*. Lewes: Falmer.

NIAS, J. (1987b). *Seeing anew: Teachers' theories of action*. Geelong: Deakin University.

NIAS, J. (1988). *On becoming and being a teacher*. London: Methuen (forthcoming).

PAJAK, E. (1981). Teaching and the psychology of self. *American Journal of Education, 9,* 1–13.

POLLARD, A. (1985). *The social world of the primary school*. London: Holt, Rinehart & Winston.

RICH, R. (1933). *The training of teachers in England and Wales in the nineteenth century*. London: CUP.

RICHARDSON, J. E. (1967). *Group study for teachers*. London: Routledge & Kegan Paul.

RICHARDSON, J. E. (1973). *The teacher, the school and the task of management*. London: Methuen.

ROGERS, C. (1982). *A social psychology of schooling*. London: Routledge & Kegan Paul.

ROKEACH, M. (1973). *The nature of human values*. New York: Free Press.

ROUSSEAU, J-J., (1762). *Emile* (trans. by B. Foxley, 1911). London: Dent.

SALZBERGER-WITTENBURG, I., HENRY, G., and OSBORNE, E. (1983). *The emotional experience of learning and teaching*. London: Routledge & Kegan Paul.

SIKES, P., MEASOR, L., and WOODS, P. (1985). *Teachers' careers*. Lewes: Falmer.

THOMAS, W. (1931). The relation of research to the social process. In Lyon, L. S. (ed.) *Essays on research in social science*. Washington: Brookings, Inc.

TROPP, A. (1957). *The school teachers*. London: Heinemann.

VERNON, M. (1955). The functions of schemata in perceiving. *Psychological Review, 62*(3), 180–93.

WOODS, P. (1981). Strategies, commitment and identity: Making and breaking the teacher role. In L. Barton and S. Walker (eds), *School, teachers and teaching*. Barcombe: Falmer Press.

WOODS, P. (1987). The art of teaching in primary school. In S. Delamont (ed.), *The primary school teacher*. Lewes: Falmer.

8 Teacher Professional Development: Perceptions and Practices in the USA and England

Mary Louise Hulbert Holly

To take a stranger's vantage point on everyday reality is to look inquiringly and wonderingly on the world in which one lives.

... and it is in wonder and questioning that learning begins (M. Greene, 1973, *Teacher as Stranger*, pp. 267–268).

Somehow, finding myself in the TB vaccination line, then moving into the high school auditorium to listen to the Superintendent introduce new policies, new faculty, and Mr Baldenstat, the new sports director and math teacher who would 'kick-off' the school year (and the football season), did not do much to build my enthusiasm and curiosity as I contemplated the children who would bounce through the classroom door the following day. Perhaps the peanut butter and jelly sandwiches and tomato soup which followed the speaker would allow some time to talk with colleagues. By three o'clock the 'in-service day' would be over and I could finally move to the classroom and let my mind wander through the children's arrival and our first day together. The year was 1969.

Years later (1982) I found that the often-quoted descriptors of in-service education used by teachers in the United States were also used by teachers in England: 'Piecemeal', 'haphazard', 'one-shot'. These words point to a common problem: the profession needs a conceptual framework that will provide direction and a context for individuals and groups of practitioners to shape continuing staff development' (Edelfelt and Lawrence, 1975, pp. 17–18). Feeling the need for 'renewal' back in the 1960s I happened on to a book entitled *Self-Renewal*, by John Gardner, and these words and images imprinted themselves in my mind as Mr Baldenstat and 'burnout' seemed to coalesce: how do we fashion 'a system that provides for its own continuous renewal' (1963, p. 21)?

Since that September 'in-service' (the January 'in-service' focused on 'behavioral objectives', kindergarten through grade 12, and featured hotdogs and Jell-O), I have continued to study professional development with Gardner's question in mind. The purpose of this chapter is to explore professional development from the teacher's point of view and also to put this point of view within broader historical and cultural contexts of England and the USA.

Though teacher perceptions are only one aspect of conceptualizing professional and staff development, they are an important one. The teacher as person, with unique life history (Abbs, 1974) and adult qualities and characteristics (Oja and Pine, 1983), and sense of self as professional (Nias, 1987), shapes educational opportunities for children. By understanding teachers, their contexts, and their perspectives, perhaps we can begin to conceptualize ways of supporting professional and staff development which take advantage of the questioning and wonder inherent in teaching and learning with young people.

Teacher Professional Development in Transition

Traditionally, the major vehicle for promoting teacher learning has been in-service education. Operationally defined, this means activities designed to improve skills, knowledge, attitudes, or techniques relative to teachers' roles, predominantly that of 'instructor' (Holly and Holly, 1983, p. 75). Long before teachers were college graduates with professional credentials 'in-service' was viewed as training which took place in institutes and lasted for a few days or in short courses which took place in the evenings. The rationale for these institutes was 'to enable teachers to bridge the gap between what they were expected to do and ... their level of knowledge and their teaching competencies' (Tyler, 1971, p. 6). 'In-service' was mandated, prescriptive, remedial, content-focused, and organized and implemented by persons in authority. During the last century, 'in-service' programs:

> reflected, above all else, the prevailing and partially valid assumption that the immaturity, meager educational equipment, and inexperience of the teacher rendered him unable to analyze or criticize

his own teaching, or, unless given direction, to improve it (Richey, 1957, p. 36).

As teacher preparation developed into professional programs and continuing education became an expectation for continuing to teach, gradually the term *in-service training* was replaced by *professional development*. Whereas training was based on eradicating the 'deficiencies' of inadequately prepared teachers, development signified (if only symbolically) the continuing nature of career and lifelong learning for teachers.

Today, we are caught between these two images. Though we know that development continues throughout the life cycle (Erikson, 1953; Havighurst, 1953: Knowles, 1978); and that effective teachers are 'searchers' who continue to grow and to become more cognitively complex and conceptually flexible (see for example: Combs, 1965; Heath, 1980; Hunt, 1978; Jersild, 1955; Lindsey, 1978; Loevinger, 1976; Oja, chap. 6; Sprinthall and Sprinthall, 1983), we continue to be influenced, perhaps unconsciously, by images of pathology and deficiency — thus, our preoccupation with 'improving' teachers. Consequently, teachers feel 'in-service' is something done *to them, not with them* (Sharma, 1982).

Over the last decade, numerous studies describing professional development from various perspectives — the school, the teacher, the administrator — have helped to differentiate more clearly the concepts of professional and staff development, and school improvement. Extrapolating from this research, Edelfelt (1983) provides a conceptual model for personnel development (Figure 8.1). He points out that historically the focus for improvement was on the individual teacher's professional development. The effect was to neglect teachers as a group and to reinforce teacher isolation (Lortie, 1975). The assumption was that improving individual teachers (e.g., writing better behavioral objectives) would improve schooling and thereby children's learning. As researchers realized that staff development was necessary to improve curriculum and teaching, the focus moved to staff development. With the growing awareness of the importance and interrelationship of other staff members, parents, community, and other educators, school improvement came to the fore. Educational improvement, according to Edelfelt, is the next step. At this time we are focusing on all levels: the individual teacher, the staff, the school, and to a lesser degree, educational improvement. *All* are necessary for educational development and change.

Figure 8.1   Four Contexts for Personnel Development

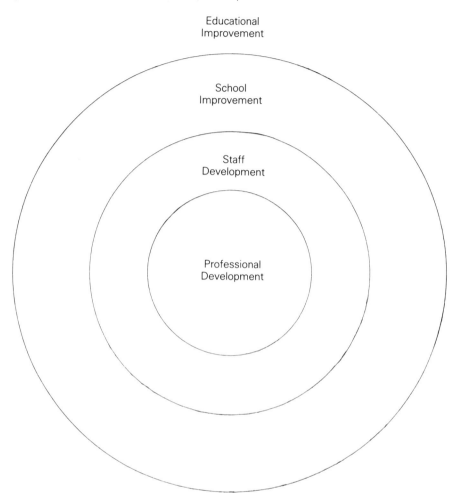

Source: Edelfelt, R. A. (1983). In-service Education: Moving from Professional Development to School Improvement, *Urban Educator, 7*(1), 102.

Perceptions on Professional Development

Line of Inquiry

Seeking to understand the teacher's perspective on possible relationships of in-service education to professional development, I interviewed 102 elementary and secondary school teachers from urban, suburban, and rural districts in Michigan (Holly, 1977). From this research I designed a phenomenological and longitudinal study of seven classroom teachers within different schools and cultural settings (Holly, 1983).

The research here builds on these studies and from previous study of teaching, schooling, and professional development in England in 1973, 1975 and 1982. After analysis of teachers' perceptions and the circumstances that appear to be conducive to professional development in the United States, a comparative study was designed to identify and analyze the perceptions of educators (including teachers, principals, headteachers, teacher center wardens [called directors in the USA], and teacher educators), on professional development in the United States and in England I anticipated that a comparative study between these two countries might provide insights into professional development. Because teacher professional development in England has been recognized and supported substantially at national and local government levels through appropriations and legislation (e.g., teachers' centers and curriculum development projects), we in the United States might learn from their experiences.

The research reported on here deals with teachers' perceptions on where they gain ideas and insights into their work, interactions with colleagues which they feel contribute to their professional development, and the kinds of activity in which they might engage if given the opportunity.

Professional Development in the United States and England

When comparing responses of teachers on both sides of the Atlantic, it is necessary to keep in mind that differences in practices and attitudes can be the result of many factors. For example, do different practices 'represent only differences in approach to the enterprise of education or ... [do they] reflect underlying cultural differences in the different countries?' (Gough, 1983, p. 71). Historical and cultural contexts surround practice; differences in terminology, teacher roles and responsibilities, and the structure of the profession exist.

Financial Support and Governance

Although education in the United States and England are financed both nationally and locally, there are significant differences (Gough,

1983). In England, local government — city or county councils — receives a government grant that is undifferentiated (i.e., a block grant) for the provision of various services, including education. Each council selects from its elected members an education committee that is allocated a budget each year from which to fund education in the area. This committee makes key decisions regarding the allocation of resources. The committee normally represents the views of the majority party on the council.

The power of the local education committee to make financial decisions seems to lessen community involvement. If the minority parties are in opposition to major decisions, they must wait until an election year to demonstrate their disapproval.

> Thus, in Britain the community is not closely and immediately involved in decision making about education. Neither is there a board of education that is directly elected. The legitimate concerns of the community may be expressed only via the elected council and its education committee, and — to some extent — through the governing bodies of schools. Each school has a set of governors ... including also a teacher governor and a parent governor (Gough, 1983, p. 72).

By contrast, educational financing and policy direction in the United States are influenced to a greater degree by the community. First, all school districts, regardless of size and complexity, are governed by a directly elected board or committee . This group is responsible to the electorate and usually encourages community involvement in setting priorities in programs, funding, and even personnel qualifications. Second, the amount of money available to be spent by the school board in any year has usually been established in prior years through tax levies or 'millage' which are voted on by local communities during government elections. Local school financing is obtained mainly through property taxes, which property owners traditionally have some role in setting. Should the electorate refuse to vote additional tax dollars for schools, then the board must live within its budget.

Organizational Structure

There are differences in the organizational structure of schools at the elementary level between the two countries. Schools in England tend to be smaller than schools in the United States. 'Nursery' schools in England span roughly the years from 3 to 5; the 'infants' schools range from 5 to 7, and the 'junior' schools span from 8 to 11. Often the infant and junior schools are housed in the same building and referred to as 'primary schools'. There are kindergarten through grade two (occasionally grade four) schools in the USA but the dominant organization is kindergarten through grade six (ages 5 through 12).

Whereas students in the USA are divided by 'grade level', students in England are divided into 'bands'.

> In Britain students normally go through their school career in age cohorts. The child in a class of seven-year-olds will, the following September, automatically progress into a class of eight-year-olds. There are no statutory end-of-year tests, still less any common delineated program indicating what a seven-year-old has to know (and hence, presumably, what a teacher has to teach) (Gough, 1983, p. 71).

Although teachers in both countries have been described as 'isolated' (Lortie, 1975; Nias, 1983), Ellis (1984) reported that there is an increasing focus in England on the school as the educational unit for change rather than the individual classroom. He attributed this to three factors: intentional de-isolation of the teacher, promotion of unity, and progression within the institution. 'Discussion and cooperation between staff members are encouraged, with emphasis on school-based professional development' (Ellis, 1984, p. 269).

In the USA there is discussion (and writing) about the school as the unit of change (Edelfelt, 1983; Lawrence, Baker, Elzie, and Hansen, 1974) and of school-focused professional development (Howey, Bents and Corrigan, 1981). Until recently collaboration among staff members, and colleagueship, have more been talked about than practiced (Goodlad, 1984). However, there is mounting evidence that these patterns of interaction and relationship are associated with successful schools (Little, 1982). There are increasing signs of movement toward collaborative practices. There is, for example, a parallel between teacher collaboration and teacher use of 'cooperative learning' for students in classrooms (Slavin, 1987). And, the National Education Association's (NEA) three-year national school improvement 'Mastery in Learning Project' (in 24 schools in the USA) has colleagueship and collaboration at its core (NEA, 1986).

Philosophical and Theoretical Foundations

Organizational structures, staff roles and responsibilities, curricular and program development and evaluation in the two countries reflect their historical, philosophical, and theoretical foundations.

The elementary school in the USA developed to support a growing and culturally diverse population. Basic skills in reading, writing, and computation formed the core of the curriculum. These skills were taught to ensure an informed citizenry for participation in a democratic and pluralistic society. The focus of learning in the elementary school was on the future — on preparing the student to be a responsible and contributing member of society. Schools started as single classrooms with multiple-aged students who learned 'basic skills' during the few hours each day they spent in school. They learned broader life skills and knowledge at home and in the community. As schooling grew to include more children and concomitantly more 'subject' areas, schools increased in size by adding classrooms, and as Lortie (1975) describes it, they developed in a cellular fashion. Children were divided into grade levels. Subject areas multiplied in the same manner, and time was divided to accommodate study. Structurally, elementary schools in the US have changed little (with the exception of adding kindergarten) since their inception.

Philosophically and theoretically, elementary schools in the USA have been influenced by at least four main themes: *positivism, business and industry, child development,* and *progressivism.* Since the early 1900s, American behavioral psychologists and business and industry have been influential in the development of measurement and competency-based education. Specifiable objectives, curriculum packages, 'teacher-proof' curriculum materials and standardized testing are examples.

Theories of child development and education, (e.g., Piaget, Erikson, Anna Freud, Montessori, Isaacs, and Dewey) have had some influence in the USA, and a few such as Montessori, have had a considerable impact on primary education (for example, child-sized materials and furniture). Thorndike, Bruner, and Tyler have had substantial influence on elementary schooling — even if indirectly through a filtering down of practices in testing and curriculum development designed for older students.

Early childhood education in England developed with some of the same influences but in different ways and with different results. Whereas primary education in the USA reflects a science and industry orientation (including delineated subject and competency areas, grading, testing, grouping, sequencing curricula, competition, and promotion tied to achievement), primary education in England reflects an emphasis on and an integration of child development and principles of progressive education.

Philosophically, British early childhood education reflects a child-centered environment, more akin to Rousseau's child as 'noble savage' than to Locke's child as 'tabula rasa'. Children are to be nurtured more than molded. Early schooling is to be 'family-like'. Children are to enjoy learning; emphasis is placed on play, creativity, and sensorimotor activity. Expression through language and the arts are key elements in nurturing the personal growth of children. Developmental influences are strong and can be seen in the respect for individual differences and learning styles. Piaget's theory of cognitive development, attention to the child's construction of reality, and qualitative changes in thinking undergird the action and problem-solving orientation of British primary schools. Dewey's concepts of experiential learning and community environments in schooling are more in evidence in British schools than in American schools. The curriculum offered primary students was to be 'thought of in terms of activity and experience rather than of knowledge to be acquired and facts to be stored' (Ministry of Education *Reports on Education*, No. 1, *The Primary School*, July 1963, p. 93). The aim was:

> to develop in a child the fundamental human powers and to awaken him to fundamental interests of civilized life so far as these powers and interests lie within the compass of childhood, to encourage him to attain gradually to that control and orderly management of his energies, impulses, and emotions, which is the essence of moral and intellectual discipline, to help him to discover the idea of duty and to ensue it, and to open out his imagination and his sympathies in such a way that he may be prepared to understand and to follow in later years the highest examples of excellence in life and conduct (Ministry of Education *Reports on Education*, No. 1, *The Primary School*, July 1963, p. 93).

Whereas independence in functioning, competition, and striving for performance in schools follow from capitalism in the USA, cooperation, interdependence and sharing bespeak the more socialist oriented England.

Roles and Responsibilities

In England head teachers (principals) and teachers have more auto-nomy in teaching and curriculum development than principals and teachers do in the USA. Head teachers have been classroom teachers and many retain instructional responsibilities as 'teaching heads'. Many 'cover' classes for teachers to release the teacher for professional development activity or curriculum development[1]. Head teachers are viewed more as instructional leaders than as managers (Holly and Holly, 1983) which is the reverse in the United States (Seifert and Beck, 1981), though there is evidence that both these views are chang-ing.

Ellis (1984) notes that there are more adults present in USA class-rooms than in British classrooms. He attributes this in part to ancillary assistance and special classes, which mean fewer children in the class-room at any one time. Whereas special teachers work with groups and entire classes (e.g., art, music, physical education) in the USA, which contributes to greater teacher efficiency, 'they may [also] con-tribute to a more fragmented curriculum' (Ellis, 1984, p. 268). Class-room teachers in England are responsible for all subject areas. 'This means that each teacher is rarely out of the classroom during the school day, and spare time is often spent working with small groups or individuals who need extra assistance' (Ellis, 1984, p. 268). Ellis suggests that this necessitates concentrated teaching commitment and it also ensures continuity and flexibility within the curriculum, with a considerable degree of autonomy for each staff member. The elementary school curriculum in the USA, therefore, reflects subject differentiation with a reliance on teacher specialization, whereas the English primary school program is based more on content integration and generalist teachers (Ellis, 1984, p. 268-9).

Curriculum, Program Development, and Evaluation

Because teachers in England have a high degree of autonomy in what and how they teach, it is not surprising to find that curriculum development is a continuing process integral to teaching. A common approach to curriculum development at the primary level is 'topical'; a theme is selected and the curriculum is designed around it. This might involve one, two, or all of the teachers in a school. It is an approach which encompasses many of what in the USA are termed 'courses' or 'content areas' such as science, art, social studies, and language arts. Perhaps one of the more surprising aspects (other than subject integration) is that it often exemplifies Dewey's (1938) philosophy of experience — the 'content' arises out of exploration of the topic — it emerges rather than most curriculum development in the United States where the content is carefully planned (and heavily influenced if not determined by textbook authors) *before* experience. Teachers in England develop topics for study using many resources. Often the children develop their own books as their study evolves. In contrast, in the United States, it is common practice to have a textbook for every subject taught. In fact, it is estimated that at least 90 per cent of class time in the USA is textbook-related (Phillips and Hawthorne, 1978).

According to Gough (1983), 'in the United States school subjects are quite distinct and the boundaries carefully drawn. The curriculum is fragmented, and the instruments for assessment reflect that fragmentation' (p. 71). He notes that 'the USA grade system and its associated assessment procedures do seem to be the source of certain rigidities' (p. 71). The practices of using 'preordained syllabi' and 'mandated textbooks' are foreign to many British teachers.

British teachers visiting USA schools, for example, are somewhat surprised and perplexed by the frequency of testing, and standardization of the curriculum, but they also begin to question the nature of their own evaluation procedures: 'How to preserve the independence of the teacher, while responding to the legitimate claims for accountability from the community at large, is something currently exercising the minds of many British educators' (Gough, 1983, p. 72).

The American visitor to British schools is often surprised at the amount of writing, speaking, listening (language arts) and art and craft that permeate the school day.

> Creative activities ... occur more frequently as the need arises in the normal classroom, rather than at predetermined periods in special rooms. Self-expression with a variety of media is encouraged as a natural extension of reading and writing ... English primary teachers also generally give writing assignments more frequently and use fewer ditto sheets and workbooks; most recording is written out in exercise books or on paper ... [there are] more opportunities for children to write spontaneously and to pursue language activities according to their interests and needs (Ellis, 1984, p. 269).

Less curriculum conformity and a wider diversity of alternative curricular materials and projects are used in England. This can be attributed, in part, to reliance on standardized procedures in the USA.

Teacher Preparation

Since 1960, formal academic teacher preparation in England has taken place in three years (previously it took two years) in special teacher preparation schools called 'colleges of education' and culminates with a certificate which, in all but unusual cases, permits teaching until retirement.

From the outset, the teacher education curriculum is focused on the application of content areas to teaching, which includes observation and teaching experiences with children. In the USA teacher preparation lasts a minimum of four years and usually includes a set of 'core courses' including liberal arts, social science, humanities, and science taken at the university at large (i.e., outside the college of education) with students who are studying in fields outside education. British teachers in preparation focus almost entirely on the application of knowledge to teaching. They begin and end their program almost exclusively with other education majors.

There is an exception to this form of teacher preparation — one that is becoming more usual in England and that is slowly becoming an option at some universities in the United States. In England it is called the BEd degree; in the United states it is a BA (Bachelor of Arts) degree, or if a five year program, an MAT degree (Master of Arts in Teaching). This is a restricted possibility in England because in order to qualify for university work the student must pass national examinations with high marks. It can be interpreted in that country, then, that teachers with a BEd degree (four years) have more comprehensive and prestigious credentials than those not obtaining a degree. However, because those students can elect to become teachers midway or later in their coursework, they are sometimes viewed as less committed to teaching and as not having adequate time for the development of teaching and management skills.

Professional Development Activity: Incentives and Opportunities

Teachers in the United States must engage in academic, professional coursework at the university graduate level to move from initial or provisional certification to permanent certification and tenure. Although requirements vary from state to state, many states require master's degrees and an increasing number of teachers obtain this degree even when it is not required. Teachers are encouraged to continue formal schooling through salary increments for additional credit hours earned, and some school systems provide teachers with partial or full reimbursement for university credit fees.

In England there is not the widespread practice of working toward master's degrees at universities; teachers are not rewarded by an increase in salary; further study is not a condition for continuing employment, nor are the same type of programs available to the 'average teacher'. There is no British equivalent of the 'three credit hour course'. A course is either a 'short course' lasting a week or two, or for a few weekends, where the teacher might reside at the institution offering it, or it is a 'long course' which is a set of planned and evolving experiences often culminating in a final research project designed and conducted by the participant. Teachers who want to progress in their careers to higher 'posts' or 'scales' (positions and responsibilities, respectively) may elect to go on a master's course or to work toward an advanced diploma, but these teachers are the exception rather than the rule. Long courses last for a year or two in which the teacher studies with a group of peers, and the typical emphasis is directed toward the teacher as researcher. Teachers and administrators taking the course develop as colleagues as they study together over time. Since the early 1970s the Open University has provided coursework leading to degrees for many teachers throughout England.

For most British teachers, incentives for professional development activity include: the potential to learn new ideas and grow in understanding of teaching and children, to work with colleagues, and to gain knowledge for curriculum development and leadership. They are 'encouraged to undertake a fair amount of in-service training and refresher courses' (King, 1973, p. 244) which are often offered through teachers' centers maintained by most local education authorities. These are short courses. They are usually 'practice oriented' and similar to what teachers in the United States would call 'workshops', though no 'credit' toward a degree accrues (as it often does in the United States). Unlike many workshops in the USA, these courses are almost always funded by the local education authority. Perhaps because teachers in England are so active in curriculum development, the authorities and administration are generally supportive psychologically and financially of these professional development activities.[2]

In England, the teacher center is a primary system for providing in-service education and support for teacher professional development as well as staff development. Teacher center wardens suggest that the teacher center is a concept which serves multiple purposes, not the least of which is to contribute to a climate of change for curriculum development. It extends to people a chance to find out about local, regional, and national news and it provides a forum for discussion (Holly and Holly, 1983, p. 81).

The teacher center concept was introduced in the McNair Report, *Teachers and Youths* in 1944. It was designed to provide support and 'neutral ground' for curriculum and program development. Centers increased from a 'mere handful in 1960 to well over 600 by 1972 (Thornbury, 1974, p. 3). This rapid growth came as a result of the expansion of schools and the reorganization of secondary schools. During this time, the Schools Council, the first national teacher center, came into being. Working papers published by the Schools Council between 1964 and 1969 (e.g., *Curriculum Development*, 1967) and other research spurred the development of more centers (Cane, 1969; HMSO, and H. E. R. Townsend: *Statistics of Education*, 1970; HMSO, *Teacher Education and Training*, 1972). Today, teacher centers are available to most, if not all teachers in England.

Centers in the United States took their impetus from the British model, but they did not seem to have the same sense of neutrality or reason for being — collaborative curriculum development and program development — nor did they have the sustained governmental, administrative, and structural support of centers in England. Federal support lasted only three years. From 1978 to 1980 federal funding was extended to 133 centers. According to Edelfelt (1982, p. 393), 'in all of them it has been the major support for funding. In most it is the *only* source of support, except for the in-kind contributions of local districts and colleges'. With a shift in political power in Washington, DC, came the termination of categorical funding, and with it, moneys for teacher centers. Many centers were discontinued when federal funding was terminated. Most centers were not institutionalized — they were not able, in the time available, to become part of a larger organizational structure for affiliation and support.

Cross-Cultural Perceptions of Teacher Professional Development

Areas of Data Collection

The data reported here were collected in three urban areas: Akron, Ohio in the USA, and Liverpool and Cambridge, England. Akron lies in highly urbanized northeastern Ohio. The Akron economy is shifting from one based primarily on manufacturing to one oriented more toward technology, services, and information. Akron suffers from a higher than average unemployment rate, largely as a result of structural shifts in the traditional industries on which its economy has been based (e.g., rubber products, transportation, machinery). A fairly large percentage of its population is considered to be 'minority' and European-ethnic in composition. Liverpool, too, is an aging center based on shipping and transportation, located in northwest England. Liverpool's traditional economic base is declining in importance, unemployment is high, the social and ethnic composition is diverse, and the social pathologies normally associated with economic depression are evident.

Cambridge, a university and service center, sits in the relatively prosperous agricultural area of East Anglia in east-central England. The regional economy is diversified, unemployment is below the national average; the population is fairly homogeneous and well-educated. The town itself is relatively affluent — with a robust local economy driven by university and tourism revenues. However, as more than one person in Cambridge cautioned: 'All the problems you find in other areas, like Liverpool, can be found here in Cambridge. There are many poor people and their problems, and the problems posed to the schools are pretty much the same.'

Sample Profiles

A total of 60 teachers agreed to an interview consisting of 10 open-ended questions related to personal and professional activities and attitudes. Twenty-eight early childhood teachers from several school systems in and around the Akron metropolitan area of northeastern Ohio, and 32 early and middle primary school teachers from the Local Education Authorities (LEAs) of Liverpool (15) and Cambridge (17) were interviewed. Interviewing was conducted in the USA during

Table 8.1   Respondents' years of teaching experience by location

	United States	United Kingdom		
Measure	Akron	*Liverpool*	*Cambridge*	*Total*
Mean	9.6	12.1	12.2	12.1
Standard deviations	5.1	6.3	4.6	5.3
Coefficient of variation (*sd/m* × 100)	52.4	51.8	37.4	44.0
Range	2–19	2–25	5–20	2–25
N	28	15	17	60

January and February 1981 and in England during May and June 1982. Each sample was drawn in a non-random fashion by a nominating process, and therefore cannot be considered representative of some larger population. Both groups were interviewed by the same interviewer with the same instrument, thereby eliminating response or interviewer bias.

The British sample draws teachers from two different sections of the country, whereas the USA sample comes from one area. What effect this may have on the outcome is unknown. In addition, the British teachers represent a broader range of age groups in terms of teaching responsibilities. Although both groups teach at the early childhood level, some of the British teachers work with slightly older children of 10 to 11 years.

The two groups of teachers were compared on the basis of experience, since this has been identified as a factor influencing teachers' professional development activities (Fuller, 1969). Younger, less experienced teachers are thought to be more actively involved in formal activities such as credit courses for degrees (in the USA) and 'hands-on' in-service education, while teachers with more years experience are less likely to feel the need for such activities (Fuller, 1969; Yarger and Mertens, 1980). Highly experienced teachers have also been found to be less satisfied and more critical of in-service education (Holly, 1977). Although the English sample averaged about 2½ years more experience, the difference was insignificant. Both means and chi-square tests failed to demonstrate significant differences. The coefficients of variation (ratio of the standard deviation to the increase) differed, with the USA sample having greater variation about the mean years of experience. The standard deviations of the two groups were almost identical, but the means varied substantially. Interestingly, the Liverpool subgroup displayed more similarity to the USA group on this measure, suggesting that older industrial areas like Akron and Liverpool have similar teaching corps with respect to range of experience. The fact that Cambridge has a relatively experienced group may be due to sample selection methods.

In both countries, workshops or specialized courses ('short courses') are made available to teachers, particularly in content and skills areas. This service is provided through graduate institutions in the USA. The LEAs, teachers' centers, and education institutes serve the same purpose in England. The USA system stresses academic preparation as well as continuing formal education, while the British system places more support and emphasis on experience and school-based professional learning. This partly explains why only a few British teachers were presently enrolled in 'a course'. The USA teachers, on the other hand, responded in the majority (17 out of 28 were currently enrolled). Somewhat surprisingly, current enrollment did not vary with experience (Chi-square not significant at 0.05). In other words, more experienced teachers were not less likely to be enrolled in professional coursework as were their less experienced colleagues (degree of experience dichotomized at the mean).

For purposes of analysis, then, the two samples are similar in experience and grade level taught. Measurement error should be small resulting from standardization of data collection. Differences in attitudes and activities between the two groups can be attributed, at least in part, to differences between the two systems in: (1) how teachers are educated, (2) organizational structures, (3) professional development opportunities, and (4) cultural patterns.

Comments on Data Analysis

Responses to each question were analyzed separately and in relationship to other questions. All responses were listed for each question and read several times. As categories emerged for each respondent, they were excerpted and grouped with like responses. Responses were tallied and presented in number and percentage. Categories were formed from actual responses. That is, if a teacher said, 'I get ideas from books', *books* was the category. If a teacher said, 'I gain ideas from reading', *reading* became the category. Thus, *Books* and *reading* are separate categories though they are both the same process. Differences become more important when we look at the category, *books*, as opposed to *magazines* (and *journals*) which are not as available in

England as they are in the USA. From teachers' responses, *Books* associated with courses in England are considered a source for ideas and insights, whereas in the United States this was not indicated.

Because the numbers of respondents is not large (USA $N = 28$; England $N = 32$) the specific percentages should not be taken too literally: 15 respondents in the US group, for example, is 54 per cent, while 15 respondents in the group from England translates into 47 per cent. The exact number of responses per category is of less importance to this analysis and discussion than are the trends and patterns. For example, it is probably not significant, in itself, that three or four USA teachers and five or six British teachers give the same response on a given question. It might become important if the differences hold up over several other questions.

Categories that appear for one sample and not for the other indicate points to consider. For example, when asked where they have gone for ideas and insights into their work, several teachers in the USA said, without hesitation, that they relied mainly *on themselves*. No British teachers responded in this way. Several did, however, mention that along with turning to other teachers, they reflected about what they did as teachers and gained insights from this process. Each of the teachers who responded in this way mentioned it in addition to other categories; they did not focus on it as the immediate response as did the USA teachers who replied *from myself*. So, while *myself* did not appear as a category for British teachers, they did note the importance of personal reflection. The absence of the category *from myself* in the British sample pointed to further analysis which suggested a trend seen when total interview samples were considered — USA teachers appear to be more independent from their colleagues in their teaching, and in their professional development. This feature will be addressed later.

Gaining Ideas and Insights into Teaching

When asked to reflect on their teaching careers, '*Where did you get ideas for your classroom and insights into your work?*' several activities were given by both groups in fairly high percentages. For example, 'other teachers' topped the list with 68 per cent and 63 per cent for the USA and England respectively.[3] After this point, the frequencies for various activities diverge with the USA teachers mentioning magazines (54 per cent), self (32 per cent), workshops (29 percent), and books (21

Table 8.2 Looking back over your teaching career, where did you get ideas for your classroom, and insights into your work?

Source	United States (%)	United Kingdom (%)
Other teachers	19 (68)	20 (63)
Magazines	15 (54)	6 (19)
Self	9 (32)	3 (9)
Workshops	8 (29)	—
Books	6 (21)	13 (41)
Courses	5 (18)	15 (47)
Reading	4 (14)	2 (6)
TV—radio	—	7 (22)
Visits to other schools	—	12 (38)
Children	—	8 (25)
In-service	2 (7)	5 (16)

Respondents: USA N = 28; England N = 32.

per cent) most often; while the British teachers emphasized courses (47 per cent), books (41 per cent), visits to other schools (38 per cent), their students (25 per cent), and TV-radio (22 per cent).

Both groups of teachers referred more often to informal activities as sources of ideas over more formal, institutionally based activities, with the British slightly more institutionally and school-based oriented. Second, the British teachers appear to make extensive use of visitations to other schools (38 per cent) which does not appear to be an option for the USA teachers.

English educators also appear to rely on radio and television for sources of ideas; American teachers do not mention these. This may be a function of USA electronic media being exclusively entertainment-oriented (public television and radio notwithstanding), while the British Broadcasting system (BBC) schedules liberal amounts of news, current events, culture and education. The USA teachers mentioned themselves and workshops more often than English teachers who, in turn, mentioned courses and their students to a greater extent. In-service activities were mentioned by American and British teachers, 7 and 16 per cent respectively. A variety of other sources were mentioned by one or two teachers in each sample.

The nature of the responses are consistent with previous research (Holly, 1977; Lortie, 1975) in which teachers most highly valued professional activity where they could selectively and directly apply their experiences to teaching. Most activity cited with 'other teachers' took place informally — chatting before and after school and on breaks from teaching although many teachers in both countries spoke

Table 8.3   If you had the time available and could design your own program for personal, professional development, what kinds of things would you include?

Activity source	United States (%)	United Kingdom (%)
Visit other teachers' classrooms and other school systems	11 (39)	19 (59)
Reading	7 (28)	6 (19)
Upgrade specific skills	6 (21)	7 (22)
Planning	6 (21)	5 (16)
Courses	5 (18)	14 (44)
Workshops	4 (14)	—
Sabbatical leave	1 (4)	7 (22)
Travel	1 (4)	4 (13)

Respondents: USA N = 28; England N = 32.

of a major benefit of workshops and courses as the chance to 'talk with other teachers'. That the British teachers sought out and found a greater diversity of resources seems reasonable with their greater responsibility for curriculum development.

Use of Time for Professional Development

Previous research often has identified *time* as an important contextual variable in professional and staff development. Teachers, head teachers and teacher center wardens interviewed in the current study (Holly and Holly, 1983) all singled out insufficient time as a constraint on teachers to expand themselves professionally. Although Stenhouse (1981) is referring to teachers in England, his works are echoed by many educators in the USA: 'The most serious impediment to the development of teachers as researchers — and indeed as artists in teaching — is quite simply shortage of time. In this country teachers teach too much' (p. 16).

In an effort to gain insight into attitudinal and temporal aspects of teachers' professional activities both sample groups were asked: *If you had time available and could design your own program for personal development, what kinds of things would you include?*[4] 'Oh! What I could do with some time!' was not an unusual response for either group of teachers. Responses to this question produced a high degree of convergence in the two groups, with *visits to other classrooms, schools and school systems* heading both lists: USA 39 per cent, and England, 59 per cent (see Table 8.3).

Again, British teachers displayed interest in a greater range of activities than did their American counterparts, yet both groups were in substantial agreement on what they would do. The USA teachers, who have found few formal opportunities to visit other classrooms and schools, and the British teachers who do, both expressed a high degree of interest in having regular opportunities to observe how other teachers operate in the classroom. This desire is consistent with their recognition of professional colleagues as sources of ideas and insights. Again, consistent with Lortie's (1975) findings, teachers in both countries were selective in what they felt would be beneficial. They seemed to want to visit other classrooms but they wanted to be the ones to sift through practices themselves, 'I'd like to visit other teachers' classrooms and pick up ideas from them, not from their telling me.' The missing element in allowing this to happen is time, as well as, in the USA case, opportunity. In England, visitation is a normal activity and highly valued if the responses of these teachers are an indicator. Interviews with teacher center administrators add confirmation to this finding as responses from both groups suggested that visitations and observations were among the most important resources for teacher professional development (Holly and Holly, 1983).

Both groups recognized the necessity for continuing their formal education through their desire to continue taking courses. Courses were a strong second choice for British teachers (44 per cent), while they were a fifth choice for USA teachers (18 per cent). The British teachers, on the whole, seemed to be more favorably disposed to take courses but they, like the USA teachers, were critical of courses that they perceived to be 'irrelevant'. For many teachers, even professionally meaningful experiences and ideas obtained outside of their classrooms and schools (courses) do not apear to be powerful enough to be implemented and sustained back in their classrooms.

For teachers from the United States mentioning courses the purpose was usually to work on a degree program, while for British teachers it was to study a subject area: art, music, drama, or environmental studies. British teachers were also more likely to suggest courses which were of high personal interest (not program or degree related). One British teacher did mention that 'It would be nice to go on a course and to receive a certificate upon its completion.' Embedded in several teachers' comments was the desire to return to professional study full time for awhile.

Other activities drawing more than a few responses included (USA and England respectively): reading (28 per cent, 19 per cent), upgrading specific skills (21 per cent, 22 per cent), planning (21 per cent, 16 per cent), sabbatical leaves (4 per cent, 22 per cent), and travel (4 per cent, 13 per cent). That more teachers in the USA cite *planning* might be predicted, given the specific and mandatory lesson plans common to most schools. The difference in mentions of sabbatical leaves is consistent with practices in both countries. Leaves are rarely, if ever, provided in USA school systems. Although most teachers do not have sabbatical leaves in England, they are not rare. There is a similar practice of 'secondment' that enables teachers to take a position temporarily, outside their normal jobs. Two British teachers mentioned their desire for secondment to teacher centers where they could act as consultants to teacher colleagues.[5]

Other teachers mentioned a sabbatical to return to college full time to work on either a degree or an advanced diploma. Several teachers who mentioned sabbatical (as did those who said 'travel') did so with the explanation that they needed to 'get out of the classroom for awhile'. 'I'd like to take a sabbatical to get away from the classroom ... to step out, and then you'll come back with vigor. After fifteen years you need to get out ... it would be good to get away from stress and look back from a fresh angle ... to see how education works in a different country.'

Certainly, many of these activities are presently available to teachers, but the demands of full time work and private lives leaves insufficient time for in-depth study. This raises the issue of whether continuing education should be part of the teachers' contractual obligations, and therefore provided by the school system, or whether it is a professional obligation to be pursued in addition to teaching responsibilities. Much of what these teachers say they would do if given ample time involves institutional aegis (for example, formal courses, planning time, visitations) and at present these are not provided under the prevailing definition of 'in-service'.

Professionally Meaningful Activity With Other Teachers

As a means of gaining insights into possible links between colleague interaction and professional development, respondents were asked to describe which activities with other teachers, if any, were beneficial to their teaching. Responses provide pictures of the kinds of experiences which teachers feel are useful. Not surprisingly, one or two respondents in each sample responded '*Nothing* with other teachers in

Table 8.4   Do you engage in activities with other teachers which you feel are beneficial to you in your teaching?

Activity source	United States (%)	United Kingdom (%)
Informal exchanges at lunch, breaks, after school	12 (43)	21 (66)
Workshops	7 (28)	
Social occasions	6 (21)	8 (25)
Courses	5 (18)	
Staff meetings	2 (7)	8 (25)
Joint teaching	2 (7)	4 (13)

Respondents: USA N = 28; England N = 32.

my building is beneficial', but the predominant response indicated frequent and valued communication and relationships with colleagues: 'We talk over a lot'; 'You are dependent upon your colleagues.'

The most frequently mentioned activities or situations are displayed in Table 8.4 with percentages given in parentheses.[6] For each sample the list is dominated by two kinds of activities. They are informal activities occurring at lunch time, breaks, in the staff room, after school, or in casual meeting: 'Chatting in breaks in the morning and afternoon'; and 'First thing in the morning — conversation at night ... we sometimes swap classes ... our coffee break at 10:20 [am] ... lunch time, 2:20 [pm] ... [colleagues are] more like friends than anything else. If we have worries about the children — "How did you find David?" We're like a big family — we've been here so long and we know the families.' The discussions often center on how to solve specific problems dealing with students, curriculum content, or teaching. Occasionally, such exchanges include principals/head teachers (British head teachers were mentioned more often than USA principals).

The other primary set of activities involved planned collaboration at courses and/or workshops. For the American teachers these were uniformly located at a local college or university, whereas for the British teachers these take place at a variety of locations: the school, teacher centers, education institutes, or local colleges.

Next in number of mentions were social occasions outside of school, either with teachers from the same school or others who were friends, and staff meetings held after the day's classes were over. More frequent mention by British teachers of staff meetings might be related to the size of staff, the frequency of staff meetings, as well as the content and procedures within meetings. Meetings tended to be less formal, smaller in the number of participants (because of smaller schools), more frequent and participatory in format — often tied to curriculum development and evaluation issues. Teachers appeared to have more influence on the agenda and participate more than their peers in the United States. This was not universally the case as two British teachers replied: 'We don't have meetings very often'; 'Our meetings are more administrative — not discussion oriented.'

Joint teaching efforts round out the list, perhaps evidence of how little it is practiced. Throughout the interview, British teachers did, however, mention 'swapping children', 'taking another's class', 'covering another's class', and 'team teaching'. These appear to happen more often in England than in the USA — at least at the time of the interviews. This is consistent with the British practice of head teachers and others covering a teacher's class to free the teacher for professional development activity.

The two groups were in general agreement on those activities or situations which provide important and productive exchanges with colleagues. They diverged on the frequency with which they were mentioned. The British teachers responded in higher percentages for informal exchanges, staff meetings and joint teaching efforts. It might be that there are more opportunities in British schools for such exchanges. It might also be that collaborative activities have been viewed as more necessary and therefore meaningful in British schools. Here too, we find a difference between the two groups when the *reasons* for working collaboratively and the *content* of their interactions are analyzed. In general, curriculum development interactions of British teachers tapped the teacher's experiences and creative abilities; the teachers collaboratively developed topics and ideas for teaching while teachers in the United States regarded their curriculum development more as adaptation and implementation methods and techniques for standardized curriculum materials. Playing with ideas, 'batting them round', and developing curricula with colleagues is different from pooling strategies for curricula implementation. The tone, context, roles and responsibilities vary considerably.

Clearly, in both groups teachers view their colleagues as valuable resources and draw heavily on them for ideas, techniques, support, and inspiration. Since teachers seem to derive as much usefulness out of informal as formal situations, it might be that increased opportunity to interact with teachers, regardless of the setting, would be perceived as beneficial by teachers.

In Summary: Comments and Questions

The perceptions of the 60 teachers interviewed in this study provide three areas for consideration of teacher professional development in both countries: *The time and opportunity to share with and learn from colleagues; the relative importance of informal interactions in contrast with more formal and structured activities (and why)*, and *the relevance and integration of professional development experiences with teaching.* The activities sought and valued by teachers are activities which connect with their experience while at the same time extend and enlarge this experience. That is, teachers seek alternative perspectives which both connect with the 'everyday' world of teaching but also move beyond it (reading, discussion with colleagues, courses, sabbatical or secondment).

Contrasting the views of teachers from the two countries brings some differences into relief: USA teachers express value for collegial interactions and ideas yet they guard (in apparent contradiction) their perceived independence and autonomy while teaching a standardized curriculum. In contrast, British teachers place greater reliance on colleagues, collaboration, and sharing while functioning uniquely and creatively in teaching and curriculum development. These images suggest fundamental questions which, as addressed, might lead to new ways of viewing and conceptualizing professional development.

In what ways do history, geography, economics, politics, and culture influence and define teacher professional development? What effects are there, for example, in living in close proximity and interdependence? In living in relative independence and spatially dispersed?

What influence does teacher preparation have on professional and staff development? To what extent and in what ways does the British system of teacher education among peers — and with collaborative field work throughout the preparation program — influence attitudes and practices of teaching, curriculum development, colleagueship and professional development? To what extent and in what ways does the USA practice of two years of university general coursework followed by professional methods courses and culminating in individual fieldwork influence attitudes and practices of teaching, curriculum development and colleagueship?

What influences do teacher roles and responsibilities have on professional and staff development? The British teachers' autonomy and responsibility for curriculum development and teaching? The USA teachers' subscription to standardized curricula, textbooks, standardized testing and scheduling?

What influences do school and curricula organization have on professional development? How might the size and physical structure of a school influence the interaction within it? What effects, if any, might teacher designed curricula or commercially designed curricula have on: teacher attitude, use of time, teaching, colleagueship?

What influences might expectations for professional development have on practice? Degree and certification requirements? What mechanisms exist to enable teachers to work collaboratively? What attitudes and values underlie institutional provisions for professional development? In-service education? The teacher center in the UK? Graduate education in the USA?

In what ways does how schooling is conceptualized influence professional development? What are the perceived and/or acted upon purposes of schooling and of professional and staff development?

Since the data collection and analysis presented here, there have been significant initiatives for policy changes at national, state and community (LEAs) levels in both countries: teacher competency testing at the state level and the development of a national examination in the USA, and new policies related to school organization, curriculum development and appraisal schemes in England (See Tickle, chap. 5), for example. The following excerpt from a recent report (MacLure, Elliott, Marr and Stronach, 1988) suggests that teacher professional development is currently in a state of transition and highly vulnerable to changing policies and practices.

Conventional notions of professional development are likely to be at risk; conditions already exist which undermine prerequisites such as collegial interchange, peer-group support amongst young teachers, mobility, promotion prospects and motivation to engage in INSET activities. The further implications for teachers' profes-

sional development of the new conditions of service, the proliferation of curriculum and examination initiatives and the Education
Reform Bill need therefore to be considered in the light of such
conditions (p. 12).

The time for reconsidering and reconceptualizing professional development is clearly present.

By comparing and contrasting professional development in different countries, we can gain distance from current practices, *and* we can
look more closely at them. We can begin to see in-service education
from broader perspectives and interpret our observations from different vantage points — to connect what has frequently appeared to be
fragmented and piecemeal, or as many teachers put it 'One-shot!'.
Although several differences become apparent when professional development is compared between countries, so do similarities, including the recent focus on accountability and appraisal (usually referred
to as assessment in the USA).

Teachers are persons who chose to work with the young, whose
experience in classrooms is shaped not only by the broad social circumstances within which they teach, and by the children within each
classroom, but also by their own life histories and aims. Their evolving identities as professionals (Nias, chapter 7) and their striving for
ever more adequate ways of teaching and learning are influenced
heavily by their opportunities for professional renewal and by the
climate and conditions within which they work. Teacher responses to
questions concerning their teaching and professional development indicate their perspectives and understandings of the complexities of
practice which are within their purviews; their 'sense' or knowledge
that 'in-services' and 'resources' are useful to the extent that these
connect and 'fit' with their professional aims and are relevant to 'this
classroom' and 'these children' and 'this child'. Other teachers, relevant courses and readings and workshops, provide opportunities for
growth which build on and contribute to professional judgment, and
which respect the complexity of teaching and engender trust while
they open possibilities and support colleagueship and perspective
transformation.

The power to pose one's own professional questions and to enter
into discussion and dialogue with colleagues and others pertaining to
these — whether or not the Board of Education or the Local Education Authority pays for the peanut butter and jelly sandwiches —
keeps alive the spirit of inquiry and the wonder of teaching.

Notes

1. Though the number of school days a year in each country are comparable, the British academic year is more equally spaced throughout the year so that they do not have the three-month vacation period in the summer that occurs in the United States.
2. It is not unusual, for example, for a head teacher to take a teacher's classroom responsibilities (i.e., 'cover a teacher's class') while the teacher participates in a course or other 'in-service' activity away from the school. Another practice relatively unheard of in the USA is the 'covering' of one teacher's class by other teachers who divide the students into their rooms (see Holly and Holly, 1983).
3. This question, posed to 102 teachers in Michigan (Holly, 1977), resulted in similar results. *'Other teachers'* was by far the most often cited response (58 per cent), followed by reading (33 per cent), university classes (24 per cent), self/experience (17 per cent), teachers in classes (14 per cent), students (12 per cent), and seminars/workshops (12 per cent).
4. This question, when posed to 102 teachers in Michigan (Holly, 1977), resulted in: reading (46 per cent), plan, prepare, organize (41 per cent), visit/observe (39 per cent), curriculum development (25 per cent), work with other teachers (22 per cent), classes (22 per cent), make things for own classroom (18 per cent), research in own area (16 per cent), work with students (13 per cent), and seminars/workshops (13 per cent).
5. One drawback to this practice is that many teachers who have been seconded to consultant positions find it so rewarding that they do not want to return to their traditional teaching positions.
6. This question, when posed to 102 teachers in Michigan (Holly, 1977), resulted in: socialize outside school (45 per cent); eat together (32 per cent); informal conversation (28 per cent); sports/camping (23 per cent); work on school outside of school (17 per cent); no (nothing I do with colleagues is professionally meaningful) (16 per cent); staff meetings/committee work (15 per cent); planning time at school (14 per cent); workshops/seminars (9 per cent); university classes (7 per cent); professional membership (6 per cent); in-service education (5 per cent); and travel (3 per cent).

References

ABBS, P. (1974). *Autobiography in education*. London: Heinemann Educational Books.

BRITISH BOARD OF EDUCATION. (1944). *Teachers and Youths*, (The McNair Report). London, England: Author.

CANE, B. (1969). *In-service training: A study of teachers' views and preferences*. London: National Foundation of Educational Research.

COMBS, A. W. (1965). *The professional education of teachers*. Boston: Allyn & Bacon.

DEWEY, J. (1938). *Experience and education.* New York: Kappa Delta Pi.

EDELFELT, R. A. (1982). Critical issues in developing teacher centers. *Phi Delta Kappan,* 62(6), 390–3.

EDELFELT, R. A. (1983). In-service education: Moving from professional development to school improvement. *Urban Educator,* 7(1), 100–13.

EDELFELT, R. A., and LAWRENCE, G. (1975). In-service education: The state of the art. In R. Edelfelt and M. Johnson (eds), *Rethinking in-service education.* Washington, DC: National Education Association.

ELLIS, P. D. (1984). American and English elementary schools: Some personal impressions, contrasts and comparisons. *Childhood Education,* 60(4), 268–72.

ERIKSON, E. (1953). *Childhood and society.* New York: Norton.

FULLER, F. (1969). Concerns of teachers: A developmental characterization. *American Educational Research Journal,* 6(2), 207–26.

GARDNER, J. W. (1963). *Self-renewal: The individual and the innovative society.* New York: Harper & Row.

GOODLAD, J. I. (1984), *A place called school: Prospects for the future.* New York: McGraw-Hill.

GOUGH, R. (1983). Professional development in London through international exchange. *Urban Educator,* 7(1), 70–4.

GREENE, M. (1973). *Teacher as stranger.* New York: Teachers College Press, Columbia.

HAVIGHURST, R. (1953). *Human development and education.* New York: Longman.

HEATH, D. (1980). Toward teaching as a self-renewing calling. In G. Hall, S. Hord, and G. Brown (eds), *Exploring issues in teacher education: Questions for future research.* Austin: Research and Development Center for Teacher Education.

HER MAJESTY'S STATIONARY OFFICE (HMSO), and H. E. R. Townsend. (1970). *Statistics of Education Special Series,* No. 2. (of three parts). London: Her Majesty's Stationary Office, Department of Education and Science, Statistics Division, (Part 1): H. E. R. Townsend, Part 2 and 3.

HER MAJESTY'S STATIONERY OFFICE (1972). *Teacher Education and Training.* (The James Report) London: Author.

HOLLY, M. L. (1977). *A conceptual framework for personal-professional growth: Implications for inservice education.* Doctoral dissertation, Michigan State University.

HOLLY, M. L. (1983). Staff development and adult learners. *Staff development leadership: A resource book.* Columbus: Ohio Department of Education.

HOLLY, M. L., and HOLLY, B. P. (1983). Toward an empirically grounded conceptualization of staff development: Reflections on professional development in Cambridge and Liverpool, England. *Urban Educator,* 7(1), 75–87.

HOLLY, M. L. (1983). Teacher reflections on classroom life: Collaboration and professional development. *Australian Administrator,* 4(4), 1–6.

HOWEY, K. R., BENTS, R., and CORRIGAN, D. (1981) (eds), *School-focused inservice: Descriptions and discussions.* Reston, VA: Association of Teacher Educators.

HUNT, D. (1978). Teacher personality, teacher attitude, and teacher behavior.

In B. Joyce, M. Brown, and L. Peck (eds), *Flexibility teaching*. Berkeley, CA: McCutcheon.

JERSILD, A. T. (1955). *When teachers face themselves*. New York: Columbia University.

KING, E. J. (1973). *Other schools and ours: Comparative studies for today*. Guilford, Surrey: Billing & Sons.

KNOWLES, M. (1978). *The adult learner: A neglected species* (2nd edn). Houston: Gulf Publishing Company.

LAWRENCE, G., BAKER, D., ELZIE, R., and HANSEN, B. (1974). *Patterns of effective inservice education: A state of the art summary of research and materials and procedures for changing teacher behaviors in inservice education*. Report prepared for the State of Florida, Department of Education. Tallahassee, FL: State of Florida.

LINDSEY, M. (1978). Teacher education: Some reflections. In E. Hunt (ed.), *Margaret Lindsey: A teacher educator speaks*. New York: Teachers College Press, Columbia.

LITTLE, J. (1982). Norms of collegiality and experimentation: Workplace conditions of school success. *American Educational Research Journal, 19*(3), 325–40.

LOEVINGER, J. (1976). *Ego development: Conceptions and theories*. San Francisco: Jossey-Bass.

LORTIE, D. S. (1975). *School teacher: A sociological study*. Chicago: University of Chicago Press.

MACLURE, M., ELLIOTT, J., MARR, A. and STRONACH, I. (1988). *Teachers' Jobs and Lives: A research project funded by the ESRC, Interim Report*, Norwich: Centre for Applied Research in Education, February.

MINISTRY OF EDUCATION. (1963, July). *Reports on Education*, No. 1, *The Primary School*. London, England: Author.

NATIONAL EDUCATION ASSOCIATION, (1986). *The mastery in learning project*. Washington DC: The National Education Association Center.

NIAS J. (1983, April). *Selves, values and reference groups: Reflections on the professional socialization of primary teachers*. Paper presented at the American Educational Research Association annual conference, Montreal.

NIAS, J. (1987). *Seeing anew: Teachers' theories of action*. Victoria: Deakin University Press.

OJA, S. and PINE, G. (1983). *A two year study of teachers' stages of development in relation to collaborative action research in schools*. Final report to the National Institute of Education. Durham: University of New Hampshire.

PHILLIPS, J.A., & HAWTHORNE, R. D. (1978). Political dimensions of curriculum decision making. *Educational Leadership, 34*(5), 362–6.

RICHEY, H. G. (1957). Growth of the modern conception of in-service education. *Fifty-sixth yearbook of the National Society for the Study of Education: In-service education for teachers, supervisors, and administrators*. Chicago: The University of Chicago Press.

SCHOOLS COUNCIL. (1967). *Curriculum development: Teachers' groups and centres*. Schools Council Working Paper No. 10. London: Author.

SEIFERT, E. H., and BECK, J. J. (1981). Elementary principals: Instructional leaders or school managers? *Phi Delta Kappan, 62*(7), 528.

SHARMA, T. (1982). Inservicing the teachers. *Phi Delta Kappan, 63*(6), 403.

SLAVIN, R. (1987). Cooperative learning and the cooperative school. *Educational Leadership*. *45*(3), 7–13.

SPRINTHALL, N. A., and SPRINTHALL, L. T. (1983). The teacher as an adult learner: A cognitive-developmental review. In G. Griffin (ed.), *Staff development: Eighty-second yearbook of the National Society for the Study of Education*. Chicago: University of Chicago Press.

STENHOUSE, L. (1981). What counts as research? In J. Rudduck and D. Hopkins, (eds) *Research as a basis for teaching: Readings from the work of Lawrence Stenhouse (1985)*. London: Heinemann Educational Books, 8–19.

THORNBURY, R. (1974). Introduction: A tumult of centres. In R. Thornbury (ed.), *Teachers' centres*. NY: Agathon Press.

TYLER, R. W. (1971). In-service education of teachers: A look at the past and future. In L. J. Rubin (ed.), *Improving in-service education*. Boston: Allyn & Bacon.

YARGER, S. and MERTENS (1980). Testing the waters of school-based teacher education. In D. Corrigan and K. Howey (eds) *Concepts to guide the education of experienced teachers*. Reston, VA: Council for Exceptional Children.

PART IV

SUPPORT FOR PROFESSIONAL
DEVELOPMENT

9 Teacher Organization Influence on Professional Development

Roy A. Edelfelt

Teacher organizations influence professional development more than is recognized. One evidence of the lack of notice is the almost total absence, in the in-service education literature, of material on the role of teacher organizations.[1] The reason is probably the nature of teacher development activity carried on by teacher organizations. It is unlike traditional study, less direct than most forms of continuing education. Except for some activities by subject matter associations, it does not fit into an established discipline, nor does it deliver a specified body of knowledge. It is usually not measured in credits or units, entails no term-paper writing, is typically not evaluated by examination, and infrequently requires a specified number of contact hours.

It involves sharing ideas and experience. It may include training on a specific topic, but it is often problem-centered and frequently engages participants directly in action steps. It addresses teaching, academic, and political issues. Teachers participate voluntarily and usually actively. In a recent National Education Association (NEA) survey, teachers rated professional development programs sponsored by teacher organizations as one of their four most prominent professional growth activities: 'Teachers were most likely to participate in system-sponsored workshops during the school year (72.7 per cent); committees (33.9 per cent) and curriculum committees (30.5 per cent); professional growth activities sponsored by professional associations (31.5 per cent) and college courses in education (21.1 per cent) during the school year' (NEA, 1987, p. 49).

Most of what teacher organizations do is meet. They hold conferences and workshops. They create task forces, committees, and commissions, and appoint people to governing boards and councils. They sponsor training sessions. Some of the activities address the business and the conditions of teaching; others, the techniques and the content of instruction. The former are usually the agenda of teacher unions; the latter, the focus of subject-matter groups.[2] Both kinds of groups deliberate on the profession of teaching (they recommend standards and professional practices).

Teacher unions help their members learn about problems of and procedures for improving salaries, achieving better working conditions, ensuring due process, and governing the profession. Activities include not only studying the content and the issues of professional standards, practices, working conditions, and rewards, but also learning techniques of board and commission interplay, political maneuvering, and collective bargaining — techniques that might enable teachers to take effective action. No other institution or agency provides training in these aspects of teaching.

Still another activity encouraged by teacher unions is direct political involvement — participation in the mainstream of political parties and civic governance. Teachers caucus to elect delegates to political conventions; to lobby school board members, local council members, state and federal legislators, governors, and the President; and to select their own candidates for political office. Although instruction may be provided, much of this kind of teacher development is learning through experience, through individual and collective action. Inevitably such experience influences teachers' behavior, as they teach students and as they work together as members of a faculty. The influence may be subtle, with cause and effect not easily distinguishable, but the result clearly is learning and development. A teacher is never quite the same after lobbying elected officials or serving on a school board, in a state legislature, or on a collective bargaining team. The knowledge that develops about the social and political system can only be acquired by being a part of an activity; watching never teaches it.

Professional development that encompasses teaching techniques, classroom management, testing, and other instructional problems is also part of teacher union in-service education. The NEA and its state units have divisions labeled Instruction and Professional Development (IPD). The NEA allocates about $4 million of a $108 million annual expenditure to its IPD division (NEA, 1986, p. 290). Outside the control of the IPD division, other units of the organization (Publications, for one) devote staff and budget to professional development.

NEA also sponsors (with local school districts and other supporting agencies) a Mastery in Learning Project that includes action projects in

27 schools (local settings) across the country. The primary thrust is to promote school-based self-renewing centers of inquiry that help teachers better serve the needs of students in their particular setting.

The American Federation of Teachers (AFT), long recognized primarily for efforts in collective bargaining, also sponsors a variety of programs to foster teacher development. Major among them are the Quality Educational Standards in Teaching (QuEST) conference, the Educational Research and Dissemination Program, and the Critical Thinking Project. QuEST has flourished for over a decade, helping members keep current on critical issues. More recent is the Educational Research and Dissemination Program, which trains Teacher Research Linkers (TRLs) to disseminate carefully selected research to their colleagues. The Critical Thinking Project, designed to help teachers help children learn to think, was launched in 1985 and has now trained 155 teachers, who will take a 35-hour program back to the local level to train other teachers.

Subject matter organizations busy themselves with a variety of activities that have impact on teacher development. Among them are efforts in recruitment and selection, promotion of standards for preparation and practice, promulgation of goals for teaching in the various subjects, data gathering (studies and surveys of status and practice), and alerting of members to materials and developments in their field. Many subject matter groups serve teachers at several levels and as a consequence offer options of membership for elementary school, secondary school, and college teachers, and sponsor a journal for each group. These associations publish a wide variety of theoretical and practical professional books, monographs, pamphlets, and cassettes. The National Council of Teachers of English, for example, publishes more than 350 such items. Resources, training materials, and instructional materials are proliferating in television form, with the advent of videotapes and videocassette recorders. Some associations are linked to ERIC Clearinghouses and advise their members on computer access to the material in the relevant data bank.

Every subject matter organization sponsors conferences, some conduct workshops and training sessions, and a few are involved in lobbying legislators in matters that promote professional standards. Relationships are also maintained with appropriate related organizations and agencies — for example, the National Science Teachers Association with the American Association for the Advancement of Science, the American Chemical Society, and the National Science Foundation; the National Council for the Social Studies with the

National Endowment for the Humanities. Further, all national associations maintain a liaison with the US Department of Education. Even though such relationships may seem peripheral, they affect teacher development in very direct ways — witness the impact of the science teacher institutes and science education curricula developed with National Science Foundation grants and contracts.

The major impact that subject matter associations have on teachers in public schools is probably through publications and conferences. These are still the major modes of communication. What the future will bring as the electronic age proceeds is yet to be seen. It could make a major difference.

Motivation for Involvement

The motivations of teacher organizations for involvement in professional development are several, and they are important to understand. Too often, they are lumped into just one category: self-serving. In the case of pre-service teacher education there is both a professional obligation — teachers should and do care about teaching – and a concern for professional survival. Teachers already in the profession want to ensure that new teachers are at least as well prepared as they are. That desire has altruistic and selfish motivations. Because they care about youngsters, teachers want education to improve, and well-prepared teachers are more likely to make this possible. They also want competent colleagues so that they are not burdened in their jobs by inept faculty members. And, of course, they are sensitive to the reputation and prestige of the profession, that it not be tarnished further.

Despite the attacks on teaching from almost every quarter these days, a clear majority of teachers have an educational and humanitarian motivation to be in education. In a recent survey, 76.6 per cent of teachers under 30 years of age (65.6 per cent of all teachers) reported that they entered teaching because they wanted to work with young people (NEA, 1987, p. 55). Teachers are also concerned about pre-service preparation and their own continuing education. Such concerns are documented in the activity of teacher organizations in working for higher standards at the state level, and in the participation of teachers in in-service education (NEA, 1987, pp. 49–51). Teachers recognize that more appropriately prepared teachers will contribute to an improved quality of life, a more productive society, and a higher civilization. Thirty-seven per cent of all teachers selected teaching originally because of the value they placed on education in society (NEA, 1987, pp. 55–7). Such goals and commitments are part of the philosophical persuasion.

Each state sets it own legal requirements for preparation and certification of teachers. Before the 1940s, such standards were largely determined by state officials in conjunction with college and university people. The practice was followed because these were the people with the apparent expertise to make such decisions. Until 1950, fewer than 50 per cent of teachers had a college degree, and teacher voice in professional matters was not the norm. As the education of teachers was extended to four years (by 1965 most states required beginning teachers to have a college degree) and as participatory democracy broadened in all walks of life (for example as blacks asserted their voting rights and women sought equal opportunities), practitioners began to demand a voice in professional decisions. They were not unlike children growing into adolescents. As they matured, became more knowledgeable, and gained confidence, they challenged the power structure. At times they overreacted. The huge interlocking organization that was the NEA at the time, for example, could not survive teachers' challenging of authority, which had for so long been in the hands of school administrators, state department officials, and college and university personnel. The NEA as an umbrella organization disintegrated. What remained was a teachers' union that could have been renamed the National Teachers Association.

Bruising as it was, teachers' assertion of power was part of the maturing of the teaching profession. It resulted in a teachers' power group that demanded, among other things, an influence in teacher education. Much of the learning that teachers achieved in the process came from participation in the activities of the revolution. In professional development one of the NEA's commissions, the National Commission on Teacher Education and Professional Standards (NCTEPS), was instrumental in promoting teacher involvement in decisions about professional development. Created in 1946, NCTEPS was committed to including all members of the profession in deliberations about the recruitment, selection, preparation, and certification of teachers and the accreditation of teacher education programs. Teacher development under NCTEPS auspices occurred largely through conferences and working committees. Teachers learned by thinking through, debating, taking action, and sometimes solving problems facing the profession. There were deliberations and battles over national accreditation. Through NCTEPS, NEA (and thus teachers) became a member of the National Council for the Accreditation of Teacher Education (NCATE). When the college-and university-dominated American Council of Education demanded more higher education representation on NCATE, maintenance of equal teacher representation was ultimately the result of teacher power, in this case exerted through the NEA.

Legal requirements for teaching received attention at the state level through teacher union success in influencing professional standards and, in some states, in establishing professional standards boards. The goal was to involve practitioners in the governance of the profession (setting standards for teacher education and adjudicating alleged malpractice, incompetence, and immoral behavior). Again, teachers had to examine (through their organization) the meaning of *profession*, the governance of professions, the essence of due process, and the legal prerogatives and responsibilities of teachers. They also had to learn political skills — how and when to use power in the battles to achieve parity with their colleagues in higher education and state government bureaucracies. No teacher education program did much with those learnings. They were not part of the curriculum. Teachers had to learn the hard way, through experience. But they would have been unable to do that without the collective unity and power of the teacher union. One problem was (and is) that too few teachers had an opportunity to take part in the governance fight and serve on standards boards or accreditation teams, and teacher organizations and higher education did little (perhaps little could be done) to disseminate such experience. Just as the learning teachers have experienced through organization activities cannot be easily disseminated, sharing experience is not enough. Teachers need to taste it. They must try it out, do it, fail, succeed, see a project written up in the local newspaper.

The motivation for this kind of learning has been teachers wanting to be somebody, wanting to have more control over their professional destiny, wanting a status commensurate with the progress made in training and competence (by 1986 essentially all teachers held a bachelor's degree, and over 50 per cent were recipients of at least a master's degree). Admittedly, progress in the empowerment of teachers has been slow — witness the fact that at this writing, only four states have legally constituted professional standards boards (several have advisory boards with no legal status). Advancement has been greater than four state boards suggest, however. The strong endorsement of the

Carnegie Task Force on Teaching as a Profession (1986) for greater empowerment of teachers in all types of decisions is evidence of that. As important as support is momentum, which also seems apparent. Legislators and education experts, along with teachers, are calling for greater teacher prerogatives in decision-making in instruction and curriculum as well as governance matters.

Still other motivations for teacher organizations to influence teacher development come from the political gain and the vested interests that are served if teachers have more voice and prestige and are more highly regarded. Professions are not necessarily valued to a degree commensurate with their worth in American society. Stockbrokers or accountants, for example, may not make nearly the contribution that teachers or nurses do, but they are more highly rewarded and rank higher in status than teachers. Rewards are earned in a free enterprise system by being productive. Supply and demand may also be a factor. Having no truly tangible product, social service professions, perhaps teaching particularly, find difficulty justifying a particular level of reward on the basis of productivity because achievement is so nebulous. However, when demand exceeds supply in teaching, publicly supported recruitment programs swing into gear and supply increases, at least enough to keep schools operating. When supply exceeds demand, teachers are left to fend for themselves. They may find one of the scarce teaching jobs, remain unemployed, return to graduate school, or seek employment in another field. Teacher unions have been the main keepers of data on supply and demand. And they have been the primary groups to bring attention to the need for better planning and record-keeping on supply and demand and improvements in the incentives and rewards offered teachers.

Quite obviously, vested interests are in play in such activities, but there is another side to it. The most poignant illustration is the teacher who loves teaching but will not recommend it to his or her son or daughter. If the conditions, rewards, and prestige of teaching were better, such reluctance would probably not exist. It is not purely selfish, then, for teachers to work for a more attractive profession.

Achieving immediate improvements, of course, quite clearly represents success in serving self. There are a few situations in which strides have been made; for example, in certain school districts, some married couples — both members of which are teachers — have combined incomes in excess of $70,000 (ERS, 1987, p. 11), without extra duties or outside earnings.

The Nature of Teacher Development Programs

The Print Media

Teacher unions and associations carry on a variety of programs that contribute to teacher development. They disseminate an enormous amount of information in bulletins, journals, monographs, books, and audiovisual material. Every teacher union and association has a publications program. Publications increasingly have striven to become more attractive to teachers. They provide new knowledge and developments in subject matter, reports of successful practice, and reviews and interpretations of research. At times, in an attempt to respond to teacher need, printed materials provide answers and recipes, but teachers are more prone than ever to seek information and ideas that will help them figure out for themselves how to deal with their own problems. Teacher organization staff, for example, report less interest and reliance on packaged training sessions and prescriptions for ways to teach.[3] Numerous printed materials also publicize and promote organizational purposes and political agendas. The more a union or association reflects teacher opinion or desire, the more effectively the publications program represents what teachers want in order to move ahead professionally. What teachers want, some would argue, is not always what teachers need. However, whether in publications or in another part of a professional development program, when teachers are introduced to something that satisfies a need, that addresses a purpose, that is timely and right, they accept and appreciate it. The artistry of that judgment for staff and leaders is knowing what is appropriate. In some instances leaders get too far away from membership, and what evolves represents more the agendas of those in power than the agendas of the rank and file.

Professional Development

Whether from the major unions or the many smaller associations, much effort goes into fostering the growth and development of teachers in all areas of professional concern. The unions, of course, add in-service education in bargaining and political action to the usual concept of professional development. The unions were instrumental, for example, in supporting teacher centers when they were first federally funded in the late 1970s. That support has continued, shifting from a national-state effort to a state-local effort after federal funding ceased in 1981. California and New York are outstanding examples of support for teacher centers in the 1980s. In both states the legislatures, with teacher union support, have increased funding for teacher centers, with technology (computers especially) as a focus.

The NEA and its state affiliates conduct workshops and conferences that address the full gamut of professional and union issues. Almost all state unions hold summer workshops, many a week in length. These workshops include leaders but are mostly for rank-and-file members, Increasingly the AFT has broadened its professional development efforts. As noted earlier, AFT's most significant teacher development program, Quality Educational Standards in Teaching (QuEST), has been conducted for over a decade. But AFT activities now go well beyond QuEST. Where formerly AFT was a union, purely and simply, its current direction is a more balanced program. Obviously both unions have made a statement in demonstrating teacher power, so that now they are part of professional deliberations at the local, state, and national levels. Such involvement includes more than collective bargaining, but collective bargaining is in place in most states where labor unions are functional.

The subject matter associations also sponsor conferences, workshops, and other professional development activities. In most cases the subject matter groups also include supervisors, college professors, state department personnel, and others with responsibilities in the area of teaching represented by the association. These associations, then, ensure the participation of scholars and researchers, but in so doing sometimes place school teachers in less than the most prominent position, at least academically. The situation is further complicated because it is easier for everyone except teachers to take time and find financial support to attend conferences and workshops. For these and other reasons teachers often do not have the dominant role in subject matter associations, but through such affiliations they do have the benefit of the best thinking in their field as well as the chance to engage directly in discussions with the experts in their subject — perhaps bringing more reality to esoteric deliberations and more substance to teacher talk of actual practice — all of which adds up to a kind of professional development for teachers and their colleagues that is seldom available in any field.

Professional development activities in teacher organizations are different from traditional, formal graduate study in other ways. They are more egalitarian and probably more democratic. That is, there is not the social distance between the provider of training and the receiver. Teachers are treated more like professionals. They participate voluntarily and can take or leave an activity that is unsatisfactory. When school district time is provided, what has come to be called in-service days, teachers can usually choose among activities. The fact is they have contracted voluntarily for in-service days and must carry out the contract.

Teachers are more active in the professional development activities of their organizations than in other in-service education. They are less the tractable, compliant, acquiescent receivers of instruction and more the involved shareholder, partaker, partner. Overgeneralizing here is a bit risky because as the professional development activities of teacher organizations become more formalized, they have a tendency to take on the most telling characteristic of traditional in-service training: didactic teaching.

Organizational activities are also more social than those sponsored by colleges, universities, state departments of education, and school districts. Working cooperatively as peers, sensing commonality as soldiers from the trenches, participating voluntarily, and living together for several days at a conference or workshop contribute to a social conviviality that has few parallels in continuing education. The learning at such sessions may not be as important as the stimulation to think, the opportunity to be away from the usual pressures of home, and the chance to reflect and gain perspective with new people. The action orientation and the sense of purpose create a special spirit of collegiality. The focus is often on what is to be done and how, as a classroom teacher or as a faculty or organization member. All of these characteristics are different from traditional in-service education. These are probably a few of the factors that cause teacher organization professional development not to be recognized with conventional professional development.

Achievements and Rewards

At first glance there are no conventional checks on achievement and no rewards for teacher development through teacher organizations. At least there are none of the usual rewards, such as academic credit, salary increments, and university degrees, and none of the typical achievement measures. Written examinations and evaluations of performance by superiors are not part of the procedure. Students do not assess a teacher's performance, and teacher behavior is not expected to alter the achievement of students. (A small exception to these observations is the practice in some school districts of granting in-service credit for workshops or training sessions conducted by teacher organizations, or for travel and study that may be under teacher organization auspices.)

A second look, however, reveals a number of different rewards. Teachers are given time and sometimes expenses to go to conferences. There is professional satisfaction in the privilege to attend, in the rubbing of elbows with fellow teachers, and in the learning offered at such meetings. Through participation, teachers earn status and recognition in their organization. They gain distinction and pride by appointment to committees and task forces and by election to office. With such assignments go perquisites: committee members and organization officers have opportunities to travel to meetings and conferences, often in distant places, with expenses paid. They get time off the job, frequently with pay, to participate in organizational activities. They gain stature as a professional or as a union member. The teacher whose name appears on a committee report or who is pictured in the paper as a leader or negotiator for the organization, achieves status. The professional recognition is often more important than any other reward.

It may be that teacher organizations are more on the mark in their approach to professional development than other institutions and agencies. In a national survey by independent researchers (contracted by NEA), when teachers were asked to rate the effectiveness of sources of job-related knowledge and skill, they rated experience, consultation with other teachers, observation of other teachers, and study/research pursued on their own as the four most effective ones (Bacharach, Bauer, and Shedd, 1986).

Notes

1. See, for example, NEA's *Status of the American Schoolteacher: Rethinking Inservice Education*, by B. R. Joyce and colleagues, as part of a 5 volume study of in-service education.
2. The term *union* applies to the American Federation of Teachers, and the National Education Association, and their affiliates. The term *teacher associations* is used to represent subject-matter organizations that are largely

made up of teachers, for example, the National Council of Teachers of English or the National Council for the Social Studies.
3. Personal interviews with state and national AFT and NEA staff.

References

BACHARACH, S. B., BAUER, G., and SHEDD, J. (1986). *The learning workplace: The conditions and resources of teaching.* Ithaca, NY: Organizational Analysis and Practice.

BRANDT, R. M., MESA, R. P., NELSON, M., MARSH, D. D., RUBIN, L. J., ASHWORTH, M. C., BRIZZI, E. N., WHITEMAN, H. V., JOYCE, B. R., HOWEY, K. R., BOYER, J., and VANCE, B. A. (1976) *Cultural pluralism and social change: A collection of position papers, Report V.* Palo Alto, CA: Stanford Center for Research and Development in Teaching.

CARNEGIE TASK FORCE ON TEACHING AS A PROFESSION. (1986). *A nation prepared: Teachers for the 21st century.* Washington, DC: Carnegie Forum on Education and the Economy.

EDELFELT, R. A., and JOHNSON, M. J. (eds). (1975). *Rethinking in-service education.* Washington, DC: National Education Association.

EDUCATIONAL RESEARCH SERVICE. (1987). *Salaries paid professional personnel in public schools, 1986–87* Arlington, VA: Author.

JOYCE, B. R., HOWEY K. R., YARGER, S. J., HILL, W. C., WATERMAN, F. T., VANCE, B. A., PARKER, D. W., and BAKER, M. G. (1976). *Issues to face, Report I.* Palo Alto, CA: Stanford Center for Research and Development in Teaching.

JOYCE, B. R., NcNAIR, K. M., DIAZ, R., McKIBBIN, M. D., WATERMAN, F. T., and BAKER, M. G. (1976). *Interviews: Perceptions of professionals and policy makers, Report II.* Palo Alto, CA: Stanford Center for Research and Development in Teaching.

NATIONAL EDUCATION ASSOCIATION. (1986). *Handbook (1986–87).* Washington, DC: Author.

NATIONAL EDUCATION ASSOCIATION. (1987). *Status of the American public school teacher.* Washington, DC: Author.

NICHOLSON, A. M., JOYCE, B. R., PARKER, D. W., and WATERMAN, F. T. (1976). *The literature on inservice teacher education: An analytic review. Report III.* Palo Alto, CA: Stanford Center for Research and Development in Teaching.

YARGER, S. J., BOYER, J., HOWEY, K. R., WEIL, M., PAIS, R. M., WARNAT, W. I., BHAERMAN, R. D., LUKE, R., DARLAND, D., JOYCE, B. R., and HILL, W. C. (1976). *Creative authority and collaboration: A collection of position papers, Report IV.* Palo Alto, CA: Stanford Center for Research and Development in Teaching.

10 Administrative Leadership in the Intellectual Transformation of Schooling

John Smyth

One of the more contentious and perplexing issues that plagues schools and teachers is that of the legitimate function of administrators in schools. For some commentators the matter is nonproblematic — schools exist, as they always have, as agents of the State and their function is to transmit knowledge through social and cultural reproduction. The involvement of administrators in the mission of schooling is construed as equally unproblematic. Schools, through the agency of teachers, engage in the reproduction of the given culture, and to the extent that they are involved in any kind of change, the function of administrators is therefore one of fostering 'planned change' which aims to *maintain* rather than *transform* deep social structures (or the nature of social relationships) that are played out in schools. All of this makes for a fairly static state of affairs in which administrators are preoccupied with 'orderly' change designed to preserve and maintain the status quo.

The view adopted here is contrary to that expressed above. It is a view that challenges and dismisses the hegemony of administrators and regards the administrative (indeed, the leadership) function within schools as having less to do with ensuring the maintenance of certain dominant structural arrangements, and more to do with finding ways in which school participants can gain a wider sense of community and give full expression to an enhanced 'possibility' of the way schools might be. As one of the major proponents of this cultural view of schooling (Greenfield, 1973) put it:

What many people seem to want from schools is that schools reflect the values that are central and meaningful in their lives. If this view is correct, schools are cultural artifacts that people struggle to shape in their own image. Only in such forms do they have faith in them; only in such forms can they participate comfortably in them (p. 570).

If schools are regarded as cultures that people seek to fashion and shape according to the definitions of reality they hold, then it follows that there will be a continual process of negotiation and contestation as they seek to give meaning and expression to the beliefs, language, rituals, knowledge, and myths that amount to the cultural resources of schools. Schools, like society, represent a plurality of values that deny *ultimate* legitimacy to any *single* view. As Greenfield (1981) put it, this has important implications for who has the right to impose their view of reality on whom:

> What we are left with ... is contention among values or, more accurately, among those who espouse different values. In this view we are all leaders in some degree. We all have legitimacy in the degree to which we act out of our own values and can involve others in them. This view rejects the idea of a simple, unitary value structure as the foundation for any large, complex social order. In this view all social orders are pluralistic and there will always be struggle and contention among those who represent the conflicting values within the structure. Those who represent the contending values are the leaders and they are in all respects human, fallible, self-interested, perverse, dogged, changeable, and ephemeral. In social possibility we are all leaders. Certainly none of us can claim the ultimate right to leadership ... (p. 27).

An Educative View of Leadership and Administration

I want to pursue here what school administration (in particular, its leadership fragment) might look like if we were to move away from a behavioral sciences view of leadership as a process of influencing others towards setting goals, and then checking on their achievement. I have in mind a more 'educative' (Fay, 1977) notion of leadership that fosters in teachers a capacity to make sense of what they do, and through an understanding of their work, to orient themselves towards reflecting on the limits they face and how those aspects that constrain their range of choice might be overcome. According to Smyth (1986), this means starting:

with the practicalities of teaching, developing a language for talking about teaching, and assisting teachers to collect evidence about the contradictions, dilemmas, and paradoxes that inhere in their work. This consciousness raising amounts to developing an inner eye so as to penetrate accepted assumptions and, in the process, isolate viable ways in which transformation might occur (p. 3).

While the deficiencies of instrumentalist views of leadership are apparent enough, what is not so clear is how to proceed in developing a more 'educative' view of the possible relationship between the theory and the practice of leadership, especially insofar as this might have relevance for schools. I am arguing for the abolition of privileged and elitist forms of leadership in schools, and for their replacement with a form of leadership that stimulates dialogue and mutual learning about teaching. This notion of leadership has as its central tenet the idea of forms-of-action that enable people in school settings to acquire an understanding of how the social and institutional circumstances of their school lives causes them frustration, and of how that anxiety detracts from the self-fulfillment of what they do. Viewed in this light, leadership becomes a means by which people 'can change their lives so that, having arrived at a new self-understanding, they may reduce their suffering by creating another way of life that is more fulfilling' (Fay, 1977, p. 204).

The educative — we may even describe it as *transformative* — perspective is predicated on the assumption that through assisting people to understand themselves and their world it becomes possible for them to engage in the radical changes necessary for them to overcome the oppressive conditions that characterize their work patterns and social relationships. Knowledge, therefore, is not construed as a means by which those in dominant positions acquire power and exert control over others; rather, knowledge becomes a means through which people are able to arrive at self-understanding and an awareness of the debilitating circumstances of their lives. Even more important, knowledge becomes the means by which people are able to identify the social and institutional constraints that make their teaching lives less than satisfying. Knowledge as a form of power emerges from and helps to sustain certain social conditions, but it also takes on a dialectical relationship in contributing towards changing the social structure that spawned it.

Because prevailing views of leadership endorse a viewpoint where there is an inequitable distribution of knowledge and expertise —

where those in elevated positions generally have important knowledge while by definition others do not — the actions of leaders is aimed at preserving the status quo. Hierarchical notions of leadership like this are grounded in a technicist and scientist view of management that is essentially conservative. Divulging information and sharing facts about the nature of reality is not in the interests of leaders, and indeed strikes at the very basis of power and influence. Investing people with the capacity to ascertain the facts for themselves, and hence to develop a critical awareness and a basis for radical change, is to create a situation of independence rather than dependence. This is anathema to traditional views of leadership.

One of the difficulties with constructs like leadership and administration is that, although they may have some generalized meaning in the management sciences, they are difficult to translate into schools in a way that is defensible. Indeed, the notion of one group (the leaders) who exercise hegemony and domination over another (the followers) is, in a sense, anti-educational. If schools are to be the inquiring kinds of places we would hope them to be, then the values espoused and the activities pursued will be as a consequence of dialogue about the nature of schooling and what is considered important in the development of children, and not as a result of bureaucratic or autocratic decree.

Central to my argument is the notion that school administrators, through the way they construe the work of teachers, might actively assist them in uncovering meaning in what they do, while investing in them the capacity to change those practices by transcending them. By starting with the 'practical' and proceeding in ways that permit and encourage 'deliberative exchanges', teachers are able to develop an increasingly powerful language for examining, speaking about, and transforming the circumstances of their working lives. By collecting evidence about the contradictions and dilemmas that plague them in their teaching, and using this evidence as a basis for dialogue, teachers are able to develop a grammar for examining their pedagogy in increasingly critical ways. Having problematized their teaching in this way and having begun the difficult process of raising their collective consciousness about taken-for-granted assumptions, teachers are able to treat their teaching as a process of social change.

Contrary to the conventional view of leadership that insists on the separation of 'leaders' from 'followers', the argument here focuses on how forms of moral assistance and consciousness raising might be provided in working towards social conditions which vest control in the hands of those affected by decisions. In schools this means teachers, students, as well as parents. Forms of consciousness raising are needed which amount to collaboratively intellectualizing about teaching, learning, and administrative experiences, with the aim of extracting meaning from those experiences and in the process generating information about new and alternative possibilities. I want to highlight briefly how these collaborative and empowering ways of working might actually be pursued. Fried (1980) expressed the meaning of empowerment as 'helping people take charge of their lives, people who have been restrained, by social or political forces, from assuming such control' (p. 8).

Because of the deafening silence that teachers are forced to endure in schools due to their subordinate status, and because of their isolation within the cellular structure of schooling, one of the most urgent needs at the moment is for educational leaders committed to a frontal attack on those silences that have come to characterize the working lives of teachers. What I have in mind involves assisting teachers to raise their voices by 'talking to one another after a long silence' (McDonald, 1986, p. 358). In particular, teachers need ways of beginning a dialogue with one another so as to penetrate the habitual taken-for-grantedness of their classroom practice and developing robust theories about their teaching. In Freedman, Jackson, and Boles' terms (1983), it amounts to teachers' 'not facing the issues alone' (p. 298), but realizing that part of being a teacher involves grappling with and collectively confronting the contradictory demands of the educational system, rather then scapegoating disaffected or incapable teachers or acquiescing to bitter and unproductive self-recrimination.

I have in mind the kind of activity that McDonald (1986) describes in his informative anecdotal account of how a group of high school teachers met regularly to discuss and explore together the insights, uncertainties, and paradoxes that arose from their teaching, Chronicling their activities, he notes how they decide to adopt the 'political aim' of transforming their role as teachers from that of 'passive recipient(s) of policy *made*, to active participant(s) in policy *making*' (p. 359). The group found that they not only had a long history of having been left alone, but more significantly, that they had come to adapt to being alone. There was a collective realization that there was more to silence than just the pernicious effect of isolation: they saw how it was a 'protective response to subordination' (p. 358). With the tightening control of curriculum prescription and its accompanying administrative supervision, it was a relatively attractive response to 'close

[our] doors and cultivate [our] own gardens' (p. 358). Through discussion and collective reflection, they came to also see that beyond their 'structural isolation' and 'hiearchical subordination', the actual dynamics of teaching itself was an even greater impediment. The inherent volatility and ambiguity of teaching, with its accompanying tension, actually made for *less*, not *more*, disclosure on the part of teachers. McDonald (1986) claims that:

> teachers' silence on matters they would seem to know a great deal about may at least partially involve their wish to protect their capacity to act. And so they leave inquiry to the theorist, who theorizes without benefit of the teacher's intimate knowledge of practice, and in time, the resulting theory comes around to the teacher in the form of some policy directive (p. 361).

The reason behind teachers' reticence may not be hard to see either when we consider that:

> Teachers in the USA, like others trained in Western habits of thought, come therefore to regard their own knowledge as inherently provisional — useful perhaps for getting through a teaching day, but not particularly worth sharing with others, nor even worth articulating to oneself. Discovering uncertainty when certainty is the measure of knowledge can only produce demoralization and perhaps paralysis of action as well (p. 362).

The punchline comes in McDonald's (1986) almost throw-away 'what-if question' when he says:

> But what if teachers, recognizing the uncertainty of their work, raised their voices instead of growing silent? And what if theorists recognized that intimate knowledge of this uncertainty was exactly what was missing from both their theories and the policies these theories provoke? (p. 362).

Enabling school people to develop ways of framing their problems and of discussing and working collectively on defining and understanding these problems, while striving to obtain the resources to solve them, is not something that happens easily or fortuitously. It is intentional in the sense that it has to be worked at. According to Kemmis (1983), empowerment of this kind occurs:

through the development of critical awareness; through the development of networks of critical, learning communities ... where people can think freely about their problems — and redefine their problems, in the light of growing experience and understanding.

To do this we must create learning communities able to act — empowered to act — and able to reflect openly on the consequences of their actions. By subjecting our experience to joint self-reflection, we may incorporate wider group understandings and create a shared language and a shared identity — an identity formed in cooperative action and cooperative self-reflection (p. 25).

The level of consciousness for teachers to begin to dramatically alter the nature of their practice may occur by starting with a consideration of *the practical*. For Schwab (1983), this amounts to a 'deliberative exchange and consideration among several persons or differing selves about concrete alternatives in relation to particular times and places' (p. 239). Sanders and McCutcheon (1986) describe this in terms of teachers' practical theories — conceptual structures and visions that provide teachers with reasons for acting and choosing as they do. In their words:

Practical theories of teaching are consciously held, and teachers are able to explicate them. Sometimes, however, though teachers may not be conscious of the reasons for their actions, they still act .... . But whether or not teachers are conscious of their reasons for action, all professional work is rational ... in the sense that it is intended to accomplish some purpose, to produce a desired consequence. Teachers may not be fully conscious of their reasoning, and they may well rely on accustomed routines without consciously thinking about them, but it is in the nature of their work that teachers are always trying to accomplish something when they act professionally (p. 55).

Getting teachers to acknowledge that they have what amounts to theories about 'what works' for them in teaching is a considerable achievement. This is because teachers historically have been treated as 'civil servants' (Bullough, Gitlin, and Goldstein, 1984) concerned with implementing agendas formulated outside of classrooms. Pagano (1987) noted that in their professional lives teachers have tended to become 'satisfied with all sorts of intolerable situations' (p. 121). To become truly empowered (Smyth, 1987a), teachers need to be assisted to pursue and ask *why* questions, rather than being contented with *how to* questions. As Pagano (1987) put it, unless teachers reflect critically upon the 'emancipatory' as well as the 'enslaving' possibilities of educational practice, then those practices 'become fact(s) of nature to be managed scientifically' (p. 119). In my own endeavours to get teachers to adopt a socially critical view of their teaching (which is to say, locate their teaching in its wider social and cultural structues), I have them confront a number of questions (Smyth, 1987b):

- Where do the ideas I embody in my teaching come from historically?
- How did I come to appropriate them?
- Why do I continue to endorse them now in my work?
- Whose interests do they serve?
- What power relationships are involved?
- How do these ideas influence my relationships with my students?
- In the light of what I have discovered, how might I work differently? (p. 20)

The kind of distinction I seek to get teachers to focus upon in their teaching is that between *receiving* knowledge versus *creating* knowledge. It is essentially Freire's (Bruss and Macedo, 1985) distinction between 'the pedagogy of the question and the pedagogy of the answer', in which the former challenges teachers-as-learners:

> to think critically and to adopt a critical attitude toward the world. It is a pedagogy that enables the learners to break the chains of alienation imposed upon them by the mechanistic nature of their daily routine. The pedagogy of the question requires that learners distance themselves from their bureaucratized daily existence, while they become more and more aware through reflection of the mythical facts that enslave them. Unlike the pedagogy of the answer, which reduces learners to mere receptacles for prepackaged knowledge, the pedagogy of the question gives learners the 'language of possibility' to challenge the very constraints which relegate them to mere objects (p. 8).

Teachers, therefore, are required to stand back from the habitualness of their teaching and to ask pointed questions about what they do and why. They are encouraged, above all, to challenge, to doubt, and to reject. In Freire's words (Bruss and Macedo, 1985):

> In ordinary life we grasp the human presence; we know we are face to face with facts, we are enveloped with facts. But we don't necessarily get a distance on those facts in order to understand the reason behind them. This is why we are normally more submerged than emerged with our daily lives. It should be possible to get distance on these facts ... (p. 10).

What this amounts to is the enactment of Shor's (1980) plea to 'extraordinarily re-experience the ordinary'. By theorising about the social, political, and cultural nature of their work in the way being suggested here, teachers can not only develop a language about teaching but an understanding that to change teaching requires altering the constraints that impose limits upon it. Through developing a more coherent understanding of what it means to be a teacher in the broadest sense, it becomes possible to encourage and foster those circumstances that permit teachers to transform their work.

Clearly, therefore, leadership in schools is not something that is exercised in a vacuum; it exists in the context and culture of the school and is grounded in instruction and pedagogy. In the past, educational researchers and scholars have been less than charitable in the credit given to teachers for creating worthwhile knowledge of and about their teaching. Indeed, there is a good deal of negativism about the alleged lack of rigor and the absence of disciplined thinking in what teachers do. Berlak and Berlak (1981, p. 235) claim that 'authorities', such as Lortie (1975) and Jackson (1968), 'assume that the experts in teaching are not the teacher but scientifically trained administrators, or educational scholars who study schooling scientifically'. Maybe what is required is that educational scholars, along with administrators who follow their advice, cease concerning themselves with teachers' apparent lack of technical language which is said to prevent them from being able to 'tap a pre-existing body of practical knowledge' (Lortie, 1975, p. 231) and begin working with teachers on their own terms.

The kind of turn-around in thinking necessary by educational leaders and policymakers is one that requires adopting a view of teachers as active creators and users of practical knowledge about their own teaching. It will also necessitate a radical reassessment of the nature of the relationship between theory and practice. Where teaching is conceived as a static process of transmitting accepted bodies of knowledge, and where the 'ends' of teaching are artificially divorced from the 'means', it is likely that there will continue to be problems of how to translate somebody else's theory into practice. Rather than theory continuing to be something that is 'put into practice' with practice being subservient to theory, the view expressed here dismisses the unnatural separation of ends from means, and focuses instead on how deliberative and reflective processes may be used to create understandings that change practice. By using concrete and practical experience with all its frustrations and contradictions as the basis upon which to theorize, teachers become agents in the creation of their own structures of knowledge in regard to a range of matters, including subject matter and curricular content, classroom organization, the strengths and weaknesses in their teaching, the interests and needs of their students, as well as the social and political circumstances of their work. Elbaz (1981) suggests that while teachers may remain largely silent about the pedagogical knowledge they possess, they do, nevertheless, have a broad range of knowledge that helps them make sense of the realities and dilemmas of teaching.

The issue, then, is one of enabling teachers to move from a situation of dependence and nonreflectivity to one of becoming active inquireers into their own and others' practices by acquiring new lenses for critically examining their teaching and its social circumstances. Doing that will involve acknowledging how teachers put together coherent views of their world. It could mean that rather than teachers instantly becoming critically conscious agents, they would first pass through a phase of 'naming' and describing their contexts — a process akin to mapping the domain (Smyth, 1987b). Gradually, as they become comfortable with describing and analyzing their unquestioned practices and how they came to be, teachers move towards the demystification of the wider social and cultural contexts in which their teaching is embedded. They do this through discussion, disclosure, and dialogue.

Focus on the Intellectual

The argument being pursued here is antithetical to recent calls for educational reform that aim to tighten control over teachers through competency testing and performance appraisal schemes. The alternative line of argument developed here is that if teachers are to enhance their pedagogy, then it will be as a result of *less*, not *more*, technical control over teaching by agencies outside of classrooms. This amounts to a call for the restoration of the 'intellectual' within teachers' work. This notion of the intellectual nature of teachers' work owes much to the recent theoretical works of Giroux (1985a–c) and Aronowitz and Giroux (1985). Giroux's discussion of the work of teachers as a form of intellectual labor represents a departure from the portrayal of teachers as 'technicians' (Scheffler, 1968) and 'civil servants' (Bullough, Gitlin, and Goldstein, 1984).

In proposing a focus on 'the intellectual', it is not being suggested that teachers become aloof, abstract, or detached from the real world of teaching — this is a misconstrual of what it means to be an intellectual. As Kohl (1983) argues, an intellectual is a person who 'knows about his or her field, has a wide breadth of knowledge about other aspects of the world, who uses experience to develop theory, and questions theory on the basis of further experience' (p. 30). Indeed, this integration of 'thinking' and 'doing' characterized by a willingness to open one's practices to critical self-scrutiny is only a precondition; it is the preparedness to engage in reasoned moral action by transcending the means and questioning the ends, that is the real hallmark of an intellectual. Kohl (1983) had this in mind when he said, 'An intellectual is also someone *who has the courage to question authority and who refuses to act counter to his/her own experience and judgement*' (p. 30, emphasis added). As Greene (1985) expressed it, there are many teachers who fail to do so:

> because the processes that go on in their institutions strike them as so automatic, there seems to be no alternative but to comply, Their schools seem to resemble natural processes; what happens in them appears to have the sanction of natural law and can no more be questioned or resisted than the law of gravity (p. 11).

To construe the nature of teachers' work as a form of intellectual labor is, therefore, to permit and encourage teachers critically to question their understandings of society, schooling, and pedagogy. It involves acknowledging the claim made by Kohl (1983) about the need for teachers to assume actively the responsiblility for theory making (and theory *testing*) or accept the fact that these will be made for teachers by academic researchers and others only too willing to assume that task. For Kohl (1983), this is inevitable if teachers bargain away their educational power by giving up their responsibility as intellectuals. In his opinion, 'When teachers fail to develop and use educational theories ... they open the door to stifling curriculum proposals devised by stodgy academics with no real sense of what goes on in the classroom' (p. 28). Viewed in this way, educational theory becomes a species of social theory. As Giroux (1985a) put it:

> Educational theory ... is not viewed as merely the application of scientific principles to the concrete study of schooling and learning. Instead, it is seen as ... political discourse that emerges from and characterizes an expression of struggle over what forms of authority, orders or representation, forms of moral regulation, and versions of the past and future should be legitimated, passed on and debated within specific pedagogical sites (p. 29).

As a way of countering the narrowly technical conceptualization of curricula, pedagogy and schooling, I want to draw on Gramsci's (1971) argument that what is important about intellectuals is not their cognitive function — often seen as existing independently of issues of class, culture, and power — but rather their political and social prowess in developing the potential to engage with and transform dominant theoretical traditions. Gramsci (1971) dismisses the notion of intellectuals as residing in a particular social class or category. He argues instead that:

> When one distinguishes between intellectuals and nonintellectuals, one is referring in reality only to the immediate social function of the professional category of the intellectuals, that is, one has in mind the direction in which their specific professional activity is weighted, whether towards intellectual elaboration or towards muscular-nervous effort.

In proposing that intellectual labor is a particular form of political work, Gramsci (1971) challenges the allegedly value-free neutral stance of intellectual work. His disavowal of intellectuals as apolitical is well put by Giroux (1985b):

> Inherent in such a view is the notion that the intellectual is obligated to engage in a value-free discourse, one that necessitates that he or she refuses to take sides on different issues, or refuses to link knowledge with fundamental principles of emancipation. Such a view reinforces the idea that intellectuals are free floating and detached in the sense that they perform a type of labor that is objective and apolitical (p. 86).

The visions of education and schooling contained in recent reports calling for schooling reforms are problematic in the chasm they create between the 'expert' and the 'inexpert'. These documents perpetrate a means-oriented view of teaching and learning that limits debate about schools and education to managerialist issues of efficiency and effectiveness. The separationist ideology embedded in these reports, between those who *think about* and those who actually *do* the teaching and learning in our schools, must itself be the subject of conjecture and debate. It could be argued that the existence of these reports represents a major problem — it is almost as if educational discourse cannot occur unless it is decreed by some technocrat who writes a report to which the educational community has to refute or respond. Yet, despite the flurry of activity on the surface as in evidence by the frenetic pace of report writing, there is an uncanny unreality about it all at the classroom level where things really matter. As one commentator (Hansen, 1986) put it recently, 'There is an inescapable sense that whatever is happening is happening *up there, out there, somewhere, but not in here, in this school, in this classroom*' (p. 21, emphasis added).

The problem with the technocratic view of education and teaching as embodied in the recent reports purportedly aimed at reforming schools is that the emphasis on 'excellence', quality', 'efficiency', and 'effectiveness' brings severely into question the ability of teachers to provide the kind of intellectual and moral leadership necessary to enable children to be educated. What these reports do is 'rehearse liturgical solutions' (Nunan, 1982, p. 37) on what is considered important in schooling. What is not opened up for debate and contestation are the fundamental deficiencies in the ways schools are conceived and organized. What we have, therefore, is what Giroux (1979) terms 'a dispensing of the culture of positivism' which serves only to bolster and reproduce the orthodox view of what schools and teaching are about. As Nunan (1982) put it: 'Education, if nothing else, is concerned with valued ends; the world view of the technocrat, on the other hand, features a deafening silence about such ends and, instead, trumpets the values of techniques, process, or means' (p. 37). The actual disservice to teachers in all of this occurs through the unquestioned acceptance of educational ends implicit in the culture of accountability. Particular educational knowledge and pursuits are unquestioningly regarded as being worthy. Enquiry and action are, therefore, reduced to and defined solely in terms of the technical criteria of economy, efficiency, and effectiveness (Van Manen, 1977).

What is most worrying about the thinly veiled demands in many of these reports exhorting teachers to 'lift their game' is that teachers themselves have been excluded (except as benign respondents) from the dialogue, debate, and critique about how teaching might be transformed. Teachers' views on what is wrong (or right) about teaching have not featured prominently — proposals for reform have originated from quarters far removed from classrooms. The not-so-subtly disguised message in most of these reports is that teachers belong to a civil servant class whose sole purpose is to act out technical agendas decided by others. The impression conveyed in *A Nation at Risk*, and other reports of similar ilk, is that teachers' work is construed as that of:

> a minor technician within an industrial process, the overall goals ... [of which are to be] ... set in advance in terms of the national needs, the curricular materials prepackaged by the disciplinary experts, the methods developed by educational engineers — and the teacher's job ... just to supervise the last operational stage, the methodical insertion of ordered facts into the student's mind (Scheffler, 1963, cited in Scheffler, 1968, pp. 5–6).

The preoccupation is with competence and how to ensure compliance. Responding to the management mentality implicit in these educational reports and the domesticated debate they purport to engage in about education, one classroom teacher (Mullins, 1985) displayed an uncanny capacity to penetrate the issues in a way uncharacteristic of the educational technocrats and bureaucrats, when he said:

> The critics have overlooked the real crisis which has come upon us. It is not a crisis of competence, it is a crisis of ideals — exactly the same crisis which has hit many other professions [for example, medicine and law] .... In teaching, this crisis has its own manifestations, and incompetence is not among them. Cynicism and frustration are .... The profession of teaching has lost conviction in its own importance and the prospects of rekindling fervor are not bright (p. 13).

This teacher is in effect arguing for a dramatic shift of emphasis in the educational debate, 'away from spurious discussions on the technical competence of teachers — they are as technically sound now as they ever were — to the broader issue of role and ideals of the teacher' (Mullins, 1985). From this particular teacher's viewpoint, what is required is a theoretical perspective that is both less impoverished and which radically redefines the nature of educational crisis — a perspective that incorporates teachers as reflective practitioners into the debate about the changing nature of teaching and that ceases to regard them as objects of educational reform.

There is an important and compelling message here. If educational leaders and policymakers are concerned about educational reform, then they need to jettison the view that schools are like factories that only require revamped inspectorial systems, outcomes-oriented effectiveness, and efficiency schemes, program performance budgeting (PPB), management by objectives (MBO), competency-based teacher education (CBTE), and other elements of the 'alphabet soup of educational reform' (Darling-Hammond, 1985). According to Darling-Hammond, (1985):

> the most critical issue [currently] facing ... education ... is the professionalization of teaching. Professionalization involves not only the status and compensation accorded to the members of an occupation; it involves *the extent to which members of that occupation maintain control over the content of their work* and the degree to which society values the work of that occupation (p. 205, emphasis added).

Summary

The theme of this chapter has not had much to do directly with educational administrators or with helpful 'how to' hints on what educational administrators should do to encourage or facilitate the professional development of teachers. This omission has been quite deliberate. What is required at the moment is not a further proliferation of formulae on how to implement the technicalities of teacher professional development. We have a nauseating surfeit of that already. What this chapter has sought to do in broad brush strokes is to begin the transformation of administrative thinking about schooling, teachers, and students. If the professional development of teachers is to occur in any meaningful way, this will have to be a crucial prerequisite. We have to get the bigger canvas in focus before embarking on the fine brushwork.

My central claim has been that if educational administrators and leaders are to have any function at all in respect to schooling, then it shall be in finding ways by which teachers can begin to shatter the structured silence surrounding their teaching. In searching for this critical pedagogy, teachers need to be continually provoked into using 'their intellect to "burrow" through the taken-for-granted, the conventional, the genteel … [so as] … to leave their thumbprints on the world' (Greene, 1986, p. 432).

References

ARONOWITZ, S., and GIROUX, H. (1985). *Education under seige.* South Hadley, MA: Bergen & Garvey.

BERLAK, A., and BERLAK, H. (1981). *Dilemmas of schooling: Teaching and social change.* London: Methuen.

BULLOUGH, R., GITLIN, A., and GOLDSTEIN, S. (1984). Ideology, teacher role, and resistance. *Teachers College Record, 86*(2), 339–58.

BRUSS, N., and MACEDO, P. (1985). Toward a pedagogy of the question: Conversations with Paulo Freire. *Journal of Education, 167,*(2), 7–21.

DARLING-HAMMOND, L. (1985). Valuing teachers: The making of a profession. *Teachers College Record, 87*(2), 205–18.

ELBAZ, F. (1981). The teacher's 'practical knowledge': Report of a case study. *Curriculum Inquiry, 11*(1), 43–71.

FAY, B. (1977). How people change themselves: The relationship between critical theory and its audience. In T. Ball (ed.), *Political theory and praxis: New perspectives* (pp. 200–33). Mineapolis: University of Minnesota Press.

FRIED, R. (1980). *Empowerment vs. delivery of services.* Concord, NH: New Hampshire Department of Education.

FREEDMAN, S., JACKSON, J., and BOLES, K. (1983). Teaching as an imperiled 'profession.' In L. Shulman and G. Sykes (eds), *Handbook of teaching and policy.* New York: Longmans.

GIROUX, H. (1979). Schooling and the culture of positivism: Note on the death of history. *Educational Theory, 29*(4), 263–84.

GIROUX, H. (1985a). Intellectual labour and pedagogical work: Rethinking the role of the teacher as intellectual. *Phenomenology and Pedagogy, 3*(1), 20–32.

GIROUX, H. (1985b). Critical pedagogy and the resisting intellectual, part II. *Phenomenology and Pedagogy, 3*(2), 84–97.

GIROUX, H. (1985c). Teachers as transformative intellectuals. *Social Education, 49,* 376–9.

GRAMSCI, A. (1971). *Selection from the prison notebooks.* New York: International Publishers.

GREENE, M. (1985, July). *Teacher as project: Choice, perspective, and the public space.* Paper presented to the Summer Institute of Teaching, Teachers College, Columbia University.

GREENE, M. (1986). In search of a critical pedagogy. *Harvard Educational Review, 56*(4), 427–41.

GREENFIELD, T.B. (1973). Organizations as social inventions: Rethinking assumptions about change. *Journal of Applied Behavioral Science, 9*(5), 551–74.

GREENFIELD, T. B. (1981, June). *Understanding educational organizations as cultural entities: Some ideas, methods, and metaphors.* Paper presented to the conference on Administrative Leadership: New Perspectives on Theory and Practice, University of Illinois, Urbana.

HANSEN, I. (1986). Retrieving and reviving the lost years. Melbourne, Australia: *The Age* (9 Sep.), 21.

JACKSON, P. (1968). *Life in classrooms.* New York: Holt, Rinehart & Winston.

KEMMIS, S. (1983). Empowering people: A note on the politics of action research. In A. Pitman, J. Parrott, S. Grundy, W. Carr, and P. Watkins (eds), *Educational inquiry: Approaches to research.* Victoria, Australia: Deakin University.

KOHL, H. (1983). Examining closely what we do. *Learning, 12*(1), 28–30.

LORTIE, D. (1975). *Schoolteacher: A sociological study.* Chicago: University of Chicago Press.

McDONALD, J. (1986). Raising the teacher's voice and the ironic role of theory. *Harvard Educational Review, 56*(4), 335–78.

MULLINS, A. (1985, January 29). Stop caning the state school teachers. Melbourne, Australia: *The Australian*, 13.

NUNAN, T. (1982). Dispensing the culture of positivism to schools. *Pivot, 9*(2).

PAGANO, J. (1987). The schools we deserve: review of 'A place called school: Prospects for the future' by J. Goodlad. *Curriculum Inquiry, 17*(1), 107–22.

SANDERS, D., and McCUTCHEON, G. (1986). The development of practical theories of teaching. *Journal of Curriculum and Supervision, 2*(1), 50–67.

SCHEFFLER, I. (1968). University scholarship and the education of teachers. *Teachers College Record 70*(1), 1–12.

SCHWAB, J. (1983). The practical 4: Something for curriculum professors to do. *Curriculum Inquiry, 13*(3), 239–65.

SHOR, I. (1980). *Critical teaching and everyday life.* Montreal: Black Rose.

SMYTH, J. (1986). *Leadership and pedagogy.* Victoria, Australia: Deakin University Press.

SMYTH, J. (1987a). *Teachers' theories of action: Course guide ETL 825.* Victoria, Australia: Deakin University Press.

SMYTH, J. (1987b). *A rationale for teachers' critical pedagogy: A handbook.* Victoria, Australia: Deakin University Press.

VAN MANEN, M. (1977). Linking ways of knowing with ways of being practical. *Curriculum Inquiry 6*, 205–28.

PART V

TEACHERS AND TEACHING:
NEW IMAGES AND DIRECTIONS

11 Teacher Evaluation and Teaching as a Moral Science

John Elliott

Within the United Kingdom (UK) there is a good deal of current interest in the development of procedures for evaluating the competence of teachers and the quality of their teaching. This interest stems largely from attempts by central government, during negotiations over teachers' pay and conditions of service, to establish a national system of teacher appraisal. A framework for such a system was eventually agreed between the government, local education authorities employees (LEAs), and their teachers' unions (see Advisory, Conciliation, and Arbitration Service (ACAS), 1986). It is now being piloted in several LEAs. The negotiations have been accompanied by a considerable amount of controversy which still reverberates throughout the educational system. Much of this controversy has focused on the purposes of teacher appraisal. Teachers have interpreted the government's proposals as a managerial tool either for legitimating their removal from their positions, controlling their deployment, or allocating merit pay to superior performers. Teachers have argued that the primary purpose of appraisal should be to foster their professional and career development. In spite of the differences about the purposes of appraisal all parties share a common concern with the assessment of teaching competence.

The central problem for those who want procedures for assessing teaching competence developed is a general lack of agreement about what constitutes competent teaching. This problem is often interpreted as something which can be resolved through normative-analytic investigation. Given a degree of consensus about the purposes of teaching — its intended learning outcomes — it should be possible through process-product research to identify the most effective methods for achieving them. Over the past decade or so there have been numerous attempts to discover statistical correlations between kinds of teaching behaviour and types of learning outcome through what is generally labeled *teacher effectiveness* research (Berliner and Rosenshine, 1977; Dunkin and Biddle, 1974). The aspiration underlying it is the discovery of general rules for defining competent practice. None of the research findings has proved very conclusive.

This is not the place for an extensive review and critique of this now considerable body of research literature. But the criticism of this research can be divided into two categories. Firstly, there is *technical criticism* emanating from educational researchers about the methods and procedures employed. For example, Neville Bennett's (1976) findings about the effectiveness of formal compared with informal teaching methods has been criticized from the point of view of both sampling techniques and statistical methods. Theorists have also pointed out the dangers of inferring causal relationship between variables from statistical correlations. Just because an outcome regularly happens in conjunction with a particular method is insufficient reason for inferring causality.

The Nature of Teaching Competence

Secondly, there is *conceptual criticism*. Doyle (1979), for example, has argued that the emphasis on quantifying learning outcomes has led researchers to neglect the qualitative dimension of learning. Teacher effectiveness research has tended to concentrate on measuring the amount of learning and ignored its quality. Doyle points out that the same content can be learned in very different ways. The manner in which the content is learned will depend upon the kinds of learning tasks pupils are given in relation to it. He identifies four major qualitative categories of task.

Recognition Where the learner has to recognize the correct response. The risk of making incorrect responses can easily be minimized.

Memory Where the learner has to recall information in the form in which it is presented. A memory task can be either simple or complex depending on the amount of the information to be memorized in relation to it. Simple memory tasks are low risk with respect to the pupil's chances of successfully accomplishing them. The risk of failure is higher with more complex tasks.

Algorithmic Problem Solving Where the learner has to apply rules, given in advance, to the solution of a problem. So long as the learner applies the rules correctly, the correct answer is guaranteed. Given a knowledge of the rules, the risk of failure with respect to this kind of task is low.

Understanding Tasks Where the learner has to exercise a high degree of judgment because what the learner) needs to do in order to accomplish the task successfully cannot be completely specified in advance. Unlike memory and algorithmic problem-solving tasks, those requiring understanding are high in ambiguity and therefore the risk of failing to accomplish them successfully is correspondingly high.

Doyle (1979) claims that teacher effectiveness research has totally ignored the task dimension of learning in classrooms, and he poses the hypothesis that its most credible correlations have only been established in contexts where pupils have been working on simple memory or algorithmic problem-solving tasks. This, he asserts, is because successful performance on such tasks is easier for teachers to predict and control than successful performance on understanding tasks. The latter depends upon factors in the personalities and life histories of learners which are difficult for teachers to anticipate and control. In the light of these considerations one should not be surprised to find that teaching methods which promote memory learning are more causally effective in raising mean test scores than teaching methods which aim to facilitate learning with understanding.

One can argue Bennett's (1976) 'finding' that formal methods are more effective than informal methods was an entirely predictable outcome of his research, given the concept of teaching competence presupposed by the research design. Are not informal methods precisely those which are designed to protect and foster the exercise of independent and autonomous judgment on the part of pupils, those qualities of judgment which understanding tasks require them to exercise? And are not formal methods precisely those which aim to secure a high degree of teacher control over learning outcomes by minimizing pupils' opportunities for independent judgment, and thereby reducing the risk of them getting things wrong?

Formal methods of teaching appear to imply the setting of memory or algorithmic problem-solving tasks. If, as Bennett (1976) assumes, *effectiveness* in maximizing quantifiable learning outcomes is the criterion of competent teaching, then it is only to be expected that those teachers who use formal methods will tend to appear very much more competent than those who use informal methods. But those who employ informal methods will tend to reject such a finding on the grounds that instrumental effectiveness in producing quantifiable learning outcomes is not a criterion of teaching competence.

Competent teaching, informal teachers may argue, is a matter of establishing the conditions which enable pupils to learn things in an educationally worthwhile manner. And they will tend to indicate criteria for what is to count as an educationally valuable learning process by using terms like 'learning how to learn', 'developing an inquiring mind', 'the experience of discovering things for themselves', and 'learning with understanding'. Although these qualities of mind cannot be realized independently of the acquisition of knowledge content, some teachers will argue that it is their primary responsibility as educators to protect and foster such qualities through the kinds of learning tasks they set pupils, and the kinds of teaching strategies they employ to help pupils accomplish these tasks successfully. This responsibility is inconsistent with the view that it is the instrumental effectiveness of teaching — producing quantifiable learning outcomes — that consitutes the major criterion of teaching competence. Teaching is not a matter of *causally determining* what pupils learn but of *enabling* them to take responsibility for their own learning.

I use the word *enabling* to indicate a different mode of influencing to the exertion of causal influence. When teachers *enable* children to 'develop inquiring minds', to 'learn with understanding' they are not *producing* certain qualities of mind in children, but establishing conditions which provide children with opportunities for developing such qualities. The enabling conditions may obtain even when children fail to realize these qualities in their learning. People can fail to do what others have enabled them to do. A medical doctor can enable a patient to walk again by healing a broken leg, but whether that patient does walk again is up to the patient. It is not within the doctor's power to determine. Simiarly, the development of qualities of mind like those indicated cannot be causally controlled through teaching, but teaching can establish the conditions which enable children to develop them.

One must, therefore, distinguish teaching which exerts *causal influence* on learning, and teaching which exerts an *enabling influence* on learning. The former will be concerned primarily with controlling the learning process to maximize its quantifiable outcomes. The latter will be concerned with establishing the conditions that enable pupils to learn in an educationally worthwhile manner. In assessing teaching competence within the latter paradigm, one will be concerned to identify teaching methods in terms of their logical consistency/ inconsistency with the qualities of learning specified by aims like 'learning with understanding', or 'developing an inquiring mind'. This is very different from identifying methods in terms of their causal effectiveness/ineffectiveness in producing quantifiable outcomes. The criteria of assessment are derived from logical analyses of process aims rather than empirical investigations of effective means of producing learning outcomes.

The Process Model of Teacher Appraisal

Let me now provide two examples of how criteria for assessing teaching competence can be derived logically from educational aims. The first is Lawrence Stenhouse's (1970) analysis of the principles which ought to guide the way teachers handle controversial human issues with pupils. Stenhouse's approach was inspired by R. S. Peters' (1968) claim that aims in education specify procedural values governing what is to count as a worthwhile process of education, and not extrinsic outcomes. Stenhouse outlines his procedure as follows:

> We attempted to analyze the implications of our aim by deriving from it a specification of use of materials and a teaching strategy consistent with the pursuit of the aim. In other words, we concentrated on logical consistency between classroom process and aim, rather than between predetermined terminal behaviors and aim (Stenhouse, 1970, pp. 154–62).

From a concept of the learning process defined as 'developing an understanding of human acts, social situations, and the controversial value issues they raise', Stenhouse (1970) derived the following teaching principles:

(1) that controversial issues should be handled in the classroom with adolescents;
(2) that the teacher accepts the need to submit teaching in controversial areas to the criterion of neutrality at this stage of

education (that is, the teacher regards it as part of a responsibility not to promote a personal view);

(3)   that the mode of inquiry in controversial areas should have discussion, rather than instruction as its core;

(4)   that the discussion should protect divergence of view among participants, rather than attempt to achieve consensus;

(5)   that the teacher as chairperson of the discussion should have responsibility for quality and standards in learning (for example, by getting discussants to ground their views in reasons and evidence).

Teaching consistent with this aim would focus on controversial issues, refrain from taking sides, provide opportunities for discussion, protect the expression of alternative points of view, and safeguard standards of reasoning. Teaching which avoids focusing on controversial matters, promotes one side of a controversy more than others, prevents discussion and the expression of alternative views, and exercises little concern about standards of reasoning in discussion is inconsistent with the aim. Teaching which is consistent with the kind of learning specified by the aim establishes conditions which enable it to be realized in the classroom. Teaching which is inconsistent with this kind of learning constitutes constraints on its realization in the classroom.

My second example is taken from the Ford Teaching Project which I directed (Elliott, 1976). The project was concerned to help 40 teachers in 12 East Anglian schools examine the problems of implementing Inquiry/Discovery approaches. All the teachers agreed that the major aim of Inquiry/Discovery teaching was to 'enable pupils to reason independently'. We then analyzed this aim into four constitutive freedoms for learners to:

(1)   initiate and identify their own problems for inquiry;

(2)   express and develop their own ideas;

(3)   test their ideas against relevant and sufficient evidence; and

(4)   discuss their ideas with others.

In order to exercise these freedoms, two sets of conditions must obtain. Firstly, pupils must be *free from* certain external constraints. Secondly, they must have opportunities to acquire the necessary intellectual capacities. They may be free from constraints on the expression of ideas, for example, but remain unable to express ideas because they have not been given access to any. So from our analysis of 'enabling independent reasoning' we derived two sets of teaching principles. The first set specified the constraints teachers ought to refrain from imposing on pupils' thinking, while the second set specified how teachers can positively influence their thinking in a manner which is consistent with the aim. They were called *negative* and *positive*, respectively.

Negative principles—Refrain from (1) preventing students from identifying and initiating their own problems; (2) preventing students from expressing their own ideas and hypotheses; (3) restricting students' access to relevant evidence and drawing their own conclusions from it; (4) restricting students' access to discussion.

Positive principles—Help students (5) develop the capacity to identify and initiate their own problems; (6) develop their own ideas into testable hypotheses; (7) evaluate evidence in the light of its relevance, truth, and sufficiency; (8) learn how to discuss.

Both examples of attempts to derive teaching principles from aims illustrate how criteria for assessing teaching competence can be logically derived from a conception of an educationally worthwhile learning process. In applying them, no reference is made to learning outcomes. Let us take some very simple illustrations of this point using the Ford Teaching principles.

Looking at a video recording of her teaching, Sally notices that she is asking a lot of *leading questions*, and feels this is wrong. Such questions are not wrong because they are ineffective in producing certain beliefs about the subject in her pupils; indeed, they may be highly effective in this respect. These types of questions are wrong because they express an intention to *prevent pupils from developing their own ideas* (procedural principle no. 2, above), and are therefore inconsistent with the kind of 'independent reasoning' Sally wants to enable in her classroom.

Another teacher, John, looking at his videotape, notices that he continuously pressures a group of children to accept a particular point of view by using phrases like 'Do you agree with that?' or 'That's a good point, isn't it?'. This *consensus-seeking strategy* may be highly effective in getting pupils to learn a 'correct' answer, but John regards it as a bad strategy because it *expresses the intention of restricting children's access to a free discussion of alternative views* (procedural principle no. 4), and is therefore inconsistent with his aim that children should learn through independent reasoning.

Finally, let me take a positive principle as an example. The teacher sets her pupils a learning task which requires them to identify a problem of applying a scientific theory, and as they work on this task they ask questions which require them to reflect about certain situations in the light of the theory. She can conclude that in these respects she has been helping her pupils to develop the capacity specified under principle no. 5, regardless of whether they make the best use of this help by developing that capacity.

Teaching as a Moral Activity

The kinds of criteria I have cited for evaluating teaching competence refer to moral qualities exhibited in a form of teaching which is consistent with an educationally worthwhile process of learning. They define intrinsic ends to be realized in the concrete actions of teachers, and not extrinsic effects to be produced as a result of such actions. Their application to teaching acts is a matter of moral rather than technical judgment.

Procedures which employ process criteria for evaluating teaching competence rest on an entirely different conception of teaching as an activity to procedures which employ criteria of instrumental effectiveness. The former view teaching as a *moral activity*, while the latter view it as a *technology* or applied empirical science. Tom (1980) has pointed out that the moral dimension inherent in teaching flows from the authority relationship which necessarily exists between teacher and learner.

> Teaching is moral in at least two senses. On the one hand, the act of teaching is moral because it presupposes that something of value is to be taught (Peters, 1965). On the other hand, the teacher-student relationship is inherently moral because of its inequality. This relationship, notes Hawkins (1973), entails 'an offer of control by one individual over the functioning of another, who in accepting this offer, is tacitly assured that control will not be exploitive but will be used to enhance the competence and extend the independence of the one controlled . . . .' (p. 9). Those who adhere to the applied science metaphor are insensitive to the moral dimension of teaching

because their primary focus is on increasing the efficiency and effectiveness of teaching (Tom, 1980, pp. 317–23).

As Tom implies, the adoption of a moral perspective on teaching does not mean that teachers have no learning outcomes in mind for their pupils in terms of content objectives. The moral dimension of teaching simply specifies what are to count as morally legitimate ways of influencing the achievement of those objectives by their pupils, and rules out *causal influence*. What counts as morally legitimate influence is not derived from an empirical analysis of means–ends rules, but from a logical analysis of an educationally desirable process for learning whatever content the teacher has in mind. It follows from this that it is teachers' moral competence at enabling pupils to learn content in a certain manner which should be assessed, rather than their technical competence at reproducing this content in the minds of their pupils.

It is this moral dimension of teaching which is totally ignored by Bennett (1976) in his comparison of formal and informal teaching. Of course, informal teachers are more likely to be less instrumentally effective than formal teachers, since formal teaching necessarily aspires to be instrumentally effective while informal teaching necessarily subordinates effectiveness to the exertion of morally legitimate ways of influencing learning.

Bennett evaluates informal teaching against criteria of technical competence when the approach itself tacitly rejects such criteria in favor of moral ones. What Bennett fails to appreciate is that one cannot compare the two kinds of teaching using neutral criteria. To judge informal teaching against criteria implicit in formal teaching implies a rejection of the moral dimension on the assumption that teaching is a technology.

Problems in defining criteria for the evaluation of teaching competence are not supply problems of identifying instrumental competencies in terms of empirical means–ends correlations as teacher effectiveness research would have use believe. What is basically at issue is 'What sort of activity is teaching?' To use Habermas' terminology (1971), is it purpose-rational action directed towards the production of certain quantifiable end-states in the learner, or is it best conceived as a form of communicative interaction governed by binding consensual norms which define teachers' moral obligations towards their pupils?

After nearly two decades of collaborative classroom research with groups of teachers, I am convinced that this is not simply an academic issue indulged in by educational researchers and theorists. It constitutes a dilemma every teacher experiences and 'resolves' in one way or another. Many teachers involved in Stenhouse's Humanities Project (1970) found it difficult to implement the project's procedural principles because they felt under pressure from parents and pupils to adopt an 'answers oriented' didactic approach in their classroom. Most of the teachers involved in the Ford Teaching Project (see Elliott, 1976) initially claimed that their pursuit of content objectives in no way constrained the capacity of pupils to reason independently. But, when they looked at their teaching more clearly they became aware of the extent to which they felt pressured to sacrifice quality for quantity in classrooms.

More recently, teachers involved in our Schools Council 'Teacher–Pupil Interaction and the Quality of Learning Project' (TIQL; see Ebbutt and Elliott, 1986) discovered that teaching for understanding was incredibly difficult in an educational system where accountability is assessed largely in terms of the extent to which they prepare pupils for public examinations successes. Examination papers, upon analysis, revealed that a concern for the quality of learning indicated in pupils' responses ambiguously expressed and rarely overrode a concern with quantifiable content.

When they take a close look at their classrooms, teachers become increasingly aware of the difficulty of reconciling in practice the moral and technical dimensions of teaching. Self-aware teachers come to effect what might be regarded as 'reasonable compromises'. But there are numerous teachers who, in practice, subordinate the moral to the technical while deceiving themselves into believing that the former is superordinate.

Professional Knowledge and Ethics

I would want to claim that the distinction between teaching as a moral practice, and teaching as a technology, has enormous implications for the status of teachers. When teachers are viewed as practitioners of an ethic then they may be described appropriately as members of a *profession*. But when their activity is viewed as a kind of technology then their status may simply be reduced to that of the *technician*. The technologist is the applied scientist who discovers the best ways of treating material in order to produce the desired effects. The technician is the operative who applies the treatments prescribed by the technologist to the material. All the technician has to do to get the desired effect is to apply the rules prescribed by the technologist. When teaching is viewed as a technology a division of labor will tend to develop between educational scientists (*technologists*) doing research to discover the best treatments and educational practitioners (*technicians*) who apply their discoveries to pupil learning.

I would argue that the idea of a professional practice can be analyzed into two interrelated components. Firstly, it involves a commitment to the practice of an ethic, hence, the term *profession*. Secondly, it involves the possession of *expert knowledge*.

What is the relationship between the practice of an ethic and professional knowledge? Let us begin to explore this question by examining what is involved in the practice of an ethic. I shall define an ethic as a set of practical principles which are logically derived from some conception of 'human good'. The practice of an ethic is the translation of practical principles into concrete forms of human action. If we relate this to the idea of teaching as an ethical practice, terms like 'learning with understanding' and 'independent reasoning' specify conceptions of the pupils' good in an educational situation. The sets of teaching principles I have cited constitute ethics which are logically derived from such concepts of the pupils' good. And, their competent implementation requires teachers to translate them into concrete teaching behaviors in their classrooms. This translation of principles into action is an act of moral jugdment. The practice of an ethic rests on the quality of the judgment exercised in the process of translating principles into action.

Now if all learning situations were the same, there would be no need for judgment. Teachers' actions could simply be governed by general rules which told them exactly what to do in any learning situation. The idea of professional judgment assumes that the human situations in which professional tasks have to be accomplished will differ so that no situation will be exactly like another. The translation of general moral principles (not rules) into concrete professional practices is therefore a matter of judging what constitutes an appropriate form of action in the particular situation at hand. And, of course, the quality of a professional judgment will depend upon the quality of the reflection about the situation which has preceded it. The competent practice of a professional ethic, therefore, rests essentially on an ability to translate reflectively ethical principles into concrete practices which are appropriate to a given situation (that is, on the ability to judge which actions conform to the principles in a particular situation).

The ability 'to judge' a practical situation depends on 'the stock of professional knowledge' on which the practitioner can draw. This will consist of generalizations which are retrospective distillations from experience. These are not causal laws from which the practitioner can predict the outcome of a certain course of action. Rather, they cite relationships between factors which, upon reflection, appear to recur in practical situations with a reasonable degree of frequency. Such generalizations draw the practitioners' attention to possibly relevant features of a present situation which need to be examined before a course of action is selected. Unlike causal laws, they do not tell the practitioner exactly what to do, but provide a general orientation for the diagnosis of particular situations. If, upon deliberation, the practitioner finds that some of the anticipated relationships do not apply, this does not invalidate the generalizations employed. They have served an important diagnostic function; namely, that of helping the practitioner clarify what is and what is not the case in the present situation. It is only when a generalization ceases to apply to the majority of situations encountered that its usefulness and value as part of a common stock of professional knowledge becomes questionable.

In the Humanities, Ford Teaching, and TIQL Projects we called these generalizations 'hypotheses' to indicate that they needed to be tested anew in each situation, rather than applied uncritically. Some examples of Ford Teaching Project 'hypotheses' are included in Table 11.1. These are relevant to the problems of translating a pair of teaching principles into forms of concrete action; namely: refrain from preventing pupils' expressing their own ideas and developing their own hypotheses; and help pupils to develop their ideas into testable hypotheses about how problems might be resolved.

Each hypothesis cites an action which, upon reflection, has been shown to constrain the realization of the principles cited in a number of teaching situations, together with an explanation for the constraining influence of the action. The corresponding right-hand column indicates the possible strategies for overcoming the constraints and realizing the principles.

In the Ford Teaching Project we generated hypotheses about problems and strategies for each pair of negative and positive teaching principles. The idea behind the Project was to develop a stock of professional knowledge about the problems of, and strategies for,

Table 11.1 Freedom to Express Ideas and Develop Lines of Inquiry

FREEDOM TO EXPRESS IDEAS AND DEVELOP LINES OF INQUIRY

	Teacher imposed constraints	*Constraint removing strategies*	*Guidance strategies*
2.1	*TOPIC CHANGES* When the teacher changes the direction of inquiry or point of discussion pupils my fail to contribute their own ideas. They will interpret such actions as attempts to get them to conform with his own line of reasoning.	Refrain from changing the direction of inquiry or point of discussion unless pupils have exhausted their ideas. Ensure that pupils have exhausted their ideas before changing by asking them if they have anything more to contribute.	Make your contributions responses to ideas as they are initiated and developed by pupils in the course of inquiry or discussion, rather than attempts by you to structure their thinking in a predetermined direction.
2.2	*PROMOTING VIEWS* When the teacher promotes his own views and beliefs it will tend to inhibit pupils from expressing their own. They will interpret such statements as attempts by the teacher to impose his own views.	Refrain from pressing your views and beliefs in isolation and from expressing them until asked by the pupils.	When pupils lack the power to produce ideas out of a vacuum introduce views, beliefs, and counter-arguments you feel are worth them considering through some medium other than one's own person, e.g. articles, stories, poems, films. etc.
2.3	*ELICITING PERSONAL EXPERIENCE* When the teacher probes too deeply into the personal lives of pupils he may prevent them from feeling free to make use of personal experiences. Such requests will be interpreted as attempts to pry into matters they have a right not to disclose.	Refrain from requesting information about the personal and private lives of pupils where this may be embarrassing for them.	Enable pupils to generate ideas from personal experience by providing them with opportunities for making sense of it through the study of depersonalized situations e.g. by asking questions about particular situations they have not experienced directly but which they can come to understand by drawing on their own experience of similar situations.

Table 11.1 (continued)

Teacher imposed constraints	FREEDOM TO EXPRESS IDEAS AND DEVELOP LINES OF INQUIRY *Constraint removing strategies*	*Guidance strategies*
2.4 *PRIORITY FOR WRITTEN WORK* The decision by teachers that writing rather than discussion should be the main medium for expressing and developing ideas can prevent pupils from expressing and developing them at all. This is because 'written work' is frequently interpreted as something done for purposes of assessing what they already know rather than as an aid to reasoning.	Refrain from insisting that writing should be the sole medium in which pupils are allowed to express, clarify, and develop ideas.	Provide opportunities for other forms of expression, e.g. discussion, art/craft, modelling, music, film, photography, dance.
2.5 *ASKING FOR DEFINITIONS* When the teacher persistently questions pupils about the meaning of terms and refuses to provide any answers he will foster 'a guessing game' (based on 'hints' and 'clues' he provides about meanings). This is because the answers to such questions cannot be arrive at through a process of reasoned thought.	Refrain from persistent questioning of pupils about word meanings when it is quite clear that they do not know the answers you want.	In circumstances where it is clear that pupils do not know the definition of a term then explain it to them. Definitions cannot be reasoned out; one either knows them or doesn't.
2.6 *ELICITING PRECONCEIVED ANSWERS* When the teacher asks a question with the intention of eliciting a preconceived answer it may prevent pupils from expressing and developing their own ideas and merely stimulate attempts to recall or guess at the answer expected. This is because such a question will be interpreted exclusively as an attempt to examine or test whether pupils know what the teacher knows rather than an attempt to get them to express and develop a line of reasoning for themselves.	If your main purpose is to foster reasoning rather than test pupils' abilities to recall items of information, refrain from asking a question with the intention of eliciting a preconceived answer.	Help pupils initiate and develop ideas by asking *real questions* (i.e. questions you don't know the answers to) and indicating a genuine interest in pupils' ideas for their own sake.

2.7	SUBJECT-CENTERED FOCUSING		
	When the teacher's questions focus pupils' attention solely on the subject-matter rather than on their own ideas about it he may prevent them from initiating or developing their own ideas. Such focusing will be interpreted as an attempt to find out whether they know what he expects them to know (exam type question).	Refrain from framing your questions in terms which draw attention exclusively to the subject-matter rather than pupils' thoughts about it.	Ask person-centered questions which focus the pupils' attention on their own ideas with respect to the subject-matter
2.8	REAL QUESTIONS		
	When a teacher tries to get his pupils to believe that he is sincerely trying to discover something about the subject-matter for himself he may be unsuccessful because pupils will tend to interpret his utterances as exam questions. Pupils may view teachers as experts on the subject-matter when they are not.	Refrain from questions which focus attention exclusively on the subject-matter rather than pupils' ideas about it.	Ask questions which direct pupils' attention to their own ideas because pupils will not expect teachers to be in a better position to know what is going on in the heads of pupils than the pupils themselves.
2.9	PERSON-CENTERED FOCUSING		
	Indications of interest in the ideas and actions of pupils may initially fail to activate or foster the production and development of their own ideas, because they may find it difficult to believe that a teacher is sincerely interested in what they originate.	Refrain from rejecting and ignoring ideas produced by pupils in response to your questions.	Respond to pupils' ideas by questions which ask them to clarify, develop and test them, remembering that this is a long term process.

Table 11.1 (continued)

	FREEDOM TO EXPRESS IDEAS AND DEVELOP LINES OF INQUIRY	
Teacher imposed constraints	*Constraint removing strategies*	*Guidance strategies*
2.10 *DISCOVERY SEQUENCES*		
Question sequences leading pupils towards a predetermined conclusion tend to be ineffective at helping them to produce and develop ideas either because:	Refrain from question sequences leading to a predetermined conclusion.	Ask questions intended to help pupils develop ideas and lines of reasoning they have initiated.
(a) pupils perceive them as a number of isolated questions designed to test their existing knowledge of unconnected facts, or		
(b) pupils interpret the overall intention as more concerned with eliciting a predetermined conclusion than with the methods by which it is reached. They will consequently pressurize the teacher to fill the gap between problem and conclusion with sufficient hints and clues for the conclusion to be guessed with a minimum of rational thought.		

2.11 *SHORT-TERM-KNOWLEDGE OBJECTIVES*

There is a conflict which arises in question sequences between helping pupils to develop and produce their own ideas at their own pace and the teacher trying to achieve his pace.

Refrain from attempting to structure pupils' responses to produce the short-term conclusions you want.

Make a distinction between short-term and long-term objectives. Pursue the production and development of the pupils' own ideals, rather than arriving at predetermined conclusions as short-term goals. (Inquiry rather than Discovery orientation in the short term.)

2.12 *INTRODUCING CONCEPTS IN THE TEACHER'S LANGUAGE*

Pupils often find it difficult to understand the terminology teachers use when they introduce concepts. Their perceptions of teacher authority make it difficult for them to feel free to request clarification and explanation.

Refrain from introducing concepts in terms which are not understood by pupils. Invite pupils to interrupt by requesting clarification and explanation of your terminology.

Ensure that new terminology is not left unexplained.

2.13 *INTRODUCTION MEANINGFUL CONCEPTS*

When the teacher introduces a concept pupils will fail to use it with understanding when they do not perceive its usefulness for their inquiries.

Refrain from introducing concepts without regard for the ends and purposes pupils are pursuing in their enquiries.

Introduce concepts when they are required by pupils to develop ideas.

(From *Implementing the Principles of Inquiry/Discovery Teaching: Some Hypotheses* Ford Teaching Project. Unit 3 Cambridge Institute of Education) implementing *Inquiry/Discovery Teaching* in classrooms. Similarly, in the Schools Council TIQL Project hypotheses about problems and strategies with respect to *Teaching for Understanding* were generated.

The 'hypotheses' cited above reflect the general ethical character of professional knowledge. They are conditioned by the values which define the aim of a professional practice and the principles of action which are consistent with such values. Professional knowledge is ethical knowledge, and the process of its development is best described as a kind of moral science. How then is it developed? What sort of activity is moral science?

I would claim that it is no more than the reflective practice of a profession. The process involves a dialectical relationship between theory (professional knowledge) and practice. Practitioners draw on a stock of knowledge distilled from past experience in this reflective translation of aims and principles into concrete practices. Since an initial judgment about the rightness of a strategy for a particular situation always involves an element of 'shooting in the dark', it is intrinsically problematic and therefore in need of retrospective evaluation. It is through practitioners' retrospective self-evaluations of their attempts to translate values into action that professional knowledge is further refined and developed. And this, in turn, generates new ways of looking at particular situations and possibilities with respect to what might count as competent action in them. The reflective practice of a profession constitutes the dialectical process of generating practice from theory and theory from practice.

When teaching is viewed as the reflective practice of a professional ethic, it constitutes a form of moral science in which teachers' self-evaluations play a central role in the development of professional knowledge. Within a moral science paradigm of educational inquiry there is no necessary division of labor between practitioners and inquirers. Nor is there any need to make a strong distinction between educational evaluation and research. As the means by which professional knowledge is developed, self-evaluation is an integral part of the research process I have outlined, as indeed are the practices which are self-evaluated.

Competent professional practice presupposes competent self-evaluation. This is why many who wish to enhance the professional status of teachers emphasize the importance of self-evaluation as opposed to external monitoring. No such self-evaluation dimension is logically necessary to competent teaching within the technological paradigm. In this paradigm there is room for a division of labor between practitioners and evaluators, and between both of these parties and educational researchers. The latter discover means–ends rules governing the production of measurable learning outcomes. The teachers apply these rules to their actions, and the evaluators monitor whether they have been accurately applied. Self-evaluation in the light of the prescribed rules may help teachers 'self-correct' their teaching, but since 'the rules' displace the need for practitioner judgment in particular situations, such corrections can, given a sufficient supply of manpower, be as easily administered on the basis of external assessments.

I would like to make one further point about the relationship between the practice of a profession and the development of professional knowledge. It is this: *the capacity of professional knowledge to support competent practice in particular situations will depend upon the extent to which it is shared.*

Dan Lortie in his famous study, *Schoolteacher* (1975), claimed that teachers in the USA lacked a shared body of knowledge and insight into the craft of teaching, and that this made them less than a professional group. The development of the professional practice of individuals is limited if they simply reflect about them in isolation from their peers. It is enhanced enormously by procedures which enable the development of shared knowledge and insight. Such development involves individuals using the collective wisdom of their professional group to guide their judgments, and then contributing to it what they learn from retrospective appraisals of such judgments. This process would be facilitated by a procedure for sharing and discussing individuals' accounts of their practices.

The hypotheses cited earlier were generated by teachers from the discussion of case study data collected in their classrooms. The hypotheses teachers generated in the TIQL Project (see Ebbutt and Elliott, 1986) about problems and strategies with respect to teaching for understanding were based on the sharing, discussion, and comparison of individual teachers' case studies. What emerged from both of these projects was a reflective distillation of shared insights: a shared stock of professional knowledge to support future deliberation and practice.

For those of us concerned with the improvement of teaching there are two alternative courses of action open to us. The first course is to develop a system for identifying and rectifying deficiencies in teaching conceived as a technology. This will involve the standardization of competency criteria as a basis for observation by external assessors of teachers, perhaps located in the administrative/managerial hierarchy which regulates and controls their activities. The second course is to develop forms of organization which are consistent with the idea of teaching as a moral science: namely, forms which support the continuous development of shared professional knowledge through the reflective practice of an ethic of teaching.

References

ADVISORY, CONCILIATION, AND ARBITRATION SERVICE (ACAS): Independent Panel. (1986). *Report of the Appraisal and Training Working Group.* Unpublished report. Department of Education and Science.

BENNETT, N. (1976). *Teaching styles and pupil progress.* London: Open Books.

BERLINER, D. C., and ROSENSHINE, B. (1977). The acquisition of knowledge in the classroom. In R. Anderson and W. Montague (eds), *Schooling and the acquisition of knowledge.* Hillsdale, NJ: Lawrence Erlbaum.

DOYLE, W. (April, 1979). *The tasks of teaching and learning.* Invited address at the annual meeting of the American Educational Research Association, San Francisco.

DUNKIN, M. J., and BIDDLE, B. J. (1974). *The study of teaching.* New York: Holt, Rinehart and Winston.

EBBUTT, D., and ELLIOTT, J. (eds). (1986). *Issues for teaching and understanding.* London: Schools Curriculum Development Committee/Longmans.

ELLIOTT, J. (1976). Developing hypotheses about classrooms from teachers' practical constructs. *Interchange, 7*(2), 2–21.

FORD TEACHING PROJECT, UNIT 3: HYPOTHESES (1975). *Implementing the principles of inquiry/discovery teaching: Some hypotheses.* Cambridge Institute of Education.

HABERMAS, J. (1971). *Towards a rational society.* (chap. 6, pp. 81–122). London: Heinemann Educational Books.

HAWKINS, D. (1973). What it means to teach. *Teachers College Record. 7*(5), 7–16.

LORTIE, D. C. (1975). *Schoolteacher.* Chicago: University of Chicago Press.

PETERS, R. S. (1965). Education as initiation, in *Philosophical analysis and education,* R. D. Archambault. New York: Humanities.

PETERS, R. S. (1968). Must an educator have an aim? In C. J. B. Macmillan and T. W. Nelson (eds), *Concepts of teaching.* Chicago: Rand McNally.

STENHOUSE, L. (1970). The Humanities Curriculum Project: The rationale. *Theory into Practice, 10,* 154–62.

TOM, A. R. (1980). Teaching as a moral craft: A metaphor for teaching teacher education. *Curriculum Inquiry, 10*(3), 317–23.

12 Professional Development and Journal Writing

Mary Louise Hulbert Holly and
Caven S. Mcloughlin

As every educator knows, professional teaching is not easy. It takes support and continuing professional development to explore, evaluate and learn from experience. Reflection on practice brings to awareness hidden dimensions of teaching and learning. Though we act purposefully on what we know and understand, much of this cannot readily be put into words. The fleeting nature of classroom life requires conscious effort to cultivate awareness of it if it is to be captured for later consideration. Writing about teaching, we suggest, is a powerful method for documenting and learning from experience. It is, as John Elliott (chap. 11) calls for, a tool for 'practitioners' retrospective self-evaluations of their attempts to translate values into action ...' and thus, a method by which 'professional knowledge is further refined and developed'.

Theory, Practice, Knowledge and Professional Development[1]

The debate over a perceived gap between theory and practice persists as theoreticians continue to construct theories, and teachers continue to lament the confusing language and a lack of practical application. Alternative conceptualizations of 'theory' and 'practice' are however, brewing. Sprinthall, for example, has written that:

> we derive practice from theory *and* vice versa — that is we can derive theory from a careful examination of practice. Practice is not a second-class activity for those too stupid to think at a theoretical level. Rather, interaction means just that. Practice and theory go

hand in hand. If we concentrate exclusively on either, both are diminished ... theory and practice are different sides of the same coin and reside in the real world, not the laboratory ... (Sprinthall, 1980, pp. 284–5).

Theory and practice are of necessity dialectical, discontinuous, and dynamic processes. Eraut (1985) makes the distinction between public theories — systematically developed and publicly known conceptual schemes for interpreting phenomena, as for example, Piaget's theory of cognitive development or Einstein's theory of relativity — and private theories — our own personal explanations and conceptual systems for making sense of experience. Our private theories incorporate those aspects of public theories that we find useful to our lives and teaching. This way of describing theory is consistent with Elliott's (chap. 11) definition of theory as professional knowledge. As teachers, we function from our own evolving personal, professional theoretical bases. We act on continuously changing schemata — structures of thought that are modified by and through our actions, and reflections about those actions. As we *act on* our world, and are reciprocally *acted upon* by it, our perceptions change. With these changes comes a restructuring of our assumptions, explanations, and theories. These are the mental images that influence our behavior.

All theories are 'partial pictures', attempts at explanation and comprehension of limited aspects of behavior, from restricted perspectives (Coles, 1981). Formal (public) theories are expressed in words which represent reality but are not themselves reality; 'ideas and words are more or less fixed, whereas real things change' (Watts, 1951, p. 45). From birth to death, understanding outstrips language. The infant, for example, is receptive to language long before the capacity to use language is developed. When asked 'why did you do that?' the school-age child often does not know in a way that enables telling about it. To the teenager, love is ineffable. Likewise, teachers *know* and *act* on their knowledge of individual pupils and experiences *in ways they cannot state, let alone explain.*

Knowing in words, and knowing in action, are both *knowing*; yet in different ways. Knowing-in-words represents but a small part of knowing-in-action. Personal knowledge includes tacit knowledge, and the diversity of ways that persons come to know themselves and the world; conscious and unconscious knowing, subtleties, nuances, and only dimly sensed realities (Polanyi, 1967). The credibility of these forms of knowing seems to be in jeopardy for the contemporary teacher. For example, while academics debate the nature–nurture controversy as it pertains to theory and practice, how teachers theorize about their practice continues to be shaped by standardized procedures and curriculum mandates, by what *others think they should know* and *how others think they should teach*. Teachers continue to be encouraged to understand well everything but themselves and their professional practice (Jersild, 1955).

Teacher Teach Thyself (Warnock, 1985) is a valid entreaty asking teachers to *know* and be able to *assess* and *appraise* themselves. To be connoisseurs (appreciating the significance of their work) and critics (making public the importance of educational processes) of teaching and learning, teachers must be given support to focus on their work (Eisner, 1985). They need time and conditions conducive to reflection in order to consider practice and the meanings of teaching. These are necessary for bringing implicit assumptions and beliefs which influence teaching and learning to a conscious level. Teachers celebrating their successes, posing their own dilemmas, or as Tripp (1985) would say 'problematizing their practice', and conducting their own action research within supportive and intellectually robust environments, engages and empowers teachers. It enables them to know what they know, how they know it, and to extend it.

As teachers gain awareness and confidence through theorizing they can engage in dialogue that helps to generate a shared culture of teaching (Lortie, 1975). Integrating knowledge of self, and knowledge of practice contributes to praxis, a dynamic state of personal and public knowledge in evolution.

> Knowledge is not something to be 'consumed' but made and remade ... the learners are invited to think ... beings that not only know but know that they know .... A creative act that involves a critical comprehension of reality ... and analyzing praxis in its social context, opens to them the possibility of new knowledge ... thought-language and objective reality (Chavis, 1978, pp. 23–7).

How do teachers gain awareness and insight into their teaching, and the larger contexts within which they teach? How do we both gain distance from the routine nature of our existence and probe more deeply into the *why* of what we do, the meanings of our professional lives? The following sections of this chapter report on a project designed to address these concerns.

Journal Writing and Professional Development

From January 1981 through January 1982 seven teachers kept personal–professional journals. This project, *Teacher Reflections on Classroom Life: An Empirical Base for Professional Development* (Holly, 1983) began as a study of teachers and the relationships between teaching and professional development. The goal was to explore teaching from the teacher's point of view — to study teaching and professional development from phenomenological and perceptual frames of reference. It was assumed that in order to facilitate growth (or at least not pose obstacles to it), we must understand the processes of teaching and professional development from the teacher's perspective. This view holds that the person cannot be separated from the professional. The teacher acts from situational perceptions in exercising professional judgment. Further, behavior is determined by a perceptual field, which is the 'universe of naive experience in which the individual lives, the everyday situation of the self and its surroundings which each person takes to be reality' (Combs and Snygg, 1959).

What might be learned about professional development from teachers? How do teachers define their reality? Several questions guided this inquiry: What are the problems and joys of being a teacher? What are the events and interactions in their daily lives which influence their development? What characteristics of the school setting appear to aid or impede their development? What do responses to these questions suggest for improving support systems for professional and staff development? Another question, which had been implicit in the proposed work, became apparent early in the project. What happens when teachers reflect consciously on their teaching and professional development? That is the focal theme of this chapter.

While diary writing was originally a method for the researcher to develop understanding of the teacher's perspective, it also became a journal for the teacher's personal–professional development, and as such, a process to study. Teachers reflected through writing during the school day. They documented their theories-in-action and created documentation to return to and reflect on. Returning to writing, it turns out, can be enlightening — both something rewarding ('What a good idea!'; 'No wonder we're tired at night. Look at what we've accomplished!'), and disconcerting ('Now why did I do that?!'; 'My actions are in conflict with my aims'). Journals became tools for reflection, analysis, and self-evaluation. Stages in writing were discovered, as well as different types of writing representing different kinds of thinking.

Personal Documents

Most writers on journals and diaries use the terms interchangeably (Mallon, 1984). For our purpose, however, it is useful to define logs, diaries, and journals in the following ways.[2]

Log A log is a regularly kept record of performance. Facts, unencumbered by interpretation, are recorded systematically. Social scientists and educators use this 'objective' and empirically based process to record facts important to their work. A teacher writes in the manner of a log when recording what happened in a class. A lesson plan is a plan for what is intended to take place, while the recording of what did take place is a factual recounting of the events (that is, a description of teaching).

Diaries A diary is defined as a record of personal experiences and observations over time. In contrast to the log, it is by definition a personal document — one in which the writer includes interpretations, opinions, feelings, and thoughts. A diary typically contains a spontaneous type of writing. Although diaries have been published, the intent is usually to talk to oneself through writing. Facts can be recorded but they are usually tied to the writer's thoughts and feelings about daily events.

Journals A journal includes facts similar to a log, and it can include spontaneous and personal thoughts and feelings as does the diary, but it is more than these. A journal is a comprehensive and systematic attempt at writing to clarify ideas and experiences; it is a document written with the intent to return to it, and to learn through interpretation of the writing. The journal, like the log and the diary, is kept over time. It is not necessarily a record of events as they happen. Patterns or topics that recur in the writer's experience can be written about. A teacher who is writing a journal about teaching might notice a pattern, and reflect on similar examples and write about these. The teacher then might use the journal to explore and work on problems in a systematic way.

Types of Journal Writing

Eight types of teacher's journal writing which appear to occur 'naturally' (that is, without direction or prompting) have been identified (Holly, 1988). They can be described as follows:

Journalistic writing is descriptive; like the newspaper journalist, the writer reconstructs events and circumstances for someone to read. In a journal, there may be an outside reader intended, but usually the reader is the writer.

Analytical writing is used when the writer wants to examine parts of a problem or situation. By writing about different aspects of a lesson, for example, a teacher can examine how these might reinforce or run counter to professed aims, and in what ways they might interrelate.

Evaluative writing generally, if not always, includes analysis. Description and understanding informs judgment and decision making. Evaluation assumes value.

Ethnographic writing is vivid, in-depth, descriptive writing. The writer is immersed in a setting and describes it graphically and contextually. It is useful to teachers in better understanding how others, usually students, view schooling and in viewing teaching and behavior in broader contexts.

Therapeutic writing is often found in diary writing. It taps the 'inner self' and can enhance personal growth. It includes humor, writing as catharsis, and writing as self analysis.

Reflective writing looks back over experiences. It can be evaluative, but it need not be. A teacher may recall in writing the work of the day, week, or year. A curious thing happens to people when they write reflectively on experiences. They find that they become more 'reflective in action' (Schon, 1983). That is, they become more aware of what they do while they do it.

Introspective writing asks 'what did I do?' and 'why?'. It looks at the writer's actions, aims and consequences, and tries to make sense of them. It can bring to a conscious level implicit assumptions and theories that undergird behavior.

Creative writing implies exploration and new ways of viewing experience. Though it can be exacting and demanding, it also stems from and fuels playfullness and curiosity. It helps the author to step out of routine and look differently at it.

The Experience of Journal Writing

People who write journals regularly usually find themselves writing in several, if not all of these ways. The writing type depends on the writer's purposes. Often these are implicit, especially in diary writing. When someone uses a journal for the purposes of exploring teaching, and as an aid to professional development, it can be useful to be aware of different types of writing. As the teacher re-reads a journal, he or she begins to differentiate purposes and types of writing. Over time this can become a conscious process. Journalistic writing, for example, can be very effective for the teacher who wants to gain understanding of a student's behavior. Recording the student's behavior on different days can provide important information for later analysis.

Descriptive and ethnographic writing presents many challenges; they depend on seeing descriptively — separating interpretation and opinions from facts. Writing freely, including inferences, feelings and thoughts, as well as facts, is another way to document for descriptive reflection and analysis. As the writer returns to entries it becomes apparent how thoughts, feelings and opinions color both the action and interpretations. In either case, separating facts and inferences or writing without regard for them, the more descriptive the entries, the richer the base for analysis and interpretation.

Writing to reflect involves a cyclical pattern of reflection: first, reflecting on experiences before or as you write; and, later, reflecting on the journal entries, which may in turn provide material for further reflection and writing, and so on.

Many of us find it difficult, even painful, to return to diary and journal writing after the event. Perhaps part of the reason is because we see our emotions and relive our experiences. We sometimes wonder how we could have been so distressed over seemingly trivial events, but when given the flow of circumstances, our behavior seems natural. Piecing together this flow enables acceptance and *then* analysis and change, as a result of changes in perceptions and understanding.

The tendency to judge — to dichotomize good and bad, success and failure — seems to be strongest when the complexity of circumstances outstrips our ability to understand them. We simplify our experiences until later when we can view them less defensively and more comprehensively. But, in a time of rapid technological change and an emphasis on *higher productivity*, it becomes hard to differentiate what *is* important from what *is not* important.

Taking time out for reflective writing and dialogue is an attractive alternative to running at speed or 'burning out'. Through the journal-keeping process, we can become more sensitive observers, more penetrating in our inquiry into 'what it all means', and more focused on our roles and directions in life.

According to Progoff (1975), there are two ways to record in a log, diary, or journal: (1) write close to the time of experiences; or (2) reflect back over the day or few days, as soon as possible, perhaps early in the morning or at night (or both), by jotting down ideas in snatches as they occur and expanding on them later. We are advised to record key words or phrases for later expansion. Writing soon after the experience is preferable, although not always possible; although, sometimes it is harder to 'selectively remember' our experiences the closer we are to them. On these occasions, it is easier to recall events more comprehensively with the distance of time. So, we might use a combination of writing as close to the time possible *and* some time later so that multiple views can emerge.

A quiet place is desirable for writing log or diary entries; it is necessary for the journal writer who wants to reflect, and to reconstruct or recapture the setting, thoughts, feelings, and all. Once an experience is recaptured, other events, behaviors, or ideas that 'fit' with it will become apparent too. The journal holds experiences as a puzzle frame holds its integral pieces. The writer begins to recognize the pieces that fit together and, like a detective, sees the picture evolve. Clues lead to new clues, partial perspectives to more comprehensive perspectives.

Autobiography, Life History, and Portrait Construction

Gaining awareness and insight into oneself and the broader contexts within which one practices are interactive and long term processes.

Writing autobiographically about significant aspects of personal and professional development brings unique perspectives for interpreting current practice. What do I remember about growing up? ... in the first five years? What do I remember about early schooling? Why did I decide to become an educator? When? Who was influential? What circumstances led to the decision? Who were the best teachers I had? ... the worst? Why? What do I remember about them? What were turning points in my education? Why were they important? What else might have happened? How do I characterize my first year of teaching? What were important points in my teacher preparation? Who am I in a classroom today? How do my experiences influence this?

Autobiographical writings in response to questions like these provide bridges from the past to the present and into the future. They can be an aid to establishing connections in practice. They are self narrations of development over time. Taken together, autobiographical entries illustrate part of the writer's life history (Runyan, 1984).[3] Seemingly important and unimportant events, when described, interpreted, and evaluated *on paper*, have a way of bringing coherence to the motion and punctuations that comprise the teacher's life.

Educational Improvement: Becoming a Connoisseur and Critic

Eisner (1985) recommends that teachers become critics of their practice — that is, they must make public what is occurring in teaching, and what needs to happen. To be an educational critic, one must first become a connoisseur, an appreciator of significant aspects of teaching and learning. The question is, 'How do teachers become connoisseurs?' and then, 'How do teachers become critics, able and committed to share their professional concerns in public forums?' Later in this chapter we will look at portraits of three teachers who are developing these characteristics. They are engaging in writing and collegial discussion as tools to analyze their teaching and learning, and to document professional development.

Whenever we write about an experience and later return to it, we gain at least two additional perspectives. As we write we are one step removed from it, and as we later reflect we are another step removed. What might not have seemed important at the time might become important (or vice versa) as we gain distance from it. We begin to differentiate those situations where our actions are consistent with our aims, from those where they might inadvertently be working against them. For example, we sometimes get caught in the motion of events and teaching specific skills and neglect to think about larger and long-term aims. Learning phonics, for example, should promote skill in reading, but not at the expense of an interest in, and enthusiasm for, reading.

Keeping a journal is a way to ponder these questions. If you have not yet written a journal, try it. It is a way to document events that hold significance, to clarify beliefs and assumptions, and further, to test these out in behavior. As you write about what happens in the classroom or school, what you do, and how you think and feel about both the students' and your own experiences, you will begin to see where your philosophy and 'theories' are demonstrated in your behavior and where they are in conflict. You will be able to work out dilemmas as you 'think on paper' about them. Merely by calling attention to 'hidden' facets of your teaching you will inform your practice. And, even more importantly, you might find yourself becoming more comfortable with ambiguity, complexity, and the unsettling nature of continuous inquiry.

In the fifth century BC, Socrates suggested that 'the life which is unexamined is not worth living'. Today, the push to teach 'more', 'sooner' and 'faster' exerts pressure for movement and action. However, if our efforts are to be consistent with our aims, we must examine both. We live in a time of 'quick fixes', but if we want the fix to work, it must fit the circumstances. Keeping a journal can help us to see the circumstances, and to document experience over time so that we can see the flow of events rather than isolated instances.

Teachers in the Process of Reflection: The Journal as Case Study

A personal/professional journal not only contains case studies, it is one. Factual information; the spontaneous pouring of words on to the page at the height of emotion and feeling; documentation of research; reactions to readings, colleagues, pupils, community and world events; and autobiographical flashbacks are each called forth and written by the author — all products of the author's experience.

What *really* happens when educators keep journals? In the following section we will survey the journals of three teachers (of seven) who used journals to reflect on their practice. Near the end of her journal Carole wrote of her renewed commitment to teaching. She, as the six others, found teaching to be more complicated and related to herself as a person than she realized before she began to write about it. Only one of the seven teachers, Jerry, wrote every-so-often 'just for the pleasure of it' before starting a journal. 'But how can I write about teaching? Teaching is like breathing, you just do it!' said Jerry.

After a few months of writing, Jerry felt a little differently about writing and about teaching. 'I can't believe I never thought about some of these things before!' Jerry was reflecting on the meaning of teaching. These teachers charted into new professional territory when they agreed to keep track of themselves over a year. Not all teachers continued to write on their own throughout the year; some continued well beyond the year. Journal writing was a way to explore their theories of teaching and professional development. Theories were implicit — and sometimes explicit — in their writing. By writing about teaching, new thoughts were stimulated. By talking with others, theories and questions were challenged and developed. By returning to the journal, they could explore their ideas from different perspectives and see how these ideas developed. They wrote about teaching in a time of the 'hurried child', when teacher isolation was a felt reality, and when the curriculum was becoming more standardized and testing an increasingly influential aspect of teaching and evaluation. The word 'reflection' was a relatively new term to education (Schon's *Reflective Practitioner* was not to appear until 1983, after the journal writing began), and the opportunity to reflect with other teachers about teaching and professional development was reason enough to agree to think on paper about it. Three brief portraits will illustrate how each teacher used the process of writing for personal–professional reflection.[2]

Portrait of a Teacher: Judy
'Writing is a chance to know myself'

At 31, Judy was in her tenth year of teaching at the primary level in a medium-sized suburban community. She and her husband, Kurt, were the parents of a two-year-old daughter. Kurt, a manager in business, had a difficult time understanding why Judy spent so much time on school work, grading, thinking, planning and constructing teaching aids. Further, he was minimally interested in discussing her teaching day with her.

Although the principal of Judy's school was affable, and Judy described herself as 'outgoing', she lamented little opportunity to engage in meaningful professional conversations at school. 'Why aren't our in-services relevant?' 'Why can't our lounge talk be deeper? More collegial?' 'Why aren't we teachers professionally supported commensurate with our responsibilities?'

Judy jumped at the opportunity to become part of a research project where other teachers and the researcher were to explore teaching and professional development over a year's time. Judy, along with the other project participants, would keep a personal–professional journal and discuss her thoughts, feelings and experiences as a teacher at weekly seminar sessions. Judy looked forward to the chance to meet other teachers and to participate in the seminar, but she began the writing with trepidation.

'What do I write about?' 'When do I write?' Because Judy was writing to explore her own teaching and professional development, she wrote as if she were talking to herself. Unlike many teachers starting from such a broad purpose, Judy immediately began to question herself on paper. She wrote of her apprehensions of working with other teachers ('I hope I'm up to working with such talented professionals!') and of dilemmas she recognized in her teaching ('Why did I do that instead of this?'). Throughout her journal are comments about her difficulty with the act of writing and especially of forming a 'writing habit', of finding time and a quiet place to reflect. She usually wrote at home at night but sometimes during her discretionary time (art, music, lunch, recess) at school.

Judy found writing to be cathartic. 'Just writing makes me feel better!' She found that she could think on paper and work out some of her problems and dilemmas. Because she wrote as she thought, her writing has an action quality. It is not always in full sentences. The more she wrote, the more she was able to see patterns in her behavior and intentions, and in her children's behavior. She found herself writing on different levels: a surface, descriptive level, and a deeper, more introspective level. She became able to differentiate when she was writing on either level. The more she wrote, the faster she was able to move to the deeper level. She also experienced significant discomfort when she 'went in too deeply' and intentionally returned to a 'surface level' until she was ready to return to 'deeper' concerns or introspection.

Writing for Judy became 'a contract with myself'. When she discovered something through her writing she felt compelled to do something about it, to act, rather than to 'push it aside like I would have done before'.

What else did Judy find out about herself as a teacher? What were some of the actions she was moved to make? She was able to view herself as a finite being; she saw the humanness of her endeavors as a teacher, and the complexity of her responsibilities. She increased her ability to accept herself, and to face and learn from her 'mistakes'. She saw how her feelings about (and affection toward) children influenced her teaching decisions (for example, a child was not retained whom she determined should have been 'if only I had written about David too'). She began to see how some children received less attention than others. As she wrote about some of her frustrations, she began to identify areas of concern that she then addressed with colleagues. She found the strength and self confidence to start raising questions and disagreeing with her administrator where previously she felt anxiety and a reticence to broach her concerns with him. On the home front, but certainly related to school, she became aware of her defensiveness and anger at her husband for his lack of interest in her teaching.

Summing up some of her thoughts on reflective writing, Judy wrote:

Writing. A chance to know myself. Yes. I know myself, after all I live with myself, but this was a chance to sit down and actually confront myself. Good and bad. *Self help*: I made promises in writing that I had to keep — levels of writing became a *way of thinking*. I've begun to think in terms of how I'd write about this. *An author* — For no one else but myself. I never knew that I could produce so much if only for me. As I look back, I realize that I needed to be more objective .... I couldn't see some existing problems. I was really close to my class. Because of writing, I'm beginning to see that again. As I look at children, I try to really 'see' them, their daily lives, what affects them. I also see things more in-depth; I analyze more. This is a major result of my writing. It's helped me to do this. I'm a better teacher. I feel more confident. I'm able to handle stress better.

Portrait of a Teacher: Carole
The writing itself was very beneficial to me
personally because it made me look at my teaching
philosophy and how I was dealing with students,
parents, and administrators. I was forced
through writing to take a look at myself.

Carole was born in a large northern city in the Midwest in the winter of 1952. The middle child of a large family, she took responsibility (like her older sisters) for her younger siblings while their mother worked domestically to support the family. 'Carole will be the teacher in this family', her mother frequently reminded them. Like many of her friends, Carole was assisted in her education by the Follow-Through Program for promising children from low income families. Her studies were difficult at the nearby small liberal arts college she attended, but with hard work and help in developing study skills from Follow-Through, she graduated and became 'the teacher in this family'.

Having taught at the primary level in two inner city schools in her hometown, Carole and her new husband, John, moved to a small college town about an hour's drive away. Carole began teaching in a system that was culturally different to her. As the only black teacher, she felt lonely though people were 'friendly'.

During her ninth year of teaching, she joined Judy and other teachers on a project to look at teaching and professional development. Very active in the local and state teacher's organization and in the minority caucus (an organization to further racial, ethnic and cultural understanding), Carole was a particularly promising candidate to explore teaching and professional development. At the time, she was separated from her husband.

Carole began writing by jotting down topics as they occurred to her and then expanding on them later. Her writing style was fairly formal. She wrote in complete thoughts and sentences and rarely, if ever, rewrote or extended her thoughts in the margins. The act of writing was not difficult, but finding time to tuck away, given full teaching and professional organization commitments, church, and an exercise schedule was not easy. She, like Judy, found writing to be cathartic.

She found herself unleashing on paper 'many of the frustrations that had accumulated during my first eight years of teaching'. She was surprised by her complaints, not realizing, she said, that she kept them inside.

When I first began writing, I cited mainly those things about teaching that were not to my satisfaction. When I look back I was very disenchanted about where I was as a teacher and my enthusiasm as a teacher. I had thought many times about leaving this profession ... just to get a break from the many demands that teachers receive from students, administrators, parents and the community.

Recording her frustrations and sharing some of them with colleagues seemed to allow Carole to concentrate on her teaching. She wrote of dilemmas and began to use her journal to record action research as she undertook to learn more from the children. She focused on reading and language arts. This had been a source of frustration for her for what she discovered to be several reasons. A reading consultant spent a day or two a week in the building, but worked with very few of Carole's children. Yet, to Carole's disgruntlement, the consultant made decisions on what individual children 'should be reading'. 'But how does she know? She doesn't even *know* these children!' Carole moaned. A new reading series had been adopted and Carole and her colleagues had their hands full mastering the more complex and comprehensive program. Not long before report card time, reading tests were administered followed by orders from the reading consultant that children were to be graded based on standardized scores on the test. 'But I could have moved the children along faster had I known before it would determine their grades!' Carole wrote of her frustrations.

Carole's journal documents her growing understanding of the reading series and of her research with the children regarding reading and language arts. 'What is reading to the children?' she wondered. So, she conducted a survey. (Examples: Q. Why do people read? *Responses*: 'It wouldn't be fun if when you grew up you can't read.' 'So if your friends give them a letter they'll know how to read it.' Q. How can you tell you're a good reader? *Responses*: 'You can read fast.' 'You know your *b*'s from your *d*'s.' 'When you don't make any mistakes.' 'If you can read four books a day.' 'If you don't have no trouble with no words.') From this and subsequent study, she learned more about how the children thought and felt about aspects of the curriculum. She began to recognize the differences in perception between herself and the children, and among the children themselves.

Another area Carole selected to study was math. She found that 'lots of times they are able to do the work correctly but very seldom do they truly understand the process they are using'. She was surprised at the children's candor and honesty in offering their opinions when she asked for them. 'They remembered [at the end of the year] vividly the times we had popcorn in math class, and the time we used lollipops for counting ... for next school year I should work on making math more fun for *all* students.'

In addition to finding out more about how her children experienced school, and increasing her knowledge about their home lives, Carole learned some significant things about herself.

> I began to appreciate myself and my contribution to education. I began to realize that it's not what others think of me as a teacher but how I view myself. Several times I wrote about the need for recognition and praise from administrators and I'm sure that this is a need that I have that many other teachers also share .... .

Carole found the 'praise' she sought in her writing and she began to appreciate the subtle (and sometimes not so subtle!) indications of growth and satisfaction from the children.

Carole feels that she is more aware and more sensitive to the needs of children and to the complexities of teaching. She learned 'that I have faults that I was not aware of. My attachment to my students affects my life outside of school and perhaps my relationship with my spouse.' She learned that there are 'certain things that I'll never be able to change'. And, especially through collegial discussion, she learned that 'the same problems I've had difficulty dealing with are common to other teachers too'.

Perhaps of greatest significance to Carole, she began to see the interactive nature of her home and school lives. According to Carole, the most influential factor in her school life was her personal problems at home. 'Because things were lacking in my marriage, I devoted much time to my teaching and became very attached to my students.' Having discovered the consuming role that teaching played in her life, Carole resolved to work toward a better balance.

Portrait of a Teacher: Jerry
'How often do we question ourselves?'

The thought of becoming a teacher did not occur to Jerry until he was 22 and had been in the Air Force for four years. In fact, the idea of college had until then been 'something for other people'. It was there he met Sue, who later became his wife. Sue is a school psychologist and, according to Jerry, 'It's great to have a spouse in a related field. She understands my job and I hers.'

Jerry has spent six years teaching in the primary grades at a kinder-garten-through-grade-two school in an upper-middle-class bedroom community (14,000 population) bordering a middle-sized industrial city. The school system has a fine reputation and Jerry feels quite comfortable working with the children.

Writing was not new to Jerry. He wrote poetry and occasionally kept diary-like notes on topics of interest, 'I enjoy writing, just for me though.' Writing about his teaching and professional development was new. 'But how can I write about teaching? Teaching is like breathing — you just do it!' Jerry began by writing about individual children. He wrote journalistically, descriptively, and subjectively. He later commented on his previous writing, 'My biases shine!' He wrote of his teaching day, of incidents that amused or perplexed him. He also wrote about conversations with his closest colleagues, Beverly, Jane, and Karen.

Writing, like his composing of poetry, working construction, and playing the guitar and singing, is a form of creative expression for Jerry. Writing is cathartic, and for the most part he enjoys the process more than the product.

He found himself taking side journeys into language, and would think on words and phrases and their meanings and values. 'What is *good*?' he mused and proceeded to define the different uses of the word 'good'. Jerry found that the longer he wrote, the more aware he became of his teaching, of happenings around the school, and of his interactions with others. Jerry felt that this increasing attention to detail and attending to events as they happened was largely due to his growing habit of looking at his teaching life 'as if I was going to write about it even when I'm not planning to'. While Jerry saw many benefits of this growing awareness, it posed some real difficulties too.

The *self-inspection* Jerry found himself engaged in was quite disconcerting. He felt the urge to return to more carefree times and places, and during one particularly difficult (and growth-producing) time, he said:

I've come back away from looking at myself because I think I went too far. I think in writing ... we are questioning ourselves ... and I think there is very little precedent set for us to do that. Yet, I think when we look at the whole concept of professional growth, that's a piece of it. Yes, you have to do it.

Commenting on his writing at the end of the project, Jerry wrote:

The journal was a close inspection. A chance, a delightful chance for me to speak my subjective mind and have someone actually read it. It makes all the differnce in the world. It was frequently a chore. I realize, now, because I didn't necessarily want to confront myself. The journal offered insights and revealed a lot of my inner self to me. It admits that I care and commits me to my observations. Scary in a way. How often do we questions ourselves?

An important concomitant to writing, for Jerry, was collegial discussion. Although he began writing *only for himself*, Jerry slowly began to share his ideas and selected parts of his writing with other teachers. Writing and discussion became interactively supportive of his professional development. Sometimes he stated his problems before he wrote about them; other times he wrote about them and then spoke with colleagues about them:

I'm glad to know I do not stand alone . . . defending one's position calls for reflection and close inspection. Even while wrestling with my own feelings and motives verbally, I was always received with compassion and understanding. No better feeling than to trust one's peers enough to strip the veneer which masks your motives; inspect yourself and redress, to face tomorrow a bit more prepared.

Jerry discovered how much of his home life influenced his school life and vice versa. He discovered the significance of professional dialogue, and how important *trust* was to enable reflection with others and with himself. "I can say I've grown reflective. I move a bit slower — to savor instead of merely taste. I enjoy. I yield. I trust myself more — it opens many doors.'

Summary Themes

The teachers' journals chronicled events, thoughts, and feelings. In general, teachers moved from 'What should I write?' to describing their teaching, their thoughts and feelings about their settings, colleagues, parents and students, to using writing as an analytical tool and a vehicle for introspection. They found writing to be therapeutic and were surprised at the intensity of feelings they found on their diary pages. All teachers experienced catharsis in writing and discomfort, which some attributed to dealing with new realizations. For some teachers introspective writing proved to be quite painful; some stopped writing.

As teachers reviewed what they had written (in the beginning with reluctance), they saw patterns in their own and their children's behavior. They connected events and circumstances and became increasingly aware of how their moods influence their behavior. Writing seemed to promote a consciousness of behavior which might otherwise have been 'just lived'.

Several teachers expressed surprise at the number of their complaints. They did not see themselves as 'complainers', yet their writing contained numerous complaints. One teacher wrote that over the year her complaints became concerns which prodded her to action. Another teacher felt that her initial months of writing were spent letting out pent-up frustrations from her first several years of teaching and that this was probably the reason for so many 'negative things' in her journal. Finally, there was movement in writing toward reflection, analysis, introspection and action.

Several themes emerge across portraits:

Teacher isolation Each of the teachers were isolated in at least one of the following ways: (1) *physical* isolation, where for most of the day they remained in their classrooms with doors closed; (2) *temporal* isolation, where scheduling determined when and with whom they could interact; and, (3) *psychological* isolation, where administrators and support persons are perceived in specific roles which rarely include conscious personal–professional development relationships. The currently prevailing media image of the teaching profession, and perceived pressure from others, seemed to exacerbate existing problems of time and stress associated with perceived curricular priorities. They experienced *social isolation*, where teachers have little opportunity to see others in other roles; *intellectual isolation* where teachers are cut off from meaningful adult stimulation and discussion; and related to the others and perhaps most basic, an *isolation from themselves*. They rarely consciously reflected on what they did and why. Maxine Greene writes that 'persons must be roused to self reflectiveness; they must be moved to search' (1982, pp. 3–4). This form of isolation from oneself, and 'the search' appears to be fundamental to all the other types of isolation.

Teachers said that one of the most important aspects of journal sharing was to come into meaningful contact with other teachers. 'Just to find out I'm not alone'; '. . . and find out that others feel this way too'. 'I never though about what I think before.' Although teachers do reflect as part of everyday life, the conscious act of reflection appears to be on a different level. Comfort with self, communication with self, appear to open and enrich communications with others (Jersild, 1955).

Self image Teachers explicity and implicitly lamented the image that they felt 'the public' held of them. They expressed resentment at the frequency with which others tell them, or imply to them, what they should be doing. Supervisors, parents, reading teachers, school psychologists, and administrators appear to neglect the teacher's perspective. 'I just wish they would listen to me sometimes.' Self-image is in part derived from the interactions teachers have with others. With whom they come in contact and under what circumstances become very important to the images they hold of themselves. When they feel 'low-man on the totem pole' they feel helpless. When they feel threatened, they become defensive and rigid in defense of their egos. Teachers are unlikely to 'face themselves' under threatening circumstances. Their constructs become impermeable (Kelly, 1955). Their images continue to be shaped by those in positions to influence them, or who have power over them.

Discrepancies between roles, responsibilities, power and control, and support While teachers perceive and define their roles as 'shaping tomorrow's future' through the children they teach — a role they often mentioned — they feel a distressing dissonance between the importance of this responsibility, and the lack of resources and control over their own decision–making and behavior. 'Teacher-proof' curriculum materials, school board mandated curricula, state and district required content and processes (with, for example, an exact number of minutes spent daily on reading), and bureaucratic procedures necessary to get assistance, each send messages and create images of teachers that are at discrepancy with the weight of caring their for children. This is clearly opposed to the training function which appears to be what is advocated through testing and mandated content. 'In-service training', which in most schools is defined as a day or two of speakers and workshops is a far cry from the staff development activity these teachers define as necessary to carry out their responsibilities. Teachers wrote about and discussed, for example, how frustrated they become when a child's problems are beyond their control, Children's social and emotional development are a top priority for these teachers, yet they find themselves 'pushing' children who are developmentally different from the 'standards' they must try to achieve. They ask: 'Who helps you to deal with the social and emotional needs of your children?'

When Educators Keep Journals

Keeping a journal which includes entries for different purposes and writing of different types provides a rich base for reconstructing experiences and constructing portraits of teaching, of oneself as well as of others. The journal is potentially a comprehensive and evolving data base and case study for summative and formative evaluation over which the writer retains control.

What happens when educators keep professional journals? The following is a summary of things that can happen:

There is a permanent record Talk, too frequently disappears into the airwaves. We can return to writing from multiple perspectives. We can plan, hypothesize, record current and past experiences, as well as plan for the future. No other form of documentation appears to be as effective and efficient for recording from the breadth of our teaching lives. Whereas a video tape captures actions, it is expensive and cumbersome and has limitations for tapping the breadth and depth of our thinking, of the meanings that lie beneath our behaviors. Talking into a tape recorder to record ideas of the moment, which can be written about later, is another potentially useful tool in journal writing. Writing has the advantage of easy access and comprehensiveness in what can be recorded.

Writing necessitates time out for reflection With all the motion and outside 'input' into teaching, most of us rarely take time to 'just think'. Reflection has been relegated to a luxury rather than as an essential part of practice. Like the fast pace clips on *Sesame Street* which are designed to keep children glued to the program we might wonder toward what end keeping teachers mesmerized in motion (that is, without the discomfort of thought) contributes either to the quality of our students' education or to professional growth.

Patterns, themes and the flow of life become apparent over time Much of teaching is filled with what one teacher describes as 'coping with 20 second holocausts', and as Jackson (1968) estimated, with making over 200 decisions each hour. There is very little time to become aware of the flows and patterns of life as they occur. We act on situational perceptions yet our perceptions are dependent on what we see and experience. Eisner makes a distinction between 'looking' and 'seeing': *looking* is a physical act while *seeing* is conscious achievement (Eisner, 1982). Or, as Tripp (1985) puts it, we tend to function on 'autopilot'. Only through time can we see patterns and themes in our lives. Writing over time makes seeing patterns and themes possible.

Learning from practice can increase awareness, self knowledge, and confidence Unlike Sisyphus, we need not keep repeating our defeats. As we record and peruse our professional experience and note patterns and themes, ways that we and our pupils influence and are influenced by our circumstances, we learn about ourselves and our pupils. We begin to understand why we do what we do, and can turn unconscious behaviors into conscious ones where we can change them when appropriate. Self knowledge and control over our actions (that is, engaging in purposeful action), promotes self confidence. There is something powerful in being able to justify what we do, and in knowing what we know. As we document, we find ourselves becoming more aware of our surroundings and the contexts within which we teach. We find ourselves anticipating and defining events rather than just responding to them.

Writing appears to bring to a conscious level much that was tacit knowledge The process of writing, whether thinking on paper or creating, or playing with words and ideas is dialectical. Images and ideas seem at times to appear magical and new, providing material for reaction. As we react other information darts in, coalesces, unrelated in our consciousness until that time when one idea calls forth others. We begin to understand how we know, what we sensed we knew.

Writing provides a comprehensive and ongoing data base for professional and collegial development as well being a part of these processes itself Using words to describe and tell the story of one's teaching enlarges the lexicon available to describe practice. It serves as an ongoing evaluation system for individual teachers, and it also provides bases for collegial discussion. Slowly, as we write and feel more comfortable and aware of our ideas, questions, and challenges, we begin to communicate with others which in turn enriches practice.

Reflecting on practice through writing can provide a rich, comprehensive, and evolving data base for the study and conduct of teaching. Not only does it enable us to gain personal insights into our work, it also provides us with ways of looking at teaching and describing it in words that we can use to communicate with and learn from others, to gain insight and understanding, and to improve the quality of communication and collaborative action necessary to bring education and schooling closer to democratic principles. Writing for different reasons, and in different ways, enables us to gain different perspectives on the multiple dimensions of practice. Influences on teaching and learning, and school life, can be explored through writing: human interrelationships and interactions, the ecology of the school including school and classroom climate, curriculum development and resources, teaching methods and processes, values, intentions, and aims, as well as school, community, and national contexts.

Self evaluation is an integral and essential part of professional development. It is dialectically formative and summative. Keeping a personal-professional journal is both a way to record the journey of teaching and growing, and to experience the processes purposely and sensitively. It is a method for exploring our inner worlds and histories; of probing the educational and cultural milieus within which we teach; and of inquiring into the meanings of teaching. Professional development provides the context within which assessment and appraisal reside and make sense — following from practice and the thoughtful and articulated concerns of professionals who choose to live and teach and learn with young people.

Notes

1. Conceptual and methodological issues related to research and presentation of life histories and psychobiographies are clearly presented in *Life Histories and Psychobiography: Explorations in Theory and Method* by William McKinley Runyan (1984). Examples drawn from accounts of individual lives over the last several centuries serve to illustrate alternative perspectives.
2. For more comprehensive portraits see Holly, 1987; 1989.

References

CHAVIS, M. (1978). Culture circle — Introduction to *Pedagogy in process: The letters to Guinea-Besseau by Paulo Freire*. New York: The Seabury Press.

COLES, R. (1981). Children and ethical concepts. Distinguished Scholar Lecture, Kent State University, Kent, Ohio.

COMBS, A. W., and SNYGG, D. (1959). *Individual behavior: A perceptual approach to behavior*. New York: Harper & Row.

EISNER, E. W. (1979). *The educational imagination*. New York: Macmillan.

EISNER, E. W. (1982). On play, the arts, imagination and the invention of mind. Distinguished Lecture, Association for Childhood Education International, St Louis.

EISNER, E. W. (1985). *The educational imagination: On the design and evaluation of school programs*. New York: Macmillan.

ELKIND, D. (1983) Accommodating variations in school readiness. Distinguished Lecture, Thirty-eighth Continuing Conference Early Childhood Education, Kent State University, Kent.

ERAUT, M. (1985). The acquisition and use of educational theory by beginning teachers. Mimeographed paper.

GREENE, M. (1982). A general education curriculum: Retrospect and prospect. Paper presented at the American Educational Research Association Annual Conference, New York.

HARTLEY, D. (1985). *Understanding the primary school: A sociological analysis*. London, England: Croom Helm.

HOLLY, M. L. (1983). *Teacher reflections on classroom life: An empirical base for professional development*. Report to the National Institute of Education, Washington, DC ERIC #????

HOLLY, M. L. (1985). Professional development, writing, and evaluation. Paper presented at the 4th Cambridge Conference on Evaluation. Cambridge, England.

HOLLY, M. L. (1987). *Keeping a personal-professional journal* (2nd edn). Geelong, Victoria, Australia: Deakin University Press.

HOLLY, M. L. H. (1989). *Teacher Inquiry: Keeping a Personal-Professional Journal*. Portsmouth, NH: Heinemann.

JACKSON, P. (1968). *Life in classrooms*. New York: Holt, Rinehart & Winston.

JERSILD, A. (1955). *When teachers face themselves*. New York: Teachers College Press, Columbia University.

KUHN, T. (1962). *The structure of scientific revolutions*. Chicago, IL: University of Chicago Press.

LORTIE, D. C. (1975). *Schoolteacher: A sociological study*. Chicago: Chicago University Press.

MALLON, T. (1984). *A book of one's own: People and their diaries*. New York: Ticknor & Field.

POLANYI, M. (1967). *The tacit dimension*. New York: Doubleday.

PROGOFF, I. (1975). *At a journal workshop*. New York: Dialogue House.

RUNYAN, W. M. (1984). *Life histories and psychobiographies: Explorations in theory and methods*. Oxford, England: Oxford University Press.

SCHON, D. (1983). *The reflective practitioner: How professionals think in action.* New York: Basic Books.

SPRINTHALL, N. (1980) Adults as learners: A developmental perspective, In *Exploring issues in teacher education: Questions for future research.* G. Hall, S. Hord, and G. Brown, (eds), Austin, TX: Research and Development Center for Teacher Education, University of Texas at Austin.

TRIPP, D. (1985). From autopilot to critical consciousness: Problematizing successful teaching. Paper presented at the Conference on Curriculum Theorizing, Dayton.

WARNOCK, B. (1985). *Teacher, teach thyself: A new professionalism for our schools.* London, England: The Richard Dimbleby Lecture, British Broadcasting Corporation.

WATTS, A. (1951). *The wisdom of insecurity: A message for an age of anxiety.* New York: Pantheon.

13 Teachers as Professionals

Mary Louise Hulbert Holly and Carl Walley

It is teachers who, in the end, will change the world of the school
by understanding it, (Lawrence Stenhouse, 1985).

Understanding teaching and schooling takes teachers into many disciplines: the Sciences, Arts, Humanities, and Social Sciences, and
perhaps most importantly, Pedagogy. From teacher preparation
through continuing teacher education, teachers are on the one hand
generalists, and on the other, specialists.

Teachers use professional knowledge although they are often unaware that this is what it is. Every day, teachers use specialized
knowledge in the areas of human development and social relationships, the content and processes of teaching, and methods of inquiry
related to decision making. Progress in teaching is often difficult to
ascertain. Much in a student's development is visible through subtle
changes that only a teacher can see; growth and development appear
to be slow, even erratic, and learning is unpredictable. Cathy, a
first-year teacher, asks, 'Am I a good teacher? Will I be able to teach
these kids so they can learn?' By becoming aware of the knowledge
she uses, uncovering the implicit theories which guide her, and
evaluating her teaching, she can respond to her own questions.

Knowledge in Teaching

Years ago, Jersild (1955) and Lortie (1975) pointed out that teaching
was complex, human and social. To teach well, they suggested,
demands self knowledge and acceptance, and openness to experience.
There is little reason to believe that this has changed. Without self-

awareness we continue to 'teach through our own biases and distortions' (Jersild, 1955). Knowledge of human development — child and adult — is essential, not only for understanding ourselves and the students we teach, but as a basis for building the interpersonal relationships that are an integral part of teaching — with colleagues, parents, administrators and community members. Teacher education, especially at the pre-service level, has been directed toward gaining knowledge of subject matter and methods of teaching. Both methods of inquiry (which refers to theorizing, testing ideas, and using research and data gathering methods necessary to making professional judgments in teaching and curriculum development) and human development have, until recently, received considerably less attention.

As teachers, we work simultaneously in three time zones: yesterday — *that must be connected with,* today — *that must be attended to,* and tomorrow — *towards which teaching must aim.* We work for several masters: ourselves, students and the students' parents (who are not always parallel), administrators, and community members. And, regardless of institutional provisions, teachers have a professional obligation to continue professional development and learning, not the least challenging of which is contributing to a professional milieu in which professional and staff development are possible.

What are the foci for teacher's continuing professional education? Teachers, unlike medical doctors, bankers, lawyers, athletes, and accountants, elect to live six hours a day, 180+ days a year, teaching and caring for large numbers of young people. Rarely are they alone. Rarely do they spend time with other adults. Most of their time is spent being responsible for the lives and learning of at least twenty children, frequently more.

With whom, then, do teachers interact? Mainly children. This has not infrequently been related to problems of isolation (Lortie, 1975), of defensiveness (Knoblock and Goldstein, 1971), and lack of intellectual stimulation (Nias, 1984). When too much time is spent with children teachers can become so preoccupied with current exigencies that larger issues and professional concerns are either not addressed or passed over with little depth in consideration.

What characterizes the intellectual lives of teachers? How do teachers learn (Jersild, 1955); in what ways do they model what they ask of their students; in what ways do they teach themselves (Combs, 1965)? Under what circumstances do teachers interact with other teachers, parents, administrators, staff members? When do teachers talk with other teachers? What do they talk about? To what extent do they talk about professional issues? According to Little (1982), successful teachers and environments are where collegial discussion centers on professional matters. What do teachers do with the time for collegial discussion that they have available? Before school, recess times, lunch, after school and during periods when they are not in their classrooms? What do teachers read? When do they read? What is the nature of professional discourse? To what extent do teachers talk about their teaching? . . . to students? . . . about other matters? To what extent do teachers rely on or seek out each other for professional feedback? Too frequently, teachers find themselves isolated from an adult intellectual life.

Whereas successful teachers have always exercised specialized knowledge and understanding, they are rarely called upon to make public accounts of their knowledge and skill. With time and support to focus on teaching and schooling, teachers can gain deeper appreciation of significant aspects of practice. It means bringing to a conscious level much of what already is known. Becoming active critics, enabling others to understand more of the complexities of educational processes, and gaining appreciation and respect for professional teachers, is a challenge. Neither the cellular organization of the school, nor the history of women in education lends support for such advocacy. Teachers have remained isolated from one another, and women, who have always outnumbered men in teaching, rarely have been in leadership positions to express and assert their professional opinions in public forums (Spender, 1982).

How do teachers understand teaching?   How do teachers make sense out of the dynamic and complex worlds of society and community, the forms of representation the culture affords and transmits through teaching? How do teachers convey, facilitate, draw out, extend, and orchestrate people and resources so that the young might come to know themselves and the world in their multidimensional richnesses? How do teachers balance the complexity of their philosophical assumptions and values, and a felt responsibility for each child's future?

If teachers are, as Boyer (1983) says, keys to quality in schools, how do they become empowered to help themselves? How do they become their own best critics and acknowledged professionals in teaching? How are they helped to find their own voices? How are teachers to be supported in their professional growth? How might educational environments be designed to promote questions, reflection, and collegial discussion of matters of consequence (Saint Exupery, 1943)? We will find responses to these questions embedded at the interface between theory-and-practice.

Making Theory and Practice Explicit

> Doubt is not a pleasant mental state but certainty is a ridiculous one
> Voltaire (Francois Marie Arouet; 1694–1778).

Ignorance might be bliss, but it contributes little to professional development or to the development of the profession. Asking ourselves *what we do* as teachers, and *why*, may make us uncomfortable, but as we begin to define and to accept our behavior and motives, we become more aware of the complexity of teaching, and thus more open to change and to alternative perspectives.

A great deal of knowledge in teaching is tacit, knowledge that we cannot readily explain with words. Sometimes it has been referred to as intuition. This is the base we consult when a child conveys, through subtle body language, needs that we cannot describe, yet to which we can react; knowing when a child needs encouragement, a new challenge or help; when a colleague is troubled; when a lesson is over, or when it should be delayed. Teaching is filled with complexities that the conscious mind does not readily contemplate. Tacit knowledge informs much of everyday teaching practice.

We are guided by our own theories of teaching, our assumptions and ideas about the circumstances of teaching, and our roles and responsibilities as teachers. Just as the young child cannot usually respond to the eager parent's question, 'What did you learn in school today?', the teacher cannot always respond to 'Why did you do that?'. Both the child and the teacher were involved and not accounting. They were thinking as they were acting; they were not thinking about their thinking. And, so it is with much of teaching. When someone asks us for an account of our behavior, 'we find ourselves at a loss, or produce descriptions that are obviously inappropriate .... Our knowing is *in* our action' (Schon, 1983).

To be advocates and educational critics, able to render in tangible forms more of what we know, we need to make explicit our theories: To think about our thinking — both for personal–professional growth, and for the development of teaching as a profession. Research on teacher thinking, and the ways teachers construct knowledge and make decisions can be useful in gaining understanding into our thinking, but, like other theories in development, they present 'partial pictures' — indications rather than explanations. The most important theories are those which guide practice. Teaching and learning, and theory and practice, are dialectical — each reciprocally influences the other. Freire (1971) speaks of 'praxis', or ethical action, a term derived from the Greek word for practice which was characterized by doing. Unlike *techne*, where the product to be made was known in advance, teaching was guided by ethics because the end could not be known in advance (Carson, 1984).

Stenhouse (19 –1982) once wrote that 'theory is gradually built up from the examination of accumulated observations. It is partial and fragmentary'. A phenomenologist might reply that a theory is always complete for the moment, that it always makes sense given the information and circumstances — that there is no such thing as a complete theory for different times and places. A theory is always partial because it reflects what the person can know and be at a given time — which from an outside perspective can never be everything. Part of the excitement of teaching, or theorizing and testing out one's theories, is that we are always working with 'fragments', or incomplete pictures. It is the weaving together of what seems disparate, making connections that allude casual, or sometimes even focused observation, that gives teaching its life as a profession. This is one of the problems with the further standardization of teaching and curriculum implementation — as our responsibilities become narrowed, so too do our opportunities to solve the non-standardized and developmental dilemmas which confront us. Since the contemporary focus is on skills and techniques (*techne*), rather than on understanding and insight, the *why* of teaching appears too frequently crowded out by the *how to*.

The more we learn about teaching, of our 'theories in use', the more articulate we become about the 'why' of what we do. The more we focus on and document teaching, the more visible is progress and the more explicit are our theories. We will never be able to finish all that we would like to accomplish in teaching, because, like our theories, our aspirations are always in transition. The sense of satisfaction and professional empowerment that can come from documenting the journey and becoming aware of the nuances that define educational practice and progress, are more important than closure on questionable products. With the ability to describe practice, the more focused and articulate we can become in discussing practice and professional issues with others, and the more likely is progress toward shared educational aims.

Evaluation as a Vehicle for Professional Development

With growing concern for 'higher quality' and 'excellence' in schools, it is not surprising to find the rise of competency testing and new forms and systems for accountability, of what is perceived to be progress in students' learning. These trends seem to be at cross purposes with the aim of a dynamic, evolving, educated and inquiring citizenry.

> The dominant metaphor for today's education is the Newtonian Machine: The school is a more or less well oiled machine that processes (educates?) children. In this sense, the education system (school) comes complete with production goals (desired end states); raw material (children); a physical plant (school building); a 13-stage assembly line (grades K–12); plant supervisors (principals); trouble shooters (consultant, diagnosticians); quality control mechanisms (discipline, rules, lock-step progress through stages, conformity); interchangeability of parts (teacher proof curriculum, 25 students per processing unit, equality of treatment); uniform criteria for all (standardized testing interpreted on the normal curve); and basic product available in several lines of trim (academic, vocational, business, general). Is this reminiscent of Fords, Apples, and Big Macs? (Sawada & Caley, 1985, pp. 14–15)

Tangible short-term results, generally related to lower level skills (for example, recalling facts), have come at the cost of less tangible and higher level mental processes (such as critical thinking). The effects of testing on curriculum development and teaching, for example, can be significant. Eisner (1985), for one, has made impassioned pleas for balance in a curriculum that he finds to be shaped increasingly be testing and political forces, rather than by professional judgment and democratic aims.

While it is not surprising from an historical perspective to see responses to calls for 'increased quality' take the form of those which can be measured easily, it also seems logical for educators to use this opportunity to take a long, hard look at schooling within present societal contexts, and to reconceptualize aims, roles and responsibilities.

The continuing push for accountability (with movement from evaluation to assessment, and toward narrower and more explicit forms of knowing) places emphasis on *knowing in words*, while ignoring and constraining knowing in any broader sense. There is the danger, voiced by Einstein (1879–1955), that 'perfection of means and confusion of aims characterize our age'. Only within the broader context of professional development can the evaluation and assessment of teaching truly be understood.

To know teaching, we must tap this tacit and functional knowledge of teachers. If teachers are a critical source of knowledge about teaching, then they are equally a critical source of knowledge for evaluation. What, for example, do teachers identify as important aspects of teaching and learning to assess? In what ways are they involved in evaluation and assessment? In what ways do assessment procedures and subsequent findings inform and advise teachers? In what ways does assessment contribute to evaluation?

While assessment instruments are being designed, we continue to neglect the most effective and complex instrument, and data source, available — the teacher. Only the teacher lives and teaches daily within the classroom. Of all the partial pictures held by persons who are interested in schools, teachers' experiences hold the most promise for vivid portrayals of the dynamic relationships within classrooms.

To really benefit from others' perceptions, assessment needs to be part of an ongoing endemic process of appraisal. Hartley (1985), for example, aptly describes how a head teacher subtly influences both the school's academic and social environments without conscious intent. As long as assessment is something *done to* teachers rather than *with* them, then hopes of broadening its scope and contributing to ongoing evaluation as part of schooling and professional life are slim.

To help in defining and clarifying the relationships between and among 'quality' and 'accountability' and to broaden the framework within which these are addressed, educators in England published a booklet in 1985 entitled *Quality in Schools: Evaluation and Appraisal* (HMSO). They set out the following definitions.

Evaluation is a general term used to describe any activity by the institution or the LEA [local education authority] when the quality of provision [educational services] is the subject of systematic study;

Review indicates a retrospective activity and implies the collection and examination of evidence and information;

Appraisal emphasizes the forming of qualitative judgments about an activity, a person, or an organization;

Assessment implies the use of measurement and grading based on known criteria (HMSO, 1985, p. 7).

In the past these terms have been used to mean many different things. Here, we see them interrelated. Assessment, appraisal, and review are part of evaluation. Evaluation, in turn, is for appraisal. Appraisal is linked to the essence of teaching: forming qualitative judgments. On what bases do we make professional judgments? Evaluation is now recognized to be at the heart of teaching and curriculum development, an essential aspect of quality and of professional practice. As Barry MacDonald once said, 'evaluation is, itself, an educative process' (1985).

'How do I evaluate what I do? Who sees me teach?' Few teachers view other teachers teaching. And, few teachers are observed even by administrators or supervisors after their first few years of teaching. Even then, observations are infrequent and for limited amounts of time. Several years ago, over 100 teachers were asked: 'If you wanted help in evaluating your work, just for your own professional development, to whom might you go?' It came as a surprise to learn that not one teacher seemed even slightly wary of this prospect. 'Boy, wouldn't that be nice. To have someone to talk to about *my* teaching!' Forty-three teachers said, 'Other teachers.' The next most frequently mentioned response was 'Students' (15 per cent), which was followed by 'Myself' (14 per cent). When asked why they offered these responses, most teachers gave reasons such as: 'It would have to be somebody who is there long enough to actually see what I do'; 'It would have to be someone who would be able to tell me about teaching in a humanistic way.' Ten per cent of the teachers said they would go to the principal (Holly, 1977).

Most frequently classroom observations are conducted for purposes of evaluation through teacher-competence rating. Qualitative judgments about a teacher's practices (that is, teacher appraisal) too often have been made on disturbingly scant empirical data. Reports have been based on limited observations of teaching, and they have incorporated biases and distortions from the evaluator's values and perceptions. Teacher evaluation has taken place mainly for retention of the teacher's position during the first few years of practice. Infrequently has it been approached as an ongoing aid to professional development, or as a way to gain competence in gathering data for making teaching decisions. To be a significant contributor to another person's professional development the evaluator would have to be, as Jersild noted, endeavoring to identify and understand:

> his own unrecognized needs, fears, desires, anxieties, hostile impulses .... The process of gaining knowledge of self ... is not something an instructor *teaches* others. It is not something he does *to* or *for* them. It is something in which he himself must be involved (Jersild, 1955, p. 14).

Evaluation is an ongoing process that informs practice and contributes to 'the quality of provision' from multiple perspectives. Defining appropriate provisions, methods and scheduling for formative and summative evaluations, where there are opportunities to integrate and discuss self-evaluations and the evaluations of others, is the scaffolding for professional, staff and curriculum development. It contributes to what John Gardner (1962) described as designing a system to ensure its own continuous renewal.

Evaluation contributes to professional development when it enables us to look more deeply into our work, and when it enables us to learn from other educators and our profession. Highly successful practical methods of inquiry such as action-research and clinical supervision are designed to help educators to study schooling systematically, and build data bases for evaluation and development.

Discussing what is salient to the teacher's work, with a view to personal–professional development, shifts the responsibility and control of these efforts to those persons who *can* make the most difference — educators themselves. For educators, reflective self-evaluation involves clarifying, thinking, and identifying underlying assumptions and beliefs, and recognizing motives and behavior. Most importantly, it helps to translate implicit theories into a format which can be pondered alone and with others. When teachers document practice and analyze what happens, they create case studies, which are, in effect, stories of their teaching and learning. According to Shulman (1987), case studies contribute to 'the professional knowledge base' for practice.

Reflection in Action

To look at everyday practice differently sounds logical and relatively easy to do. In practice, however, the tacit and unpremeditated nature of much of teaching makes this complicated.

When studying teachers, artists, psychoanalysts and other occupational groups with teaching responsibilities, Donald Schon described what many educators believed implicitly, and others might have suspected — that teachers are reflective, they 'reflect in action'. In *The Reflective Practitioner: How Professionals Think in Action* (1983) he presented case studies of how practitioners 'think-in-action'.

When asked why they taught as they did, people often could bring to their own awareness, as well as to Schon's, the reasons for their behavior, *even though they had not been conscious of these reasons at the time*. Teaching, for them, as for most of us, is transactional. Communication between teacher and student, or therapist and psychoanalyst, was the medium through which thinking-in-action could be documented. As, for example, when an architecture student talked with her teacher about a drawing she had made, he asked her questions about the drawing and about why she had drawn certain features as she had. His teaching was based on her drawing and their conversation. It evolved through their interaction with her work.

Stated differently, teachers rely on situational perceptions and their own evolving theories. From this perspective it no longer is tenable to explain the perceived discrepancy between teachers' actions, and theories 'taught' them, with 'teachers are *atheoretical*'. The problem lies not with educators who do not learn theories, or use them, but with becoming aware and articulating theories-in-use. It means challenging much that is taken for granted; defining problems where none were seen; stepping out of practice and looking at it.

Perspective Transformation   Mezirow writes of perspective transformation which enables us to imagine ourselves in different contexts, and to transcend our everyday histories and circumstances (1977; 1981). He argues that adult learning differs from young peoples' learning in at least one fundamental way: 'Adults are capable of being consciously critical or *critically reflective.*' In contrast, the young are 'critically unselfconscious and usually unaware of how circumstances have contrived to indicate their relationships . . . .' Becoming conscious of:

> *why* we attach the meanings we do to reality, especially to our roles and relationships — meanings often misconstrued out of the uncritically assimilated half-truths of conventional wisdom and power relationships assumed as fixed — may be the most significant distinguishing characteristic of adult learning. It is only in late adolescence and in adulthood that a person can come to recognize being caught in his/her own history and reliving it (Mezirow, 1981, p. 24).

Each professional educator has the obligation to be what the philosopher Camus (1913–60) defined as an intellectual: *A mind that watches itself.*

One of the learnings basic to perspective transformation is 'the discovery that all has context' (Broughton, 1977); that conventional wisdom and power relationships exist within social and historical circumstances. This means that educators must step out of their everyday circumstances to examine them from different perspectives. How, for example, can I facilitate other peoples' learning if I cannot see and understand something about both my own and their circumstances? I must be able to imagine myself in different contexts, and be able to view students in theirs. This *does not* mean that I must experience the student's world as the student does to make new connections to teach, but it does mean that I must understand different perspectives and broader contexts than I understood when I was the student. Teaching necessitates being able to take multiple points of view, to hypothesize what *might have been* as well as to form ideas of *what is* and *what might be.* This is why educational and developmental theorists emphasize the importance of cognitive complexity and psychological maturity over more traditional goals such as training in techniques for professional development programs.

According to Mezirow, there are two paths to perspective transformation:

> one is a sudden insight into the very structure of cultural and psychological assumptions which has limited or distorted one's understanding of self and one's relationships. The other is move-

ment in the same direction that occurs by a series of transformations which permit one to revise specific assumptions about oneself and others until the very structure of assumptions becomes transformed. This is perhaps a more common pattern of development. The role transitions themselves are only opportunities for the kind of self-reflection essential for a transformation (Mezirow, 1981, p. 7).

In Levinson's longitudinal study (Levinson *et al.*, 1978), he found that transformations are often triggered by 'marker events' (or what Mezirow describes as disorienting dilemmas). These are problems for which we have no solutions — our usual ways of making sense and problem solving no longer work. The process itself is similar to what Kuhn (1962) describes as a 'paradigm shift'. It necessitates Piaget's process of accommodation.

Gaining perspective can be facilitated by communication. 'Human experience is brought into being through language. Restricted language codes can arbitrarily distort experience ...' (Mezirow, 1981, p. 3). Unfortunately, as Lortie (1975) and Waller (1932), among others, have pointed out, professional language in education is restricted by the history, structure, and organization of schooling, curriculum, and, the profession of teaching. The cellular organization of the school, the compartmentalization and fragmentation of the curriculum, the focus on narrow and short-term competencies for accountability, and the widening distance between teachers and administrators, all pose barriers to the kind of personal and collaborative, critical reflection from which a professional lexicon can develop. Awareness of these circumstances is a step toward overcoming the constraints they pose. Another step occurs when one understands the importance and interrelationships of action, of reflection, and the use of language to personal–professional development.

Bruner sees a universal direction of intellectual development moving from action — knowing *by knowing how to do* — to symbolic representation which primarily involves the use of language with rules for forming and transforming propositions and permitting representations *not only of what is, but also of what is not and what might be*. This requires the development of self consciousness which permits one to make the crucial distinction between one's own psychological reactions and external events. This self-awareness is a precondition for developing the capacity to categorize the same stimuli according to several different criteria or points of view.

Through symbolic representation one can dialogue with oneself, and, in imagination, construct the perspective of the other person. Perspective taking then becomes an indispensable heuristic for higher level cognitive and personality development (Mezirow, 1981, p. 19; emphasis added).

Professional reflection, critical reflectivity — the kind of self-reflection essential for a transformation — is difficult, if not impossible, unless we make time for it. Seeing the need to protect time, whether precipitated by an event or an evolving consciousness, is the necessary first step.

To make use of their 'intuitive' knowledge, teachers need support in constructing the realities of classroom life. Outside theories, while potentially important, help only in so far as they augment teachers' own developing explanations. While teachers continue to use their energies trying to protect themselves from growing public criticism, and in sifting through the academic theories of 'experts', they have found little energy, time, or enthusiasm left to explore their own ideas on teaching. Not only do teachers have limited license or incentive to uncover and present their views, either personally or collectively, many have little confidence in their ability (Lortie, 1975). Nor have they sufficiently concerned themselves with professional dialogue with others — another essential ingredient of professional development.

Curriculum Change and Perspective Transformation

In the section which follows we present portraits of two experienced teachers who, for different reasons, decided to participate in a major curriculum change in the school system where they taught. Though their questions and reservations regarding the curriculum 'innovation' (literature based reading, LBR,[1]) were different, they both found the processes of collegial curriculum development and implementation to be transformative in the way they taught reading, and also in the way they viewed teaching and themselves as teacher.

The first teacher, Mary, might tell you that she was 'slow to change from tried and true methods'. But she would also tell you that she always wanted to try the kinds of methods that she heard about in college classes. For example, her classroom contained the largest collection of children's books in the school but she never allowed the children to use them because she felt guilty taking time away from the basal reader. Bill, the school principal, was looking for volunteers to pilot the LBR program and selected Mary as a highly likely candidate for two reasons. On her own volition, she had become familiar with the new program and felt a strong affinity for it, and, she was a very competent and knowledgeable teacher. He knew her well enough to know that she would not 'jump at the chance' to be involved, and that she would need a nudge to join the group. As he thought about the program and the staff he surmised that 'She was the only logical choice.' Mary was skeptical, 'I just know he chose me because I was the only one available', but she agreed to participate. She had strong reservations about the program because she doubted her own ability to develop and implement it. The traditional reading program, the basal reader, was 'textbook oriented' and structured so that teachers would follow an explicit teacher's manual. The literature-based system relied on teachers to develop their own reading curriculum using literature and writing as major components to the program.

The project included 8 teachers at the early elementary level, 2 each from 4 schools. Four taught first grade for developmentally delayed youngsters; 4 taught heterogenously grouped second graders.

Karen, one of the first-grade teachers, not untypical of other teachers in the district, described her six years of teaching reading:

> I've always taught the bottom group and we never had a chance to teach the fun stuff. It was always drill, drill, drill — there was no fun for me or the kids. But instruction was so easy when I used the basal. The manual told me what to do and it wasn't my responsibility if it failed.

While Karen felt absolved of responsibility for the students' failures, her relief came at a premium. In her words, 'By my third year I was ready to quit teaching. I was so bored.' Ruth, a second-grade teacher with nine years of experience concurred with Karen's story of frustration. Ruth tells of feeling that for years 'I *did* reading to my kids. They hated it and so did I.' In an interview Ruth was asked about these expressed feelings toward reading instruction. This was not an easy topic to discuss because reading is generally regarded to be the heart of the curriculum, or, as Holdaway describes it: 'Reading has enjoyed the unassailable pre-eminence in schooling in the modern age ... it is the only doorway to Western, linear culture — the very symbol of education' (1979, p. 25). As if in pain, Ruth slowly and softly responded to a question asking her to expand on her statements about reading, 'I found it hard to drive to work a lot of mornings. I loved the kids, but I hated what I had to do to them.'

Project teachers were not unusual in their concerns about teaching reading. They were unusual because they had the opportunity and the support to develop a new program and to discuss their practice as a group every other week. A curriculum consultant (not evaluator) acted as facilitator and liaison between schools in the times between meetings.

In the two portraits which follow, we present what happened to two of the teachers as they developed and implemented the new program. Each of the eight teachers has a unique story, any of which could be represented here. Mary and Elizabeth were selected to show how two teachers with very different orientations and styles of teaching in the same school opened themselves to curriculum change, and perspective transformation.

Mary   Mary began teaching in Cambridge, the district's New England style community, in 1970. Cambridge is dominated by the corporate headquarters of a large investment company and many of the school's students are children of the corporation executives. Abutting the southwestern corner of the town green sits Cambridge Elementary School. A tall red brick building constructed in the 1920s stands in sharp contrast to the white colonial facade of the much newer corporation headquarters nearby. Inside Cambridge Elementary the marble halls glisten as an observer imagines children's voices of generations ago echoing back through time. Not much has changed in seventy years, physically or instructionally.

Mary's second-grade classroom is tucked away on the school's upper floor. She has been here her entire career: eighteen years. Mary describes herself as intensely shy and still unsure of her abilities. During the project's initial stages she tried to isolate herself from colleagues and voiced concern about her job security to the curriculum consultant. In time though, she accepted a new level of professional responsibility and sought involvement with fellow teachers. Mary's story portrays a teacher developing a new image of her professional competence and responsibility.

Despite her love of reading, Mary began the new reading program with what could be called fear and trepidation. Though her heart told her one thing, nagging uncertainty and self-doubt plagued her throughout much of the project as she held on to one concern, 'Are the children learning?' Fear that the students would not progress in achieving 'skills' led her to shelter herself from fellow teachers. Mary's door was always closed, its windows covered by paper. No one was invited in and few entered.

Mary was the only one of the eight project teachers to use the basal reader in combination with children's literature books. She juggled the two methods of reading despite her belief teaching both was counter-productive. She said, 'I skip pages in the basal reader. I'm not doing well in either method because I'm spread too thin. This is very frustrating.' She continued to teach this way despite of her belief that it was inconvenient for her and unproductive for the students. Mary used the literature-based reading to teach reading and she used the basal reader as an insurance policy. In her words, 'I believe in whole language, but I don't want to take a chance that I might be wrong. With the basal, if I fail, no one is going to criticize me.' Another form of insurance dealt with reporting progress to the parents. While other project teachers developed narrative evaluations to report student progress, Mary continued to give letter grades and to write narratives. It was as if Mary was teaching two classes simultaneously. Juggling two reading systems doubled her work, but it also provided security. Gradually Mary's security came from another source: teacher support seminars. The bi-weekly meetings were held to assist the pilot teachers. The meetings followed an informal agenda which stressed sharing concerns, hypothesizing and developing possible solutions, and sharing new ideas and experiences.

Mary shared knowledge about teaching reading and told of interesting projects she used to accompany books. Over time she gained confidence in sharing her ideas and questions; and, the group helped her to wean herself from her reliance on the basal reader. When she heard veteran teachers, especially respected teachers her age (49), report their successes and the risks they felt, Mary drifted from the teacher's manual. Initially she taught the basal three days a week and the alternative system two days a week. In December she reversed this and taught LBR three days per week. In February, Mary abandoned the basal system completely.

Two factors contributed to the demise of the basal in Mary's room. Bill, the principal, again sensing the circumstances, suggested to her that she shelve the basal text. She felt that this absolved her of responsibility and allowed her to feel less threatened. If she had shelved it before and failed, she was on her own. Now that the principal suggested she give it up, they were in it together.

Second, Mary had slowly begun to redefine her definition of achievement. What started out simply as 'success = high achievement on a standardized test', broadened to include student motivation and response to reading. The support group was important to one another in redefining success. One teacher said, for example, 'I don't care even if the test scores come out low (which they won't), my kids are just loving to read. And they never felt that way before!'

As Mary tried out new ideas and shared these with the other teachers who were also experimenting, they reinforced each others' 'risk-taking' and, they heard themselves talk about teaching and learning. What, in Mary's case, had started as 'a very shy voice', a teacher uncomfortable talking in a group of eight, became a strong voice talking about what she had always cared most about: *teaching*. She had never had the confidence before, nor had she thought that her work would be of interest to others. Here, at last, she not only could talk with others about teaching, she could talk with them about teaching reading. But, most importantly, she learned in a safe environment that teaching involves trying out, testing, and evaluating. And, that her feelings of uncertainty were an acceptable part of being a teacher.

Mary changed visibly when she converted solely to LBR. Her door was open most mornings, and volunteers welcomed into the room. Initially, visitors were a few trusted confidants such as the county curriculum consultant and a university graduate student. Eventually Mary sought out other educators including the school art teacher and fellow second-grade teachers. She invited colleagues into the room to see how the system worked, because, she indicated, she hoped that they would choose to try LBR the following year. By the end of the year, Mary had four volunteers working in her room on a regular basis.

In addition to opening her classroom door, Mary began to redefine her image of a 'professional teacher'. By wresting control away from the teacher's guide, she became a more important member of the classroom and school. She assumed responsibility for selecting and developing reading materials and for choosing and teaching skills. In addition, Mary believes her classroom environment changed. She says,

Reading books, sharing books and stories and poetry, makes my classroom more like a family than a 'reading class'. We have more discussion, more writing, more self-expression, and increased out-lets for creativity. We also have a lot less teacher control. I sometimes feel I have lost all control of my students. I'm not fond of the feeling, but it probably is good for the students.

For eighteen years Mary defined her professional responsibilities entirely through her actions with students. The support groups helped her to discover that she had knowledge to share with other educators. She felt that she benefited personally from the support given to her from her colleagues. She asked herself, 'If I benefited from their help, wouldn't others benefit from my experience?' Mary began to realize the power of collegiality and her life as a teacher began to change.

In June of the following year (1987) the project teachers gave a three-day workshop for colleagues wishing to use the new reading program. Mary was a major contributor. She said, 'I can't believe I'm doing this!' The following schoolyear Mary continued to open the classroom doors. She invited three teachers from a nearby city to visit the classroom. In addition, she regularly invites administrators, parents and colleagues to attend special presentations by her students or to observe the classroom in action.

In part, Mary's professional growth resulted from a redefinition of what constitutes knowledge. She recognized that achievement was more than a numerical score on a standardized test and that the aims of her work included children learning to enjoy reading and to become lifelong readers. Mary realized she could help others professionally, and that her responsibilities stretched beyond her classroom. For Mary, focusing on teaching, on knowledge as transactive and 'uncertain' as well as 'defined', and as a process for professional dialogue which defines the development of teaching as a profession, were interwoven to help her to develop a new vision of herself as a teacher.

Elizabeth   While both Mary and Elizabeth genuinely 'love teaching', and highly respect one another as teachers, they are very different in philosophy and orientation to teaching, methods of teaching, appearance and personality. Where Mary is a large woman who walks slowly, quietly, and consciously about the classroom, Elizabeth is petite and glides, with remarks punctuated by sharp laughter. While Mary joined the pilot group at the principal's request, Elizabeth volunteered. Mary began the project believing that the method would work but doubting her ability as a teacher to change and use it successfully. Elizabeth began with self-assurance, but questioned parts of the program which she felt might be inappropriate for the children in her classroom who were considered to be developmentally delayed. Both are highly experienced and respected teachers.

At the time of the project Elizabeth had taught in the district for twelve years. In her second year she studied to work with 'developmentally delayed' children. The approach she learned relied heavily on prescriptive reading methods where skills are broken into particularized units. Elizabeth used this method but two issues concerned her. First, the children lacked motivation to read. Most learned to decode words, but they did not like to read. She felt that the ways the children had to plod through the segmented curriculum discouraged them from being involved with language. Elizabeth feared that the children lost gains that they made in class because they did not read for recreation — they did not seem interested in reading anything other than what they *had* to read. Second, the procedure was a chore to teach. The methods were so prescriptive that she felt little enjoyment from teaching. The decisions were all made for her. Her desire to find an alternative teaching method moved her to serve on the district's reading committee. The committee explored a variety of reading approaches and she liked what she heard about Literature Based Reading. She volunteered eagerly to pilot the program.

During a workshop for the program Elizabeth developed several concerns. She accepted readily the power of children's literature to motivate children and realized the enjoyment they would experience from the shared book groups. She was just as sure, however, that certain program elements would not work. In particular, Elizabeth argued forcefully that her children would not be able to write until very late in the year. Session leaders attempted to convince Elizabeth that this was not necessarily the case. They gave her articles which substantiated young children's abilities to write. Nevertheless, she continued to doubt the program's potential efficacy in this area.

Meanwhile, despite her reservations, she decided to give her children opportunities to write. In Elizabeth's words, 'I'm not sure this is going to work, but if you all think it will, I'll give it a try.' In the fall Elizabeth started the students in journal writing and making stories based on books they were using during shared book time. Elizabeth found that the children could write, but she also changed in her understanding of what writing was. She learned to accept 'invented spellings', a stage of writing where children spell words following their own rules rather than the conventions used in adult writing. Elizabeth also learned to accept drawings and scribblings as writing.

She learned to see progress in the children's work in ways that she had not recognized before. After a short while, she became a 'missionary' for children's writing and eventually convinced the kindergarten teacher that her students, too, could write.

Elizabeth's quick conversion to children's writing and literature-based reading seemed to be the result of several factors. First, her natural curiosity led her to read extensively on the subject over the summer. She started the year armed with a good background in the area (though she was one of the few project teachers who did not have a specialized education background in reading) and an eagerness to try the methods she learned. Second, she maintained an open mind to the potential of her students. Elizabeth was willing to support their efforts, and, most of all, she was surprised and delighted in their products. She enjoyed showing visitors the children's writing. The students responded enthusiastically to writing and wrote even more. Third, Elizabeth felt that she benefited from her relationships with colleagues. She was an important member of the support committee and her opinions were respected.

Elizabeth, unlike Mary and some other teachers, was not reluctant to bring her doubts to the group. For example, she was the first to question if children were merely memorizing the words of stories in the shared book time. With help from her fellow support group members, she answered her own question. Together they established five stages the children move through in acquiring mastery over a word; this launched the group's first (but not last) attempt at action research. Through this activity Elizabeth and her colleagues learned that they could pose their own professional questions and that they had the means to respond to them.

Elizabeth voiced concerns early in the project. These eliminated barriers to taking risks with the new program. Elizabeth learned to accept the children's writing and to seek answers and ask for help regarding her concerns as they developed. Her transformation was deeper than changing her understanding of spelling and of defining stages of word acquisition though these were significant learnings. She assumed power and responsibility for the curriculum in her class-room and she learned to work collegially.

The benefits to the children were equally impressive. They were able to define writing on their own terms; to use their own language. They learned to read and write based on natural developmental patterns rather than according to standardized guidelines and procedures from the basal texts. Elizabeth's enthusiasm, based on her attention to teaching and learning and the energy which ensued from the children's learning and enjoyment, combined with her continuing discussion with colleagues, to support further exploration.

Professional Teachers in Professional Environments

The school must be a growth environment for the teacher if it is to be an optimal growth environment for the student (Eisner, 1985, p. 376).

A teacher's work is by nature problematic. It demands the flexible use of intelligence and what Elliot Eisner (1985) describes as an educational imagination. Knowledge is used and made in classrooms. As teachers focus on what they do in classrooms and schools, and as they probe *why* they do what they do, new questions arise, and new possibilities emerge. As experienced teachers like Mary and Elizabeth come together to explore new ideas and to try new ways of teaching, and relating to children, and to each other, they rediscover — or discover for the first time — why they became teachers. And, children benefit. The 'innovation', or reason that they come together, is less important than both their aims of making schooling better for children, and the processes of exploring professional matters together. Professional judgment develops through experience, by identifying challenges, by turning problems around and around, and by exploring alternative solutions and trying them out.

There are no methods for school improvement better than serious observation and professional deliberation. As John Dewey put it, 'All that the wisest man can do is to observe what is going on more widely and more minutely and then select more carefully from what is noted just those factors which point to something to happen' (1916, p. 146). Thoughtful, reflective practice takes time and courage. To be reflective, to understand children, curriculum development and teaching, and to teach well is a tall order. To contribute to the profession is another. Teachers understand teaching 'by trying to change it' (Schon, 1983, p. 151), by stepping back from the action and gaining perspective. The rewards that accrue from providing teachers with the time and resources to work with others are the rewards of professionalism. Professional teachers are those who discover and act on their judgments and who develop ways of working collaboratively to make schools better places for children, and perhaps, the profession a better place for all.

Notes

1. Literature based reading was developed by Don Holdaway, a New Zealand educator. It is based on a 'whole language' philosophy in which language skills are treated in unity. Speaking, listening, reading, writing, for example, are all part of the program and interdependent. There is no 'text' nor a segmented skills approach as there is in basal reading programs.

References

BOYER, E. L. (1983). *High school: A report on secondary education in America.* New York: Harper & Row, and The Carnegie Foundation for the Advancement of Teaching.

BROUGHTON, J. (1977). Beyond formal operations: Theoretical thought in adolescence. *Teachers College Record, 79,* 87–9.

DEWEY, J. (1916). *Democracy and education.* New York: Macmillan.

CARSON, T. (1984). *A hermeneutic investigation of meaning of curriculum implementation.* Unpublished doctoral dissertation. Edmonton. Canada: University of Alberta.

COMBS, A. W. (1965). *The professional education of teachers.* Boston: Allyn & Bacon.

EISNER, E. W. (1985). *The educational imagination: On the design and evaluation of school programs.* New York: Macmillan.

ELKIND, D. (1983). Accommodating variations in school readiness. Thirty-eighth Continuing Conference Early Childhood Education, Kent State University, Kent.

FREIRE, P. (1971). *Pedagogy of the oppressed.* Translated by M. B. Ramos. New York: Herder & Herder.

GARDNER, J. W. (1962). *Self-renewal: The individual and the innovative society.* New York: Harper & Row.

HER MAJESTY'S STATIONERY OFFICE. (1985). *Quality in school evaluation and appraisal.* London: Croom Helm.

HARTLEY, D. (1985). *Understanding the primary school: A sociological analysis.* London: Croom Helm.

HOLDAWAY, D. (1979). *Foundations of literacy.* Portsmouth, NH: Heinemann Educational Books.

HOLLY, M. L. (1977). A conceptual framework for personal–professional growth. Implications for inservice education. Unpublished doctoral dissertation. East Lansing: Michigan State University.

HOLLY, M. L. (1983). Teacher reflections on classroom Life: Collaboration and professional development. *Australian Administrator.* 4(4), 1–6.

JERSILD, A. (1955). *When teachers face themselves.* New York: Teachers College Press, Columbia University.

KNOBLOCK, P. and GOLDSTEIN, A. (1971). *The lonely teacher.* Boston: Allyn & Bacon.

KUHN, T. (1962). *The structure of scientific revolutions.* Chicago, IL: University of Chicago Press.

LEVINSON, D., DARROW, C., KLEIN, E., LEVINSON, M., and McKEE, B. (1978). *The seasons of a man's life.* New York: Knopf.

LITTLE, J. (1982). Norms of collegiality and experimentation: Workplace conditions of school success. *American Educational Research Journal,* 19(3), 325–40.

LORTIE, D. C. (1975). *Schoolteacher: A sociological study.* Chicago: Chicago University Press.

MACDONALD, B. (1985). Personal communication.

MEZIROW, J. (1977). Perspective transformation. *Studies in Adult Education.* 9(2), 153–64.

MEZIROW, J. (1981). A critical theory of adult learning. *Studies in Adult Education.* 32(1), 3–24.

NIAS, J. (1984). Definition and maintenance of self in primary education. *British Journal of Special Education,* 5(3), 267–80.

SAINT EXUPERY, A. (1943). *The little prince.* New York: Harcourt, Brace & World, Incorporated.

SAWADA, D. and CALEY, M. T. (1985). Dissipative structures: New metaphors for becoming in education. *Educational Researcher.* 14(3), 13–19.

SCHON, D. (1983). *The reflective practitioner: How professionals think in action.* New York: Basic Books.

SHULMAN, L. (1987). Knowledge and teaching: Foundations of the new reforms. *Harvard Educational Review.* 57(1), 1–22.

SPENDER, D. (1982). *Invisible women: The schooling scandal.* London: Writers and Readers Publishing Cooperative Society.

STENHOUSE, L. (1975). *An introduction to curriculum research and development.* London: Heinemann Educational Books.

WALLER, W. (1932). *The sociology of teaching.* New York: Russell & Russell.

Epilogue

Professional development Where do we begin?

'Begin at the beginning ... and go on till you come to the end — then stop,' said the King to the White Rabbit in *Alice's Adventures in Wonderland* (Lewis Carroll, 1832–98).

Well we've begun, but we're not near the end.

We started by conducting general *in-service training*, and we've moved to conceptualizing and developing conceptually relevant *professional and staff development*.

We started as *isolated practitioners* and we've moved to persons in *collaboration and colleagueship*.

We've moved from *'no lexicon'* to *reflecting-on-practice* and *discussing it, writing about it.*

We've moved from principals as *managers*, to principals as *facilitators and participants*.

We've moved from *one way of preparing teachers* to *alternative programs for teacher preparation*.

We've moved from an *induction of 'sink-or-swim'* to *supported, systematic inquiry based entrance* into the profession.

We've moved from research *on* teachers to research *with* teachers, and latterly to research *by* teachers.

We are moving toward a profession which develops its own system for continuous renewal through the ways it structures and supports the inquiry which defines it as an educational profession.

Notes on Contributors

Jane H. Applegate Associate Professor, Teacher Development and Curriculum Studies, and Assistant Dean for Teacher Education, College of Education, Kent State University, Kent, Ohio, USA.

Jane H. Applegate began her career as a junior high school English teacher. She received her doctorate from Ohio State University with an emphasis in teacher education. She served as a consultant with the Ohio Department of Education's Division of Teacher Education and Certification, and directed a teachers' center for staff development in Columbus, Ohio. Dr Applegate's publications address teachers' personal and professional development. Results from her research on the role perceptions of educators involved in early field experiences have been published in national and international journals of teacher education. Currently, she is studying the effects of an inquiry-oriented teacher education program.

Normand R. Bernier Professor, College of Education, Kent State University, Kent, Ohio, USA.

Normand R. Bernier also lectures in Human Values and Medicine at Northeastern Ohio Universities College of Medicine. His specialization is the cultural foundations of education. He is the co-author (with Jack E. Williams, 1973) of *Beyond Beliefs: Ideological Foundations of American Education* and co-editor (with Jack E. Williams, 1973) of *Education for Liberation: Readings from an Ideological Perspective.* Dr Bernier's publications deal with teacher education and the preparation of educators for non-school settings. His major research interests are in ideology and education, and multicultural education.

Charles A. Blackman Professor of Teacher Education, College of
   Education, Michigan State University, East Lansing, Michigan,
   USA.

Charles A. Blackman has been on the faculty since 1956. His special
interests include curriculum development and related professional development. He has held leadership positions in several professional
organizations and has also been active on a local board of education.
His early education as a student in the Laboratory School at Ohio
State University stimulated a lifelong interest in teaching, curriculum
design, and professional development. He taught at the middle school
level, then returned to Ohio State University for graduate study in
Curriculum and Instruction. Dr Blackman is a contributor to publications of the Association for Supervision and Curriculum Development
and an active participant in the National Council of States on Inservice
Education. His current research addresses colleague relationships and
multiple or extended roles for teachers.

Roy A. Edelfelt Partner, Edelfelt-Johnson, Chapel-Hill, North Caro-
   lina, USA.

Roy A. Edelfelt is now a private consultant who offers services in
teacher education, particularly staff development and school improvement. He is a former teacher and university professor, also a former
executive secretary of the National Commission on Teacher Education and Professional Standards. Before becoming a free-lance consultant and writer, he was staff associate in the National Education
Association's Division of Instruction and Professional Development.
He is the author of numerous articles and has written or edited several
pamphlets and books, including *Rethinking In-service Education* (with
Margo Johnson, 1975).

John Elliott Professor of Education, Centre for Applied Research in
   Education (CARE), School of Education, University of East
   Anglia, Norwich, England.

Following five years of classroom teaching John Elliott was a member
of the UK Schools Council/Nuffield Foundation Humanities Project
under the directorship of Lawrence Stenhouse. He moved with the
project to the University of East Anglia in 1970. From 1972 to 1974
he directed the Ford Teaching Project — the Classroom Action-
Research project which has been a major stimulus to the development

of theory and practice in the UK and worldwide. In 1976 he moved to the Cambridge Institute of Education as Tutor in Curriculum Studies where he directed several major pieces of funded research. In 1984 he returned to CARE. His publications have dealt with topics such as educational action-research, curriculum planning and evaluation, and accountability.

Martin Haberman   Professor of Teacher Education, College of Education, University of Wisconsin–Milwaukee, Wisconsin, USA.

In addition to extensive publications, media involvement, and research, Martin Haberman has played a significant role in shaping teacher education: MAT programs, the original NCATE standards, the National Teacher Corps, the Training of Teacher Trainers (TTT) Program, NDEA Institutes, Professional Development Centers, Alternative Certification programs and, currently, a range of pre- and in-service programs. Professor Haberman is concerned with issues of access and equity, and in making education — for pupils as well as for teachers — a means for more fully realizing life opportunities. His primary focus is on preparing teachers for urban schools at the pre-service and in-service levels. His work is characterized by several themes: broadening access to educational opportunities, improving programs offered teachers, and involving classroom teachers as senior partners in teacher preparation and school improvement efforts.

Mary Louise Hulbert Holly   Associate Professor, Teacher Development and Curriculum Studies, College of Education, Kent State University, Kent, Ohio, USA.

Mary Louise Hulbert Holly has been an art teacher of students ages 5 to 55 years, and a primary school teacher. Since 1978 she has been a faculty member in early childhood education. Her research on teacher professional development explores teachers' lives and careers using psychosocial, life history and biographical methods. She has written on professional development, staff development, and journal writing. Her most recent work is *Teacher Inquiry: Keeping a Personal-Professional Journal* (1989), from Heinemann Educational Books.

Averil E. McClelland   Assistant Professor, College of Education, Kent State University, Kent, Ohio, USA.

Averil E. McClelland has served as an Educational Consultant at Cuyahoga Community College, designing professional development courses in administration and management for directors of volunteer programs in health, education, and human service agencies; as Field Evaluator for a major community education project; and as Coordinator of the Educational Studies Program at Kent State University. Dr McClelland has published articles on the preparation of educators for multiple settings and on education in the community. Her research interests are in social networks and women's issues.

Caven S. Mcloughlin Associate Professor, College of Education, Kent State University. Kent, Ohio, USA.

Caven S. Mcloughlin received his professional preparation as a teacher, a counselor, and school psychologist in England and the USA. His current primary responsibility is in the preparation of school psychologists with an early childhood specialty, and in the preparation of interdisciplinary personnel who provide service to handicapped infants and their families. He is Editor of the journal *School Psychology International*, and Associate Editor for several other publications. He has edited/authored *Childhood Disorders: Preschool and Early Elementary Years* (1983); *Young Children in Context: Impact of Self, Family, and Society on Development* (1984); *Educators, Children and the Law* (1985); *Parent Teacher Conferencing* (1987); and *Getting Employed, Staying Employed: Job Development and Training for Persons with Severe Handicaps* (1988).

Sharon Nodie Oja Associate Professor, Department of Education, University of New Hampshire, Durham, New Hampshire, USA.

Sharon Nodie Oja teaches courses in human learning and development in the University of New Hampshire five-year MAT/MEd program in teacher education where she is an Associate Professor in the Department of Education. She has consulted with teachers in staff development projects and been an evaluator for various local, state, and national groups. Her research has investigated adult development as a deliberate goal of staff development projects with teachers. She is the principal investigator of two federally funded projects: A National Institute of Education (NIE) project titled *Action Research on Change in Schools* (completed in 1983), and *A Collaborative Approach to Leadership in Supervision* (now in the third year) which investigates adult development, alternative models of supervision, and collaborative action research with teachers and administrators.

Jennifer Nias   Tutor, Cambridge Institute of Education, Cambridge, England.

Jennifer Nias has taught, at various times in different parts of the world, children from three to 15 years, and adults from 18 to 56. Before moving to Cambridge in 1977 she was Tutor to the primary PGCE course at the University of Liverpool. Presently, Dr Nias works with experienced teachers, especially from primary and middle schools, on in-service courses and consultancies. Her current research interests are primary teachers' lives and careers, and inter-adult relationships in primary schools. These interests are discussed in many papers and book chapters as well as in *Seeing Anew: Teachers' Theories of Action* (1987), *Primary Teachers and their Work*, (1988) and *Understanding the Primary School as an Organization* (with Southworth and Yeomans; 1988).

John Smyth   Associate Professor, and Chairperson of the Education Studies Centre, Deakin University, Victoria, Australia.

John Smyth has served as Deputy Dean at the School of Education; taught at the University of Alberta, Canada; the University of New Zealand; and Papua New Guinea University of Technology, previous to which he was a secondary teacher in Victoria. His work at Deakin has been in pioneering off-campus (at-a-distance) studies in social and administrative studies in education. He is developing an innovative field-based model of providing nurse education. He is author of a series: *Commerce in Papua New Guinea* (1974), as well as *Learning about Teaching through Clinical Supervision* (1975), and *Educating Teachers: Changing the Nature of Knowledge* (1987). His latest work (with A. Gitlin, 1987) is entitled *Beyond Teacher Evaluation*. He is founder and editior of *The Australian Administrator* and his current interests are in ways of assisting teachers to theorize about their practice and develop their professional knowledge.

Les Tickle   Senior Lecturer, School of Education, University of East Anglia, Norwich, England.

Les Tickle started teaching in 1965 and has taught in primary (elementary), middle, and high schools. After conducting in-service work while teaching full time, he moved to teacher education at the University of East Anglia in 1981. He is currently involved in initial teacher education programs and in in-service teacher education and research. Current responsibilities and research foci include the development of induction programs for new teachers, and attempts to understand how they can make substantial contributions to their own induction through their own action-research. The major concern of his book, *Learning Teaching, Teaching Teaching: A Study of Partnership in Teacher Education* (1987) is improvement in professional development for student teachers.

Carl Walley Curriculum Consultant, Elementary Education, Medina
    County Board of Education, Medina, Ohio, USA.

As a consultant to teachers and administrators Carl Walley facilitated curriculum development and implementation in primary and elementary schools. He is a former teacher, principal, and consultant for special programs. He frequently offers in-service education to teachers and administrators on writing and language arts. Carl is a doctoral candidate at Kent State University where his research focuses on the processes of change, and the relationships between curriculum development and teachers' concerns. He has also, recently, taken on the Principalship of an elementary school.

Author Index

Subject Index

accountability 24–5, 30, 86, 96
Action Research on Change in
  Schools (ARCS) 128–48
administrative leadership 10–11,
  219–34
adult development, ages and stages
  of 119–24
  see also teacher career cycle
Akron (Ohio) 187–99
American Educational Research
  Association (AERA) 100
American Federation of Teachers
  (AFT) 209, 215
appraisal, defined 294 *see also*
  teacher evaluation
assessment, defined 294

Bell, Dr Andrew 93
Bible study 68
bilingual/bicultural education 25
British and Foreign School Society
  93, 95
Buber, Martin 157
'burnout' 59, 174

California, teacher centers in 215
Cambridge Elementary School (New
  England) 301
Cambridge (UK) 187–99
Camus, Albert 297
career cycle, teacher *see* teacher
  career cycle
Chicago, University of 70

child development theory 180
Civil Rights movement 25
cognitive-developmental stage *see*
  under adult development; teacher
  career cycle
Collaborative Research Office
  (University of New Hampshire)
  128
collegiality and collaboration, teacher
  7–9, 13, 179, 194–7, 223, 225, 258
Concerns-Based-Adoption-Model
  (CBAM) 125
Council for the Accreditation of
  Teacher Education (CATE) 95,
  106
Critical Thinking Project 209
culture
  bureaucratization of 35–6
  organizational 43–4
curriculum
  autonomy in setting 158
  basic skills 64–5, 67
  change and perspective
    transformation in 299–307
  context modification of 111–12
  in elementary/primary schools
    182
  general studies 68–71
  science 46
  see also following entry
curriculum development 3–4,
  182–4
  and leadership experience 112

Davies, Don   21
Department of Education and
   Science (UK)   156
Department of Education (US), and
   teacher organization   210
'desegregation'   25
Dewey, John   181
diary writing *see* journal writing

East Anglia (UK)   246–60
education
   defined   31–2
   public   27
Education Center Inc.   113
Educational Experiences Inventory
   128
educational policy and reform
   23–5, 47–8
   and school effectiveness   33
Educational Research and
   Dissemination Program   209
Einstein, Albert   262, 293
elementary schools   42, 180–2
   reading instruction in   64–5
   staff development programs in
   46
Eliot, Charles (President of Harvard
   University)   57

Ford Teaching Project   246–60
   hypotheses   252–8
Freshman Field Experience program
   82
Freud, Sigmund   164
Froebel, Friedrich   157

handicapped children   25
Harvard, University of   57
head teachers *see* principals
Her Majesty's Inspectors of Schools
   (HMI)   156
   and new teacher evaluation   108
Holdaway, Don   309
Humanities Project   250–2

identity *see* self-identity
in-service training *see under* teacher
   education/training

individualism   56–62
infant schools   179
Instruction and Professional
   Development (IPD) division   208

Jackson, Andrew   63
James, William   161, 167
journal writing   169–70, 261–83
   autobiographical   268–9
   benefits of   281–3
   personal documents defined   265
   as reflection process   266, 270–1,
   283
   teacher descriptions of   271–83
   types of   266–7

kindergarten   179
knowledge, sociology of   28

Lancaster, Joseph   93
leadership   9–13
   administrative   219–34
   and curriculum development   112
learning   39
   qualitative and quantitative
   dimensions of   242–5, 249–50
liberal arts   56–62
life age/cycle *see under* adult
   development; teacher career cycle
literature based reading (LBR)
   299–304
Liverpool (UK)   187–99
Locke, John   181

McNair Report   186
Man: A Course of Study (MACOS)
   98
Mastery in Learning Project   179,
   208
Mayflower Compact   68
Michigan, teacher roles in   4–5
monitorial schools   93
Montessori, Maria   180

National Commission on Teacher
   Education and Professional
   Standards (NCTEPS)   20, 211,
   212

and general studies curricula
67–73
history of 93–5
and individualism 56–62
pre- and in-service 20–1, 27–8,
32–7, 173–7
teacher effectiveness research *see*
following entry
teacher evaluation 108, 241–60,
292–6
process model of 245–8
research criticism of 242–5
teacher isolation 2, 43, 179, 279,
289
teacher organization 207–17
achievements and rewards
216–17
and development programs
208–10
motivation for involvement
210–13
teacher professional development
1–13
comparative study between US
and UK 177–99
cultural influences on 55–75
history of 19
inhibitors to 29–48
policy formulation 22–8
social contexts of 19–48
time constraints in 192–4
see also adult development; journal
writing; leadership; new
teachers; teacher evaluation;
teacher organization; teachers;
teaching
Teacher Research Linkers (TRL)
209
Teacher-Pupil Interaction and the
Quality of Learning Project
(TIQL) 250, 258
teacher-pupil relations 157
teachers
collegiality between 7–9, 13,
179, 195–7, 223, 225, 258
duty contracts 6
and financial rewards 5
isolation of 2, 43, 179, 279, 289
and personal fulfillment 4

and perspective transformation
296–9
professionalism of 287–307
qualifications 107, 184
reflection and self-appraisal by
111, 277–8, 296–9
roles and responsibilities 1–13
self-identity of 155–68, 280
Teachers and Youths (McNair Report)
186
see also following entry
teaching 26–7
developmental 82–4
different patterns of 110
formal/informal methods 242–5,
249–50
gaining ideas and insights into
190–2
'inclusive' 159–60
Inquiry/Discovery approaches
246–8
intellectual transformation of
219–34
knowledge-based 86–9
and learning 37–40
as moral activity 248–60
natural acquisition of 80–2
and perspective transformation
296–9
professional culture of 41–6
readiness for 79–90
skill-based 84–6
Stenhouse's principles 245–6
theory, practice and knowledge in
261–3, 290–2
see also teachers
Texas, University of, Research and
Development Center for Teacher
Education 125
textbooks, use of 183

United States
comparative study with UK
177–99
Senate Subcommittee on
Education 21

Virginia, University of 56
Voltaire, Francois 290